THE INFERNAL MACHINE: INVESTIGATING
THE LOYALTY OF CANADA'S CITIZENS

Current historical orthodoxy contends that Canada was startled
into implementing security screening in September 1945, when
Soviet cipher clerk Igor Gouzenko defected in Ottawa, bringing
with him sensational evidence that a Soviet espionage network
existed in this country.

The Infernal Machine challenges that conventional view. In the
course of rewriting Canadian security and intelligence history,
Larry Hannant marshals evidence from previously classified documents to show that systematic security screening was launched
fifteen years before Gouzenko. It was initiated because the Russian
Revolution in 1917 and the formation of the Communist International in 1919 caused Canadian authorities, particularly the RCMP,
to view many citizens with suspicion.

The heart of the security-screening system was a unique Canadian experiment in mass fingerprinting. During the Second
World War the RCMP received and checked over two million sets
of fingerprints. This was both unprecedented and illegal.

Because fingerprinting offended popular opinion and legal
authority, surrendering their fingerprints was always 'voluntary'
for employees at war plants. The RCMP acknowledged that the
procedure could be subject to abuse – and abused it was. People
identified by security checks as having criminal records or even
personal peccadilloes were fired and denied jobs. Some of these
people protested their treatment, and in internal memos the
RCMP commissioner fretted that the force was acquiring 'a
Gestapo reputation' among Canadians.

The Infernal Machine presents a compelling new chapter in Canadian history. Hannant has produced an authoritative and dramatic
examination of the Canadian state's deep fears of its own citizens
and of the arbitrary measures taken against those citizens.

Larry Hannant, PhD, is a historian and journalist living in Victoria.

LARRY HANNANT

The infernal machine: Investigating the loyalty of Canada's citizens

UNIVERSITY OF TORONTO PRESS
Toronto Buffalo London

© University of Toronto Press Incorporated 1995
Toronto Buffalo London
Printed in Canada

ISBN 0-8020-0448-2 (cloth)
ISBN 0-8020-7236-4 (paper)

Printed on acid-free paper

Canadian Cataloguing in Publication Data

Hannant, Larry, 1950 –
   The infernal machine : investigating the loyalty
   of Canada's citizens

   Includes bibliographical references and index.
   ISBN 0-8020-0448-2 (bound) ISBN 0-8020-7236-4 (pbk.)

   1. Internal Security – Canada – History – 20th
   century.   2. Intelligence service – Canada.
   I. Title.

JL86.I58H35 1995   354.71001'3242   C95-930481-9

This book has been published with the help of a grant from the Social Science
Federation of Canada, using funds provided by the Social Sciences and
Humanities Research Council of Canada.

University of Toronto Press acknowledges the financial assistance to its publishing program of the Canada Council and the Ontario Arts Council.

Contents

ACKNOWLEDGMENTS   vii

Introduction   3

1
The last recourse of liars: Testing loyalty before 1919   17

2
The politics of identification: Fingerprinting to 1939   41

3
The birth of state vetting: Security screening in the interwar period   63

4
The infernal machine: Security screening during the Second World War   83

5
Reds under the khaki: Screening the military and merchant marine   119

6
'Gathering information regarding communistic chaps': The system's political rationale   139

7
Engineers of conduct: The system's technical rationale   163

8
Security affairs: Liaison with the Allies and provinces   183

9
'The first to come under suspicion': Popular response to security
screening   211

10
Outcomes, developments, and significance   241

APPENDICES

Appendix 1 Application for employment   255
Appendix 2 Non-criminal fingerprint form   257

NOTES   259

PICTURE CREDITS   317

INDEX   319

Acknowledgments

This book began as a PhD thesis, although I have tried very hard to take it beyond being merely a thesis. During my time in doctoral servitude at the University of British Columbia history department I had printed a sweatshirt that reflected my frustration with the process. It read: 'I'd rather be writing my book.' At the time, my attitude must have seemed highly presumptuous and the prospect of success in the venture dubious indeed. So it is gratifying to see the sentiment become fact.

If I have succeeded in bringing what I think is an important historical issue – and an interesting story – to Canadians, it is only because of the considerable assistance I have received over the years. My mother and father, Elenora and Ted Barber, and my sister and brother-in-law, Sandra and Glen Heming, have given me vital financial support on the many occasions when it seemed that lack of means would effectively prevent my finishing. They and many other people have dispensed wise counsel and emotional sustenance through the years. Among them was Elizabeth Lees, whose self-effacing humour and fortitude in the face of death invariably bolstered my resolve to see this project through. Others who have sympathetically stood by me include Maggie Thompson, Jim Hamm, Avril Torrence, Barbara Winters, and Susan Kennedy. I wish also to acknowledge a grant from the J.S. Ewart Memorial Fund which assisted me in one of my many research visits to Ottawa.

In Toronto, Salah Bachir and Tom and Gina Cody opened their homes and extended enormous hospitality to me while I wandered the city in search of elusive records. Paul Marsden and Linda Goldthorpe did the same in Ottawa.

I especially wish to thank Peter Ward of the University of British Columbia history department, a just man and a careful scholar who unflaggingly persevered in curbing my penchant to 'write like Time Magazine.' The threads of *Time* style which remain in this tapestry reflect not failure of purpose on his part but incorrigible recidivism on mine. In ways beyond mere style this work is far better than it would have been without his advice and suggestions. Ivan Avakumovic, Charles Humphries, and Stephen Straker, all of the same department, have also contributed considerably to this project.

Several other people have read the whole or parts of this work and offered helpful comments, including Reg Whitaker, Wesley Wark, John Lutz, and Anna Russell. Two anonymous readers who reviewed the manuscript for the University of Toronto Press and the Aid to Scholarly Publications Programme of the Social Science Federation of Canada offered many useful suggestions which have immeasurably improved this book. My editors at University of Toronto Press, Gerry Hallowell and Rob Ferguson, have judiciously proposed a number of beneficial changes, as has copyeditor Mary McDougall Maude. In the latter stages I had the able research assistance of John Keelor, Paulette DeKelver, and Lise Murray. Any shortcomings and errors that remain in this book are, of course, my own responsibility.

Staff members at the National Archives of Canada, the Archives of Ontario, the Ontario Hydro Archives, the British Columbia Archives and Records Service, Queen's University Archives, the Walter Reuther Library of Wayne State University, the University of British Columbia Library and Special Collections Division, and the University of Victoria library have shown keen interest in and have greatly aided my work. Although it would be impossible to thank all by name, I particularly want to acknowledge the aid of Carol White, who, along with other Access to Information archivists at the National Archives, has speeded and facilitated my access to records that had previously been closed.

RCMP historians Stan Horrall and William Beahen and Roger Sarty at the National Defence Directorate of History have given me both encouragement and invaluable assistance by pulling nuggets of information from their files. Claire Culhane generously allowed me to use material obtained by her under the Access to Information and Privacy Act.

Interviews with several former members of the Royal Canadian Mounted Police have helped me to understand the nuances of life within the force in a way that paper records alone could not do. Among those who have been particularly helpful are R.W. (Tony) Wonnacott and W.C. Bryan.

In the time since I began this work my daughter Caila has grown from infancy to childhood. Her sense of fun, her maturity, and her love have been a treasure to me over the decade of this project's life. I dedicate this work to her, cautioning her that if she's inclined to follow her dad into print, she not wait as long as he did.

The guiding spirit of the RCMP's Criminal Identification Bureau,
Inspector Edward Foster, surveys the troops in 1923. Inspector H.R.
Butchers, who would oversee the vast fingerprinting operation during
the Second World War, sits alone at the third table back.

Security intelligence relations between the RCMP and the FBI were put on a more formal basis in 1937 when RCMP Commissioner James H. MacBrien (*left*), uncharacteristically out of uniform, visited FBI Director J. Edgar Hoover (*right*) in Washington. The meeting had been initiated by MacBrien's queries to the FBI about how to monitor the movements of Canadian communists across the U.S. border.

Under the watchful gaze of an unsmiling supervisor, women civil servants in the RCMP Fingerprint Section type reports based upon fingerprint forms during the Second World War.

First World War veterans would be 'about as hard a gang to handle as imaginable,' RCMP Inspector Clifford Harvison warned in July 1939. Nonetheless, at the beginning of the Second World War they were pressed into service, after being fingerprinted and put through a rudimentary criminal record check, guarding sites considered to be susceptible to sabotage. Two such guards patrol a power station in Nova Scotia, their only uniform being armbands labelled 'Police.'

Comparing the arches, tented arches, whorls, and loops on fingerprints often required the use of magnifying glasses. An RCMP officer searches through stacks of employment and fingerprint forms of wartime munitions workers.

A civilian clerk and an RCMP officer are engaged in the tedious chore of checking industrial workers' fingerprint forms at the RCMP Fingerprint Section. Labels on the file doors below give the names of companies whose employees were being checked: General Engineering in Scarborough, the F.T. Hepburn company, and Inglis.

By the Second World War IBM keypunch and sorting equipment was commonplace in business offices. But using the machinery for fingerprint processing was introduced into the RCMP Fingerprint Section only in 1942. In a 1944 photo, a civilian clerk operates a tabulating card keypunch.

The RCMP's fingerprint-tabulating card was virtually identical to the FBI's, indicating the direct connection between the two police forces in their electromechanical processing of fingerprint data.

An IBM gang card-punch, which the RCMP used to transfer coded information about fingerprints from the left-hand side of the card to the right-hand side (the selector code area). This facilitated the operation of the IBM card sorter, seen against the wall to the right.

The image of business efficiency is deceptive: each time someone used the elevator in the Justice building, home of the RCMP headquarters, electrical circuits overloaded and the sorter stopped working.

The enormity of the wartime screening system is laid out before an RCMP officer as he contemplates stacks of industrial workers' fingerprint and employment record forms.

Italy's entry into the war in June 1940 cleared the way for Canadian authorities to collar Benito Mussolini's sympathizers in the Italian-Canadian community. RCMP Sergeant René Noel, carrying books seized from the Maison d'Italie in Montreal, leads a suspect away for internment.

Crowds gather in downtown Montreal in June 1940 as police round up fascist sympathizers and load them onto buses to be taken to temporary detention centres.

THE INFERNAL MACHINE

Introduction

Security intelligence lacks the common touch. Plain folks are seldom to be found in this nether world. Its protagonists are members of an elite – senior politicians, devious spies, brilliant but reclusive code-breakers, lonely moralists pursuing sordid moles. They are all too aware that, among the people in whose name they claim to toil, their craft and sacrifice is at best misunderstood. Indeed, it must be so, for secrecy is security's byword. The less public knowledge about it the better. Hence little or nothing about it will be apparent to the Montreal lathe-operator who mills parts for high-pressure pumps or the Washington typist who prepares invoices for the Department of Transport. Yet for one aspect of security intelligence, these uncelebrated citizens are central. Security screening, the subject of this work, counts such people as its essential raw material, its focus. Compared to other security intelligence branches, security screening is less arcane because it affects the livelihoods and political rights of millions of working people.

At heart, security screening is an attempt to accomplish the seemingly impossible. It is a procedure that seeks to establish people's trustworthiness, often on short acquaintance or based upon rudimentary or fragmentary information. But if determining loyalty is difficult, describing the screening process is not. The 1969 Canadian *Report of the Royal Commission on Security*, the Mackenzie Commission, offered an overview of what constitutes security screening when it proposed measures to prevent

those who in the judgment of the government may constitute a risk to the security of the state from entering the state, becoming citizens of the state, entering public employment or having access to classified information.[1]

The commission identified five aspects of security screening. These are control of (1) who enters the country (visa and immigration curbs); (2) who becomes a citizen (restrictions on citizenship); (3) who leaves the country (withholding of passports); (4) who works for the state (loyalty testing or vetting); and (5) who has access to classified information (security clearance).[2] The focus of this study is on the constraints exercised over who may take public employment or work for an employer with a contract to supply some commodity to the state. Some attention is also paid to security clearance and immigration restrictions, since in Canada they were developed in conjunction with a broader security-screening apparatus.

Various means have been devised in the quest to assess the loyalty of those in public employment. Oaths of allegiance were used for this purpose for centuries, and survive still. But latterly, the activity has become more complex and burdened by technology. The Mackenzie Commission described two steps to the process: 'first, the acquisition of data about the past history of an individual; and secondly, an attempt to forecast the individual's future performance or reliability on the basis of this data.' For most of the twentieth century the first of these two phases has received primary attention from security agencies, who have striven mightily to obtain greater and greater amounts of information about more and more people. Increasingly, science has been brought to bear on the problem. The outcome has been a complex battery of devices and tests – card indexes, records searches, fingerprinting, electromechanical and electronic search aids, interviews, reference checks, and active background investigations. In observing this trend, this study devotes considerable attention to the development of scientific methods to collect and analyse the information that serves as a basis for security screening. I see in them an intriguing example of the use of technology for political control.[3]

If I pay less attention in this study to the second part of security screening mentioned by the Mackenzie Commission – the effort to predict an individual's reliability and performance – it is only because security agencies themselves have mostly failed to acknowledge its importance or to resolve the conundrum it presents. Echoing a common complaint throughout the history of loyalty testing, the Mackenzie Commission lamented in 1969: 'It would be an ideal situation if it were possible to process an individual through a series of more or less mechanistic tests, and arrive at an objective judgment of the subject's future loyalty, reliability and character. Unfortunately, we are informed that this is not possible, nor likely to be possible in the foreseeable future.'[4] The dim prospect of inventing such a machine – to say nothing about how 'ideal' it would be – has not impeded the search for it. Indeed, the quest for a method to sound out human beings' true loyalty – seeking a device to delve into the human soul – is a significant theme of this work.

In sum, state security screening involves efforts to collect and process information about people perceived to be threats to the state, especially in times of national conflict such as wars. Security screening is the state's way of assessing the political opinions, behaviour, and trustworthiness of many of its citizens and those who wish to become citizens – civil servants, armed forces personnel, industrial employees, and naturalization applicants – and to use that assessment as a criterion for matters such as employment and citizenship.

Although security screening is a child of the complex marriage of security and intelligence, it does not figure prominently in the family photographs.[5] In fact, security screening is distinguished mostly by being the clan's neglected descendant. By some definitions of security intelligence, security screening does not even rate mention beside more acclaimed aspects like spying, covert action, and code-breaking. Roy Godson's description of the nature of intelligence, for example, leaves only a small niche for security screening within the category of counter-intelligence; John Bruce

Lockhart also buries it there.[6] Their definitions only serve to underline a pervasive attitude among those who write about security intelligence: that security screening is considered an unimportant part of the enterprise. The prolific British popular writer and latter-day member of parliament Rupert Allason (alias Nigel West) alluded to one reason why security screening has been neglected by researchers when he wrote that the vetting department of Britain's internal security intelligence agency, MI5, 'was regarded by some as the most junior of the Branches, since it was a dull post, best suited for bureaucrats with tidy mindsand an acceptable social presence.'[7] The same contempt is exhibited by others who write about security intelligence. They tend to value spy-catchers and their prey – heroes and villains – higher than the millions of people labouring in industry and the public service who are the subjects of security screening.

Another important aspect of security screening is the matter of who initiates it and who falls under its scrutiny. Security screening has been found expedient by states of all descriptions – monarchies, republics, dictatorships and liberal democracies – and by private employers. In the twentieth century, specialized state security agencies have emerged to assume the burden of responsibility for the process. Prior to the twentieth century, relatively few people were investigated to ascertain their political loyalties. Most of them were senior government advisers or other civil service appointees. As this century has proceeded, screening has embraced more and more people, even in countries that pride themselves on their respect for individual liberty and democracy. States have imposed it on many or all of their civil servants, and also on potential immigrants and naturalization applicants. And, increasingly, the state has cooperated with employers to ascertain the political outlook and behaviour of private sector workers. The practice has become so ingrained that it is rarely, if ever, questioned, either by large public sector unions whose members must submit to the procedure as a condition of employment, or by individals such as international airport workers who face the same requirement.

This study has five key aims and themes. First, it explains the evolution of motives and methods for investigating people's loyalty. The impulse behind security screening has existed for centuries. The persistence of loyalty oaths over the years attests to that. But only in the past century has a new urgency to ascertain loyalty led to the systematic application of science and technology to the subject.

After 1919, security concepts were profoundly transformed in Canada as in other industrial countries. Even as late as 1914 the recently arrived stranger – embodied in identifiable ethnic groups – was regarded as the primary threat to British, American, and Canadian security. That attitude started to erode with the triumph of Bolshevism in Russia in 1917 and the formation in 1919 of the Communist International to spread proletarian revolution beyond the borders of the Soviet Union. Ideological dissent assumed a new, threatening importance to the capitalist world. The state's problem was how to identify and isolate the carrier of the plague. This was no small task, since communist ideology is as transparent in the dissenting individual as capitalist ideology is in the host society. Nothing about a person's appearance or speech need betray the political or social attitudes he or she holds.

After the end of the First World War, the handy target of prewar suspicion and surveillance – the outsider – began to decline in importance as a perceived threat. It is true that ethnicity did not disappear as a convenient label of political danger. State and popular fears of the dangerous foreigner persisted into the 1930s. Nonetheless, the prevailing intelligence paradigm was shifting dramatically. State security agencies began to see the population as a whole as the primary object of attention, and as a result security screening grew to become a comprehensive system. By the Second World War the state felt the need to scrutinize many people, not just those identifiable by ethnic origin.

My second aim is to describe the creation of a Canadian state security-screening system, culminating in the huge operation of the Second World War.[8] By 1945 it had become a machine with the power to affect the lives of hundreds of thousands of Canadians. I chart the evolution of this system, illustrate its characteristics, and explain the reasons for its creation. In the process I examine various approaches to security screening, assess its effectiveness, and measure its impact. This approach paints a novel picture of Can-

ada in wartime, casting new light upon this country's regard for
civil liberties.

Before 1984, the Royal Canadian Mounted Police performed a
dual role as a police unit enforcing federal laws throughout the
country and as the Canadian state's primary political police.[9] The
RCMP is the subject of dozens of popular books and films, many
of which have helped to erect and embellish its romantic image.
Among the score of scholarly books on the RCMP, most concentrate on its policing role and only briefly address security issues.
The best of those that do deal with security intelligence were
products of the controversy about RCMP law-breaking in the
1970s, and in most cases they rely on testimony from two commis-
sions of inquiry into those crimes.[10] Only one of them, John
Sawatsky's *Men in the Shadows*, examines the security arm of the
RCMP in any depth, and it treats security screening in one page.
Hence there is no comprehensive history of security screening in
Canada in the twentieth century.[11]

Furthermore, only a handful of academic articles have
appeared on the subject, and they show a curious agreement
about the origin of the Canadian government's security-screening
program. Reginald Whitaker and Lawrence Aronsen, scholars
with conflicting interpretations of the Cold War security-screening operation, concur that such vetting did not begin until after
the Second World War.[12] Wesley Wark also asserts that after 1945
'the reach of security investigations and concerns broadened into
new and previously untouched areas of civil life: in loyalty programs within the Civil Service, for example ...'[13] This approach is
shared by the McDonald Commission's survey of the history of
the RCMP Security Service, which bluntly, but quite erroneously,
asserts: 'In 1946, in response to the Gouzenko revelations, the
Canadian government introduced a program of security screening in the federal public service.'[14]

Historical vogue claims not just that Canada implemented
security screening only after September 1945 but that it was
pushed and embarrassed into doing so by Igor Gouzenko's revelations about Soviet espionage. According to this scenario a
vacillating Canadian government, bolstered by recommendations

from a royal commission, reluctantly approved it. The RCMP, without relishing the assignment or having any practised skill at it, took over the task of vetting civil servants.

In fact, security screening of civil servants commenced in 1931. It was initiated to address criminal problems but quickly evolved into a means to deal with domestic dissent. The emergency of the Second World War created a situation in which screening couldbe greatly expanded to include most civil servants, all armed forces personnel, and merchant seamen. Other important targets of the RCMP's wartime inquiry were hundreds of thousands of private citizens who were placed under scrutiny primarily because of their work location. They were employed in some 500 companies supplying vital material for the Canadian war effort. Thus, security screening on a vast scale was already in effect when Gouzenko defected. In other words, the discovery of spies within the Canadian state did not launch security screening; it had existed for fifteen years before Gouzenko. This new information demands a reinterpretation of the motives behind vetting and of the practices of the Canadian state's domestic security intelligence apparatus. This book undertakes to provide that reinterpretation.

Tracing the origins of this intrusive procedure properly takes us to, but not beyond, 1945. Its early history ends there, at the moment when the security-screening apparatus was in place, ready for subsequent development. Its existence was not new, nor were the reasons for its existence; even its methods and their applicability to the screening of millions of people had been proven during the Second World War. To the extent that I sketch the system after 1945 at all, it is only to explain how similar were the postwar trends to those that had been evolving from the 1920s.

The third aim of this work is to explore the security intelligence connections between Canada, Britain, and the United States, which helped to shape the screening system here. In passing, it examines the British and American systems to discern how they were similar and different. Cooperation in security matters between these three North Atlantic countries is regarded as an important feature of the past half century. Indeed, the Second

World War is credited with irrevocably breaking Canada's old patterns of intelligence sharing and with establishing new levels of cooperation between the three states.[15] By 1945 a high level of joint effort characterized the relationship between Canada, Britain, and the United States. In Wesley Wark's opinion, Canada's wartime work on cryptanalysis explains its acceptance into the great powers' intelligence fraternity. Peter St John endorses this view, but adds that teamwork with British Security Co-ordination (BSC) was also partly responsible for elevating Canada's intelligence status.[16] Both of these factors relate to foreign espionage, a plot within the security intelligence field that is intensively cultivated and, judging by the production of articles and books, especially fertile.[17] This cooperation in espionage and counterespionage was doubtless influential in Canada's accession to the allied intelligence community. But it was not the only factor. Another significant joint international intelligence project was the surveillance of domestic dissent and its concomitant activity of security screening. This work explains the evolution of collaborative efforts between security agencies in Canada, Britain, and the United States in the security screening arena. This is an overlooked factor in the growing security intelligence integration of the three countries.[18]

Despite the voluminous writing on security matters since 1970, a comparative inquiry of this scope has never been undertaken before. Indeed, comparative studies of security intelligence history, issues, policies, and agencies are rare, although a recent overview of trends in the field contains a plea for them.[19] Furthermore, althoughthere is a substantial body of secondary literature on security agencies in the United States and Britain, most of it barely mentions security screening.[20] In the United States, some discussion about security clearance has arisen from works on an associated subject, McCarthyism and the Cold War, but the subject is secondary to other security intelligence facets.[21]

As for national comparisons, one early American study of loyalty testing and McCarthyism glances briefly at Britain, and one book on vetting in Britain also superficially contrasts British and American practice.[22] Both emphasize the differences between the two countries. No work examines several countries ov course of an extended period covering peace and war. Ana looks at how official policy and practice has been influencea by scientific methods or at how evolving technique and social changes are linked to new initiatives in security screening.

A fourth aim is to fit security screening into a technical context. In its broadest sense, state and industrial security screening must be seen as a politico-technical response to new opportunities and challenges in the twentieth century. The opportunities were primarily those presented by the adaptation of science to human identification and management, the most important of which was fingerprinting. Fingerprinting represented the application of science to an age-old identification problem. At least to its advocates, it was a solution with fabulous potential. Fingerprinting promised universal, quick, and irrefutable identification, a vital aspect of security screening. By the 1930s, it was being used as a security-screening tool, and in the same decade it was married to electromechanical tabulating equipment manufactured by the International Business Machines Company. This hybrid tool, used initially in the United States and then passed on to Canada, represents the first significant intervention of machinery into the collection and analysis of political intelligence. Recognizing the central importance of mechanization to loyalty testing helped lead me to the title of this book. The phrase 'infernal machine' has come to refer to a saboteur's bomb, a device whose malicious purpose was often hidden beneath a benign exterior. I apply the phrase to the screening system, a system founded on utter faith in the infallibility of science and technology and the merit of using it to change human behaviour. The Canadian state presented this system as beneficial to all Canadians. But it became a menace to Canadians' political rights, a blot on this country's democratic record.

Finally, this work probes the reaction of Canadians to the emergence of a new means of state surveillance. In the course of imposing this security screening, the Canadian state violated the civil liberties of hundreds of thousands of citizens. The fingerprinting of civil servants, which began in 1931, was contrary to the law, and that violation was compounded during the war.

Before 1946 no Canadian government authorized the RCMP to screen Canadian citizens. This disregard for civil rights also prevailed in the United States, where security screening was conducted without statutory authority beginning in the 1920s, contravening earlier legislation which forbade political investigations of civil servants and their dismissal for political reasons. In Britain's case, vetting proceeded from the late 1930s without explicit governmental acknowledgment. This is one significant way in which the issue of security screening calls forth adiscussion about the relationship between the state and its citizens, particularly during a period of war.

This study reveals much about the nature of the Canadian state in the twentieth century. It also casts new light upon the evolution of the security intelligence arm of the Canadian state, the RCMP, and the relationship of the federal government to the RCMP. It adds another dimension to our knowledge of the Canadian state in wartime. We know something about the Canadian state from evaluating its war policies vis à vis conscription, military priorities, production of war materials, fiscal policy, and a host of other subjects. These have all been investigated by scholars and popular writers. But we learn something quite new about the Canadian state by examining the huge operation it conducted to investigate its own citizens during the war. This study speaks to the changing nature of the relationship between the state and its citizens. In probing security screening and Canadians' response to this new state initiative, we enrich our understanding of the nature of politics as practised by the Canadian state and people.

A NOTE ON SOURCES

In the United States, the 1974 amendments to the Freedom of Information Act of 1966 fuelled an explosion of studies of the security intelligence process, particularly because the changes made it more difficult for government agencies to exempt records on the grounds of 'national security.' What Congress hath wrought, however, the executive has rent asunder. Since 1980 appropriations to cover the administration of the act have not kept pace with requests, greatly slowing the release of documents including those I requested. As compensation, I have benefited from the work of scholars who were able to use the act earlier. Their work has provided me with basic information about the United States security-screening operation, allowing comparisons to be drawn with Canada and Britain. I have also been able to use some primary source material released earlier under the act. Britain has no similar legislation to assist its researchers. Still, despite that deficiency, and the byzantine strictures of the Official Secrets Act, British writers have been able to produce several splendid security intelligence studies, upon which I have relied for the British side of the security-screening story.

Canadian historians have been slow to take advantage of the 1983 Access to Information Act. To date, few significant projects related to security intelligence in Canada have used the Access to Information Act.[23] This work, by contrast, has made extensive use of it. In researching it I have made Access Act requests of the RCMP, the Canadian Security Intelligence Service (CSIS), the departments of National Defence, Justice, Transport, Labour, and External Affairs, the Public Service Commission, and the National Research Council. I have also used the act to open volumes of material in the National Archives of Canada that were previously closed. Through this act more than 2500 previously unseen pages of records have been opened to me by individual departments. Several thousand more pages have been released at the National Archives.

The Access Act, however, is far from perfect. It was not written to provide researchers unrestricted access to government records. The act contains provisions which have allowed government agencies to withhold records relevant to this study. In my case, CSIS, the RCMP, and other government departments have informed me that, in total, they have kept at least 1200 pages of material from me, and they have censored parts of another 900 pages, citing various sections of the act. Complaints to the Information Commissioner have yielded little satisfaction.

It is impossible for anyone outside those state agencies to assess the extent to which the records I have seen represent a complete picture of the security-screening apparatus in the period up to 1945. In using the Access to Information Act, researchers must place their faith in organizations whose mandate is retaining rather than releasing hitherto confidential information. That faith, however, is not blind. The act authorizes agencies and departments to withhold records, but only under certain circumstances. While the justification for exemptions are numerous, the list of those that would apply to this study are relatively limited. They include sections that prohibit the release of the following: information obtained in confidence from the government of or an agency of a foreign state (section 13(1)); information the disclosure of which 'could reasonably be expected to be injurious to ... the detection, prevention or suppression of subversive or hostile activities,' (section 15(1)); and information which contains personal information as defined in the Privacy Act (section 19(1)).[24]

In denying access to material for this study, agencies often cited sections 13(1) and 15(1) to delete information completely, while section 19(1) tended to result only in the striking out of individuals' names. Section 13(1) unquestionably limited the extent to which this study could present a complete picture of the interactions between international security intelligence agencies with regard to security screening. Fortunately, that section has not prevented an examination of Canada's domestic security-screening apparatus. The application of section 15(1) was undoubtedly most injurious to this project. While I think that very little information fifty or more years old could 'reasonably be expected to be injurious to ... the detection, prevention or suppression of subversive or hostile activities' in contemporary Canada, CSIS and other agencies clearly did not agree, and they used this section to withhold much material. Open sources of information, including records in the National Archives of Canada, which have been presented to the archives by various government departments and agencies, have been used frequently to supplement the evidence acquired through the Access Act and compensate for the strictures of the act.

All told, then, this book represents the most ambitious and

comprehensive portrait of the origins of the Canadian security-screening system yet written. The Access to Information Act has been an invaluable tool in dislodging the locked door to the fusty intelligence underworld. Through this opening we may behold a previously hidden and fascinating aspect of Canadian history.

1
The last recourse of liars:
Testing loyalty before 1919

In September 1915, when it was obvious to combatants and civilians alike that the only soldiers who would arrive home from the front for the second Christmas of the war would be those incapable of savouring the celebration, the British minister of munitions, David Lloyd George, committed his ministry to the construction of a huge new shell factory immediately outside London. National Filling Factory No. 7, despite its pedestrian name, was a monumental undertaking. The site, at Hayes, Middlesex, was carefully chosen for access by rail, road, and canal, and proximity to an ample labour pool. No effort was spared in its construction; at the peak, some 2500 men laboured to build it. Just six weeks after the first sod was broken, the plant's deadly product was being prepared.

Security precautions for the model enterprise were exacting. A military guard took up duty in December 1915. Barracks were erected for the colonel, captain, three subalterns, and 190 non-commissioned officers and men who patrolled the premises. The whole of the facility, 397 buildings spread over 200 acres, was enclosed by a six-foot high corrugated-iron fence almost five miles in length. Those metal battlements were breached by only four gates.

At shift change, the four gates were the conduit for a surging tide of workers; 7500 men and women laboured on each shift. To enter, each worker passed through a barrier and was handed a pass by an officially designated 'recognizer.' A few steps further on, a policeman admitted only those with a pass. Without being recognized, no worker was allowed to enter the factory.[1]

The significance of this security-screening method at the flag-ship of the British munitions plants at the beginning of the First World War should not be lost. To the minds of those who thought about such things, security meant erecting walls and guarding them vigilantly to exclude those who posed a threat from *outside*. The burden of reviewing those who were *inside*, ironically, fell to a tiny corps of people whose mind-numbing duty required them to place the seal of safety upon the faces of thousands of people streaming pell-mell through a plant gate in the chaotic and fretful moments of shift change.

The essential elements of this approach to security screening are evident. One is its total reliance upon human agents. If the problem of ascertaining the trustworthiness of employees was registering on those who concerned themselves with such matters – and it was beginning to – applying mechanical methods to ease the burden was but a scheme in the minds of visionaries. The overt, obvious, and oppressive physical security precautions – impressive as they appeared – were still utterly rudimentary. A second element is that suspicion was still focused on those out-side the organization. Those inside were, by and large, trusted. By the end of the war, that method was already breaking down; within three decades it would be changed totally.

In some ways, the humble factory recognizer was peculiarly British. In the twentieth century, Britain did not see the paranoia and loyalty testing which swept the United States in the First and Second World Wars, and again after 1945. Indeed, it was not until 1948 that Britain officially began a civil servant–vetting program. But the recognizer, and the security-screening method he epito-mized, was more characteristic of his time than he was exclusive to his country. In the United States, too, security screening up to the end of the First World War relied on human agents – but many more of them and acting in different capacities. And there, too, attention was directed towards those deemed to be outsiders. But beginning in the First World War, and decisively after 1919, secu-rity screening changed irrevocably wherever it was practised. The recognizer of National Filling Factory No. 7, even as he granted the cachet of security to a young woman from London who he hoped was a new packer in No. 20 Clean Room, symbolized an obsolete system.

In a review of security-screening practices in Britain, the United States, and Canada before 1919, several trends come forth. One of them is the constant demand for some objective method to ascertain the loyalty of state and private employees. A second is the transition in concepts of loyalty and loyalty testing which emerged about the beginning of the twentieth century. The third is the common orientation towards loyalty in the three Anglo-American countries. The fourth is the sea change in views of who constituted a threat to security which was initiated by the Bolshevik Revolution and the popular response to it in capitalist countries. The last is the arrival of professional agencies in Britain, the United States, and Canada, which were charged with safeguarding the state from this perceived revolutionary threat, a responsibility that included security screening.

SECURITY SCREENING IN BRITAIN

Looking at how loyalty has been tested throughout history, we see that the British recognizer was in good company. For centuries, objective standards have been sought to resolve the dilemma of which noble, servant, or apprentice to trust. Indeed, the problem of assessing the loyalty of employees and civil servants was addressed in one of the first manuals of political security and intelligence, which was written more than two thousand years ago. Kautilya's *Arthasastra* describes the security problems inherent in the Indian feudal political culture of his time. Loyalty to the king was of paramount concern. In this era before vast bureaucracies, it was the inner sentiments of senior advisers that had to be examined. And the test methods – individual, conspiratorial, manipulative – were appropriate to an age of personal loyalty.[2]

Similarly, the feudal era in Europe, with its emphasis on personal fidelity, saw a preoccupation with individuals' loyalty. In Goran Therborn's memorable words, bonds based on personal loyalty 'constituted the fundamental technology of feudal rule.'[3] In fact, the bonds themselves were but the social trappings of loyalty. The testing mechanism (the technology) characteristic of feudalism was the oath of allegiance. According to Marc Bloch, a prominent historian of the feudal millenium, loyalty queries in feudal Europe embraced virtually everyone from lord to peasant, unlike those in ancient India, which were reserved for the highly placed. Scrutiny of loyalty was one part of an efficient system of social control in which the constraints imposed by chief upon subordinate facilitated the obedience of both of them to the king. As Bloch notes, the value of this system was equally evident to Charlemagne as it was a thousand years later to Tsar Nicholas I, who 'boasted that in his *pomeshchiks* (lords of villages) he had "a hundred thousand police superintendents."[4] The oath was also grounded ideologically by a common faith in a Christian god. But important as the appeal to divinity was, rulers invariably found it expedient to engage a secular guarantor for their subjects' loyalty. The eyes and ears of Nicholas's *pomeshchiks*, therefore, were essential checks on his subjects' public words.

In England, the period of shifting and confused religious and political affiliations ushered in by Henry VIII's break with Roman Catholic ecclesiastical domination produced an obsession with loyalty. More important, the Tudors derived an apparatus to verify it which would survive in various forms until the twentieth century. Henry VIII introduced a series of tests, based on oaths, to gauge the trustworthiness of his subjects. These were refined under Mary Tudor and Elizabeth I to improve their enforcement and were so successful, in the words of Harold Hyman, that 'By the end of Elizabeth's reign, England was honeycombed with a network of justices of the peace, pursuivants, civil courts, militia units, ecclesiastical investigating commissions, spies, informers, *agents provocateurs*, and port officers, all empowered to administer the current loyalty tests to all Englishmen.'[5]

Oaths remained the favoured method to assess loyalty until late in the nineteenth century, when several factors combined to sap their perceived effectiveness. One was the growth of the state and the civil service. The prevailing ideology of the political élite remained *laissez faire* liberalism, but nineteenth-century Britain nonetheless saw a remarkable extension of state intervention in society. Parliament passed many laws intended to change the behaviour of individuals and corporations, and, more importantly, it also enacted legislation to enforce such acts. Regulation of poor relief, public health, and factory conditions were but three issues which required supervision by a state bureaucracy. As a result, the size, complexity, and reach of the state increased considerably throughout the century.[6]

Efficiency, economy, and ideology also demanded an end to political interference in the choice of civil servants. Reforms passed throughout the nineteenth century paved the way for a professional and non-partisan public service that was free from patronage appointments.[7] Casting off the oath as a functional test of civil servants' loyalty occurred at the same time that patronage began to be phased out. By 1870 open competition for civil service jobs prevailed in most British government departments.[8] About the same time, British reformers observed America's unhappy experience with oaths during and immediately after its Civil War and concluded that Britain's own statute books ought to be purged of obsolete and useless oath requirements.[9]

Monarchs were not alone in wishing to ascertain and ensure the allegiance of their subjects. A kindred impulse emerged among employers, who even by the seventeenth century attempted to determine that they hired none but the most tractable workers. The merit of this kind of surveillance must have been early apparent to capitalists. In a system which requires a free market in labour, an obvious immediate problem is how to ensure that the factory hand who has arrived from elsewhere in response to an employer's call is reliable, responsible, and, perhaps most importantly, not radical.

An early case of industrial vetting occurred at the close of the seventeenth century in London, where journeymen hatters, who were organized into protective clubs, took action against their employers' efforts to reduce wages. Master hatters retaliated in 1697 with a scheme for each journeyman to obtain a 'character note' or 'leaving certificate' from his employer, with the enjoinder, in the words of Sidney and Beatrice Webb, that 'no master should employ a journeyman who did not bring with him a certificate from his previous employer.'[10] With the Industrial Revolution, reviews of workers' political and shop-floor practice became widespread, and some of these were held against them in their attempts to work elsewhere. In some instances, the scrutiny was extended into a blacklist. This kind was especially prevalent within the vital railway industry. One example took place in 1839, when the chief engineer of the Grand Junction Railway wrote to another company advising that several enginemen had been discharged for insubordination. In urging that the men be refused employment, the chief engineer pointed out 'the importance of possessing efficient control over this class of men, in which all railways are equally interested ... '[11]

Victorian Britain was, however, remarkably free of state-sponsored political policing and security screening, an innocence founded on a curious paradox, according to Bernard Porter. To Victorians steeped in the benefits of liberalism, political systems were defended most effectively by having no defences at all. 'The best way to disable "liberation" movements is to persuade people that they are already free; and the much-vaunted absence of a British political police branch went a long way to doing this.'[12]

This sense of confidence began to ebb in the 1880s and was gravely wounded before Gavrilo Princip fired a bullet into Europe's heart in June 1914. Bernard Porter dates the beginnings of the 'secret state' in Britain to the half-dozen years before the war. In the period from 1909 to 1911 a number of key security measures were launched. The domestic security intelligence agency, MI5, and its foreign arm, MI6, were founded. The Special Branch of the London Metropolitan Police was revamped, bringing it close to being a regular domestic counter-subversive agency. The modern Official Secrets Act was passed.[13] The political environment of the day had much to do with why these decisive developments occurred then. Rising demands from workers, women, and Irish nationalists caused conservative members of the establishment to believe that Britain was coming close to disaster. Basil Thomson, who became assistant commissioner in charge of the London Metropolitan Police Criminal Investigation Department in June 1913, was heard to remark then that Britain was headed straight for revolution 'unless there was a European war to divert the current.'[14] The war, when it occurred, had an effect contrary to Thomson's wishes, except perhaps in one regard. Its impact on the composition and scope of the domestic secret service in Britain was greater than any other event for one hundred years.[15] Porter argues that, while Britain did not have a political police before the First World War, within a few months after August 1914 Britain did have 'a proper political police.' The speed of the transformation indicates to him that conditions had been prepared for this outcome in the years before the war. 'The pieces were all in place.'[16]

Wartime conditions further strengthened security intelligence centralization and coordination. Initially, temporary organizations sprang up, among them the Ministry of Munitions Labour Intelligence Division, a title later changed to the Parliamentary Military Secretary Department No. 2 because the first title conveyed too much information about the branch's function. But PMS2 was plagued by overzealousness and inefficiency. Moreover, an American military attaché in London bemoaned the impossibility of getting information from the several agencies operating in Britain. So the government amalgamated its intelligence efforts under the umbrella of the Special Branch of the London police and its own domestic security agency, MI5.[17]

The First World War also whipped up a search for enemies. A register of aliens was begun secretly in 1911; by 1913 it included nearly 29,000 names.[18] As the war marched along on its baleful course, foreign residents became a particular focus of hostility. By the Aliens Restriction Act of 5 August 1914, all foreign citizens had to register. Eventually more than 100,000 would do so. Registration, in turn, led to internment, beginning in May 1915.[19] By war's end more than 32,000 people were interned and 20,000 had been sent back to their home countries.[20] This internment and deportation shows that security practice was relatively unrefined in the First World War. Faced with a group of people whose loyalty was uncertain, authorities interned large numbers of them, since they had neither the interest in investigating each individual nor the capacity to do so.

As the British political fabric began to rip because of the war, the targets of security inquiries shifted. Before 1916 espionage and sabotage had been the pre-eminent security problems. As the war dragged on, political subversion – 'general war-weariness, the greater activity of pacifist groups and the rumbling of industrial unrest' – emerged as grounds for anxiety.[21] The state's preoccupation with subversion was further heightened by the Bolshevik Revolution, which dramatically polarized political life in the world.[22] Some saw it as the signal hope for the future, others as the death knell of civilization. However it was viewed, the revolution's international appeal was, especially in the early years, the foremost Soviet impact on the western world.[23] With Britain the main bulwark against the spread of Bolshevism and its major espionage target until 1945, the British security agencies became preoccupied with this new menace in their midst.[24] By the last year of the war they were directing more effort into investigating Bolshevism than they were into counter-espionage and the control of enemy aliens.[25]

Seen in retrospect, the years immediately before the First World War and the war itself wrought deep changes in the security environment in Britain. Fears of espionage and sabotage directed from abroad gave way to concern about domestic subversion. Still, the war did not see the introduction of systematic security screening for British citizens. That measure would arrive as the country prepared for the century's second world conflict.

SECURITY SCREENING IN THE UNITED STATES

Given its preoccupation with verifying loyalty, it is no surprise that, when England began its colonial expansion early in the reign of James I, loyalty oaths and testing were part of the cultural baggage of the North American colonists. At each change of monarch from 1689 to 1776, colonial administrators were required to renew their pledge of allegiance, a practice which also carried over to the territories added to British North America through conquest of

French colonies.[26] Loyalty oaths to the monarch reflected the prevailing doctrine of the relationship between the individual and the state. As a subject, each individual had a personal relationship to the monarch, not a generalized membership within a political community.

The political instability and shifting fortunes of British and American forces in the American Revolutionary War stimulated a firmer demand for loyalty oaths as a way to distinguish Tory from Whig. Since both sides insisted on such declarations, it became common for thousands of confused or intimidated people simply to bend with the exigencies of the moment. Benjamin Franklin vividly captured the prevailing contempt for oaths when he declared that 'I have never regarded them otherwise than as the last recourse of liars.'[27] The fact that thousands on either side had a minimal attachment to the oaths they had sworn, however, created a nightmare after the war for British and American loyalty commissioners, whose task was to sort out the tangle of conflicting claims for compensation. Harold Hyman's study of the period led him to conclude that 'more than a decade of calm, unhurried postwar investigations by able parliamentary commissions into the realities of loyalty-testing in the American Revolution proved that no loyalty test, British or American, was adequate to prove loyalty.'[28] In the anti-authoritarian atmosphere of the new republic, the passion for universal loyalty declarations soon subsided. A decade after the end of the Revolutionary War, Americans had put aside loyalty oaths and testing.

That resolve did not survive long. When another convulsion of violence seized the youthful country in 1861, fear of traitors within the federal civil service instantly boiled to the surface. By the second week of the Civil War, Lincoln's cabinet had already demanded an oath of allegiance to the Union from everyone in each government department – 'from the head Secretary to the lowest messenger,' in the words of the attorney general.[29] A congressional committee of five members was quickly struck to investigate government employees who were suspected of disloyalty or who refused to take the oath. Cabinet's decision, meanwhile, had been confirmed by Congress, which passed similar legislation in August 1861.[30] Two more such laws were passed the following year.[31] Civil servants were not the only ones subject to what came to be called, in a reflection of the newest naval technology, the ironclad test oath. By the war's end, also under scrutiny were military officers, newspaper correspondents accompanying the Union army, telegraphers, judges, pensioners, and postal contractors. The end of the bloodshed in 1865 brought not a relaxation in security testing but an extension of it even to civilians throughout the rebellious states. These oath laws were not repealed until 1884.[32]

The Civil War and Reconstruction experience left many Americans disenchanted with loyalty oaths as a method of determining loyalty. This attitude was accurately summed up by a Union officer who confided to having 'a dislike for test oaths, and [I] preferred to make conduct the test ... '[33] This postwar distrust of oaths carried over into the creation of a new regulation protecting the privacy of American civil servants. Civil Service Rule 1 of 1884 forbade any inquiry into the political or religious opinions or affiliation of any applicant for the federal civil service.[34] This enlightened policy, however, did not prevent a recurrence of the loyalty inquiries. When another war threatened, civil servants and others again were required to reveal their political sentiments.

The U.S. Civil Service rule of 1884 which forbade the political or religious screening of federal civil servants was violated in the First World War. America's brief participation in that war touched off an intense spasm of loyalty investigations by state and private citizens alike. President Woodrow Wilson instructed the Civil Service Commission to remove any employee whose commitment to the state was cast into doubt 'by reasons of his conduct, sympathies, or utterances' In 1917 and 1918, the commission conducted 2672 loyalty investigations, and in 1918 barred 660 applicants from employment. Military personnel were also individually screened. Every officer granted a commission was investigated, as were thousands of Red Cross workers, religious volunteers, and entertainers.[35] Educators were particular targets of patriotic zealotry. David Caute reports that university professors suspected of pacifist or pro-German sentiment

were shown the door, and between 1917 and 1923 charges of disloyalty were levelled against teachers in thirteen states, leading
to firings in eight of them.[36]

There was cause for some of the fear of foreign agents. From
1914 to 1917 the German government mounted a destructive
campaign of sabotage against the United States, which was a
major arms supplier for the Western Allies. A comprehensive
list of cases compiled years later documented ninety-three incidents of German sabotage in North America from January 1915
to January 1917.[37] Two incidents alone, an explosion at a munitions storage site at Black Tom, New Jersey, and a fire at a shell
factory, at Kingsland, New Jersey, killed scores of people and
caused almost $40 million in damages.[38] The sabotage ceased
after the American government expelled German embassy officials several months before the United States entered the war in
April 1917.[39]

Once the country was at war, there were numerous security
excesses, mostly perpetrated by zealots who, while formally outside the state, operated with the blessing of the administration.
Two organizations, the American Protective League (APL) and
the Loyal Legion of Loggers and Lumbermen (LLLL), carried out
a witch-hunt on behalf of the federal government and private
employers. With the personal encouragement of U.S. attorney
general Thomas Gregory, the APL grew to a force of 300,000 volunteer detectives who, under the guise of semi-official spy-catchers, conducted over 3 million character investigations for the
government. These checks were conducted and transmitted without due regard for discretion and the consequences of the reports
for the careers of people under investigation. Harold Hyman has
summed up the APL's legacy in this way: 'Everywhere, personal
feuds, political enmities, financial opportunism, racial, religious,
and class prejudices – all the ills of power almost unrestrained by
effective authority – resulted in innumerable acts of terror,
unmeasurable injuries to individual self-respect and dignity,
incalculable and unnecessary fear.'[40]

By 1919, the American Protective League had outgrown its use-
fulness to the state and to the Wilson administration. The govern-

ment found it could not tolerate an agency that had become too brazen and too powerful for its nominal master. When the end of the war stripped the league of its raison d'être, a new attorney general, A. Mitchell Palmer, seized the opportunity to distance the government from its upstart child. Palmer, then in the process of leading an official campaign of anti-red purges, rebuffed private patriotic groups, declaring that aid from them was 'entirely at variance with our theories of government.' As Hyman noted, 'amateur internal security operations would destroy public confidence in constituted authorities, upset community life, and imperil standards of objectivity and justice.'[41]

Born in the same spirit as the APL, the Loyal Legion of Loggers and Lumbermen was another venture into loyalty testing by semi-official organizations. Its ostensible objective was to seek out and prevent industrial sabotage in the lumber districts of the American Pacific Northwest. Set up in November 1917, the legion was a combination of company union, security-screening body, and central clearing-house for blacklists of Industrial Workers of the World militants.[42] Helping to maintain control of dissatisfied workers made the LLLL, like the APL, valuable to employers and the state. David Davis has concluded that by 1918 disciplining labour and suppressing radicals were those organizations' major functions.[43]

The security method represented by groups like the APL and the LLLL was characteristic of the United States prior to 1919. It is true, as Davis has written, that 'the history of American intelligence operations has been marked by decentralization, amateurism, and jurisdictional rivalry, all of which were encouraged by the constitutional division between state and federal powers and by a native preference for private enterprise.'[44] But in focusing on what he calls 'participatory sleuthing,' Davis fails to acknowledge the important organizing function of the American state. Even the zealous amateur spy-catchers of the First World War did not operate without the sanction of the state. In fact, they acted as semi-official agents of the cabinet, and sometimes of rival members of the cabinet. Moreover, the authority provided by this link to the federal government was essential to the success of the APL and the LLLL.

SECURITY SCREENING IN CANADA

Like the United States, Canada began its life as a colony at a time when loyalty oaths were common in the European countries. The application of oaths was reinforced by this country's troubled infancy. Wars due to economic and political competition between European powers scarred the period before England's conquest of New France in 1760. Nor did the conquest settle matters. The period from 1760 to 1867 was highly troubled, marked by an influx of Loyalists, the immigration of people with sharply varying political views, war with the United States from 1812 to 1814, uprisings in 1837–8, and invasions by Fenians. Similar challenges in the republic to the south sparked, as we have seen, near hysteria and swift recourse to loyalty testing. It would be surprising to see a different pattern in the fledgling northern sibling, and in fact Canada pursued a parallel course. Canadian political authorities at first relied upon oaths as loyalty tests but found them increasingly unsatisfactory.

The Acadians are the best-known victims of the colonial preoccupation with loyalty guarantees. The story of the Catholic, French-speaking Acadians whose settlement of the Bay of Fundy shores was cut short by their deportation in 1755 has entered the realm of Canadian mythology. The crux of the issue was conflict between the Acadians and their British governors over the validity of loyalty oaths. The importance of such oaths is indicated by the fact that, in the four years after the 1713 Treaty of Utrecht awarded Acadia to Britain, colonial officials commanded the inhabitants to swear oaths of allegiance on five separate occasions. Each time they refused, declaring that their neutral practice was sufficient proof of their loyalty. But in 1755, when a proxy war between France and England broke out in North America, Charles Lawrence, lieutenant governor of Nova Scotia, insisted upon a formal oath. In the absence of such an attestation, Lawrence ordered the Acadians' deportation.[45] The Acadian case demonstrates the importance of the loyalty oath as a ritual of allegiance.

After the conquest of New France, the British administration demanded oaths of allegiance from their new subjects, a process that affirmed their fidelity to a new crown.[46] But this passion for loyalty oaths subsided in the absence of any threat of reconquest by the French and because of the population's manifest acceptance of British rule.

The Loyalists who flooded into Britain's Atlantic and Quebec colonies after 1783 had seen their loyalty challenged in the United States. Even though their departure from the United States was, for many, a ringing affirmation of devotion to the British crown, the Loyalists who arrived in Canada were themselves subject to loyalty tests. Everyone who received a land grant in the colonies of British North America (BNA) was required to take an oath of allegiance.[47] This stipulation did not, however, deter Americans in large numbers from taking advantage of the free land opened up just over the border. By 1812 Upper Canada had some 100,000 inhabitants, of whom about 80 per cent were Americans. Loyalist Richard Cartwright had warned the lieutenant governor as early as 1799 of the dangers inherent in this influx. In doing so he pointed out the dubious value of an oath as a test of faithfulness: 'Now, it is not to be expected that a man will change his political principles or prejudices by crossing a river, or that an oath of allegiance is at once to check the bias of the mind ... '[48]

This flaw in the procedure notwithstanding, oaths of allegiance were frequently demanded in British North America in the first half of the nineteenth century. By mid-century, however, the dispute over loyalty was largely resolved and the immigration of Americans of the first decades of the century ended; the 1850s and early 1860s proved to be a period of peace and prosperity in BNA. In these circumstances, the need for loyalty oaths significantly declined and little more was heard of them in the nineteenth century.[49]

In the late 1860s, however, two events produced a renewed interest in ascertaining allegiance, although it was significant that measures other than oaths emerged as the primary means to address the new threats. One was a direct military threat from American territory. In the 1860s and early 1870s, Irish republicans organized into Fenian brotherhoods were drilling and collecting arms in American border towns as a prelude to invading British North America. Several attacks were launched. The second stimulus to new security measures was the assassination of D'Arcy McGee by a Fenian. McGee, a Father of Confederation and an Irishman who espoused Canadian nationalism, was shot and killed near the parliament buildings in Ottawa in 1868. These events provided the pretext for the first organized security intelligence activity of the Canadian government. Collecting information through the use of undercover agents among the Fenians, the government of Sir John A. Macdonald used the intelligence to screen persons entering Canada or applying for government positions.[50] Even if the government had been inclined to use the traditional method of assessing loyalty – the oath of allegiance – the Fenian problem was not conducive to being resolved by such a measure. Thus, by the 1860s, Canada took tentative steps to reverse its earlier method of assessing loyalty and to gauge the reliability of citizens and civil servants in a different way. The new instrument was a secret security and intelligence force, which relied on clandestine methods. True, it was a halting beginning; in 1981 the McDonald Commission report described the federal security intelligence operation before 1914 as 'intermittent.'[51] But already it was using intrusive techniques, like opening mail, which in Britain were officially regarded as beneath contempt until the 1880s.[52]

As in the United States and Britain, the First World War was a turning-point in Canada's security practice. Initially, the primary security threat appeared to be the familiar one – people of foreign birth. Alarmists both inside and outside the government were apprehensive at the presence among a population of just 8 million of some 500,000 people who traced their ancestry to Germany or the Austro-Hungarian empire. While most of the former had been long established in Canada, about 30,000 Germans and another 100,000 people from the sprawling Hapsburg empire had come since 1901. At least theoretically, they remained faithful to their former rulers, and so were the focus of intense fear and scrutiny.[53] In August 1914 the Canadian government issued a series of proclamations addressed to Germans and Austrians, which prevented military reservists from leaving the country and threatened to arrest those who attempted to defy the ban but which promised to release those who would sign an undertaking to refrain from acts of hostility. By the end of October, some 10,000 had made such an oath or had been imprisoned.

Like the United States, Canada was the object of German sabotage plans in the First World War. In February 1915, for instance, Franz von Papen, the military attaché in the German embassy in Washington induced a German reserve officer to attack the international bridge at Vanceboro, Maine, which linked Halifax with American munitions suppliers. The officer made a farcical and unsuccessful bid to carry out his instructions. One of few cases of attempted or actual sabotage in Canada, it must certainly have heightened public fear.[54] Even at the beginning of the war the public mood was such that the Canadian government had to adopt a firm stand with regard to enemy aliens; in October 1914 an order in council required enemy aliens to report to local registrars, who decided whether or not to intern individuals. By the end of the war over 80,000 enemy aliens had registered, and 8600 more were interned.[55]

Although internment was intended to mollify public hysteria about sabotage and espionage, it was not enough.[56] As in the United States, amateur spy-hunters found and reported sedition suspects aplenty. This caused no end of additional work for the director of internment operations, General Sir William Otter. The public also assiduously assumed the role of security assessors, deciding, for example, that two senior civic officials of German origin in Toronto and London were security threats. In 1916 the Anti-German League in Toronto dedicated itself to driving Germans from the public service, exposing twenty who had managed to cling to their jobs.[57]

As the war ground on, labour took advantage of full employment to recoup its wage and bargaining losses of the prewar recession.[58] In Hamilton, these efforts culminated in a bitter strike at the Steel Company of Canada which divided the work force and the community. Stelco management responded to the bid for better working conditions by employing a spy system to keep track of troublemaking workers.[59] What made this novel, however, was state involvement. Imperial Munitions Board (IMB) representatives, for a short time, acted as a clearing-house for an informal blacklist system by feeding the names of union activists to the Stelco management. IMB chairman Sir Joseph Flavelle quickly repudiated these 'indiscretions' when unionists complained.[60] The Canadian state was not ready, yet, to use security intelligence to coordinate private employers' efforts to scrutinize their workers. But it would do so with considerable vigour in the Second World War.

There is, similarly, no indication that it operated a systematic security-screening operation for civil servants or industrial workers during the war. Indeed, as the McDonald Commission noted, the state's security intelligence activities at the time were not well coordinated or centralized. By the fall of 1918 the federal government was receiving reports from four security intelligence agencies. This lack of coordination was not rectified until the Mounted Police absorbed the Dominion Police in 1920, creating a single federal security police agency.[61]

As in the United States, the labour ferment which struck Hamilton and many other Canadian cities in the war stimulated a rash of charges that foreign agitators were fomenting trouble.[62] Disloyalty was again equated with foreign birth. But a new security threat had emerged. Political radicalism – labelled at the time as Bolshevism or communism – had by war's end assumed pre-eminence in the pantheon of demons.[63] The new threat would, in the estimation of RCMP historian S.W. Horrall, 'lead to a complete re-organization of the entire system of internal security.'[64]

The security agencies and their political masters were unanimous in their hatred of Bolshevism.[65] The founding of the Communist International in March 1919, a direct result of the Bolshevik triumph in Russia in 1917, signalled a new departure for Western security agencies as much as it did for revolutionaries. The Soviet Union's encouragement of world revolution presented security agencies with an unprecedented menace. The Soviet Union was advocating and promoting an international class war. This threat gave Western security services a unique opportunity to link internal dissent with a foreign antagonist, as the RCMP commissioner took particular pains to point out in his 1921 report. A.B. Perry observed that a 'Communist Party of Canada' had been organized that year 'under the direct orders of the Third International at Moscow.' The party's efforts at fomenting rebellion, he declared, represented 'the execution of plans conceived outside the country, and furnished to and imposed upon our agitators from abroad.'[66] No security intelligence agency could fail to rise to the challenge posed by communism.

THE STATE OF SECURITY SCREENING IN 1919

In 1919, the Western world was at a transition point in its appreciation of loyalty testing. The assessment method, which custom and faith had deemed effective for centuries, had lost its punch. The belief was quickly waning that a loyalty oath had the power to fuse a solid bond of fidelity. In separate countries, Benjamin Franklin and Richard Cartwright had long before perceived this flaw. By the twentieth century its ineffectiveness was obvious. In all three countries under review, oaths had begun to be treated, in the words of Harold Hyman, as 'obsolete indexes to patriotism.'[67] People still took them, although with less frequency, and much less credence was attached to their value.

New conditions in the early years of the 20th century helped to undermine existing methods of and criteria for ascertaining loyalty, and created a demand for a new loyalty-testing mechanism. The new method was security screening. It represented a development on and improvement over oaths. Its superiority was founded upon its objectivity, which stood in contrast to the oath's subjectivity. For instance, the oath of allegiance had no verification mechanism attached to it, although, as earlier indicated, astute rulers tried to ensure that a local agent was on hand to supervise the subject who had affirmed his loyalty. Security screening, however, promised to provide confirmation of loyalty, not just affirmation of it. The screening system sought to accumulate and have readily to hand intelligence that would corroborate the subject's allegiance. Science, most particularly in the form of fingerprinting, was brought to bear on the problem of comparing subjects (applicants for citizenship or the civil service) with people considered to be risks. Perhaps most importantly, the system would be operated by specialized, highly organized, and centralized security intelligence agencies.

One of the new conditions in the twentieth century that stimulated security screening was the growth of the state and of a civil service to administer it. By the late nineteenth century reform was overdue in public services, especially in Canada, where patronage was rife. When reform did occur, it introduced a new ethic into the appointment process. Patronage, for all its flaws, at least had the advantage of ensuring that public officials were known personally to the politicians. The patron-client relationship at the root of patronage was strikingly feudal. The merit system of hiring, which in Canada was given a strong push by the patronage abuses of the First World War, fractured the personal relationship as the foundation of government bureaucracy.[68] In the United States, the merit system allowed people with more education to enter the public service for the first time. Suspicion of them harboured by politicians and their constituents probably hardened as they attained influence within the government.[69] So a larger, impersonal, and educated civil service, which no longer had a personal relationship to political parties, might have contributed to the perceived need for some better way to determine loyalty than oaths.

The Bolshevik Revolution in 1917 also helped to force a change in the method of ascertaining and ensuring loyalty. It did so by shifting the focal point of loyalty. Proletarian internationalism put forward a new object of veneration. Workers' true devotion ought not to be lodged with a monarch or a nation but with the world revolution, whose standard bearer was the Soviet Union. The Kellock-Taschereau Royal Commission, which in 1946 investigated the Gouzenko revelations, captured well what had troubled Western leaders for three decades: 'the courses of study in the [communist] 'cells' undermine gradually the loyalty of the young man or woman who joins them ... In some cases the effect of these study courses seems to be a gradual development of a sense of divided loyalties, or in extreme cases of a transferred loyalty ... Thus it seems to happen that through these study-groups some adherents ... transfer a part or most of their loyalties to another country ... '[70] This sense of transferred loyalty, British Prime Minister Clement Attlee concluded in 1948, 'can be inimical to the State.'[71] Speaking in 1944, the U.S. civil service commissioner, Arthur Flemming, carried the issue of a communist's loyalty to its extreme conclusion, declaring: 'A member of the Communist Party or a follower of the Communist Party line has clearly indicated that his primary loyalty is to a foreign political group owing its allegiance to a foreign government, and that there is therefore a strong presumption in favor of his willingness to take steps designed to overthrow our Constitutional form of Government if directed to do so.'[72] According to this way of thinking, adherents of communism had transferred more than their loyalty; they had placed their rationality and will in the hands of a foreign power. Asking such a devotee to affirm loyalty to his or her own capitalist government was at best futile, at worst dangerous.

Not only was the established *method* of loyalty testing shattered by the radically new conditions which emerged around the First World War, the established *criteria* of loyalty had changed. Defining what constitutes a legitimate threat to security and fixing criteria for assessing an individual's actions in the light of this definition had been a consistent security-screening problem throughout the centuries. Almost constantly in the period before 1919, foreign birth was a reliable criterion of suspicion, even in a country like Britain where immigrants were relatively few. This extreme fear of foreigners was perhaps most vehemently expressed in December 1915 by American President Woodrow Wilson, who inveighed against 'citizens ... born under other flags ... who have poured the poison of disloyalty into the very arteries of our national life.'[73] Even as this obsession was peaking, however, it was being undermined by a new fear, requiring a different, and much more subtle, criterion of disloyalty – ideology. Moreover, this new definition of disloyalty challenged all conventional methods for identifying dissidents. No one has phrased this more succinctly than RCMP historian S.W. Horrall: 'In the past, disloyalty was usually associated with a person's racial origin, religion, language, or social class, characteristics not easy to hide. The commitment to Marx was an ideological one. The converts came from every race, social group, profession and creed. If necessary, their conversion could easily be kept from sight.'[74] No litmus test existed to analyse a person's thoughts and place them on the political spectrum. The mission for security intelligence agencies was to devise one.

This transformation in the criteria of disloyalty corresponded with larger social changes. Following the rapid influx of Europeans before the First World War, immigration to Canada and the United States fell.[75] The easy equation of foreign birth with disloyalty was not only no longer possible, it was no longer useful.[76] The crude reductionism that foreign birth equalled disloyalty came into doubt. But this gave security screeners no easier work. If anything, it complicated their task, since it demanded more complex criteria of loyalty. That challenge would be the weightiest problem for security screening during the next half century.[77]

By the end of the First World War, then, the flaws in the established loyalty-testing method and the familiar criteria of disloyalty called for a substantial reform of the bodies charged with assessing political reliability. This did not mean a new interest by the state; it always had sought to ensure its own survival. However, as Hinsley and Simkins point out, preserving security was previously a chore performed 'informally, not to say casually, at the margin of the main machinery of state, by authorities whose activities were shielded from popular curiosity.'[78] In the twentieth century, security moved from the margins of the state to assume a more central place within it.

This was but one new feature that emerged by 1919. Another initiative was the amalgamation of the myriad security units, divisions, and branches into a single, coordinated, centralized security agency. Proliferation of security efforts plagued Britain, the United States, and Canada before and during the war. In each country the state took the opportunity during the war or immediately at its end to set up a single security unit. In Britain PMS2 was closed and its work was given to existing security organizations. In Canada centralization took place in 1920, with the reorganization of the Royal Canadian Mounted Police. Improving security intelligence was one of the principal reasons for the restructuring.[79] In the United States the Federal Bureau of Investigation carved a niche for itself in the First World War by investigating and cataloguing the political opinions of Americans, and then followed up by founding its Intelligence Division in August 1919. J. Edgar Hoover, its first director, had, since 1917, been in charge of counter-radical activity as special assistant to the attorney general.[80]

A tradition of amateur security investigation persisted in the United States into the twentieth century. But even in that bastion of free enterprise, security screening as an individual endeavour began to fall under the sway of organizations. The efficacy of human agents and amateur efforts to enforce discipline and loyalty became at best suspect. Unpaid local officials were inadequate to the task of being the eyes, ears, and hands of the security apparatus.[81] In some cases they acted subjectively. In some places they were simply too vulnerable to retaliation from neighbours, and they sometimes shared local hostility to central authority. In times of crisis they were likely to side with their fellows.[82] Similarly, by 1920 RCMP commissioner A.B. Perry, 'the Father of Canada's present Security Service,' had lost faith in ordinary citizens as a reliable source of intelligence. Local police were also distrusted because of their flirtation with unions.[83] The dubious trustworthiness and vulnerability of human agents – especially unpaid ones – demonstrated the need to make security intelligence agencies more professional, bureaucratic, and regular. This development was already occurring within public services. Paying security intelligence officials provided some guarantee of consistency, efficiency, control, and loyalty.

By the First World War, state agencies in Britain, the United States, and Canada had begun to cooperate by sharing intelligence and experience in security methods. There were some exceptions to this trend: Britain ran agents in Canada in the war, and Canada did the same in the United States.[84] But as Horrall has observed about the RCMP, the war stimulated 'closer links with

British and American security agencies than ever before.'[85] After the war, the level of cooperative action between the three North Atlantic countries continued to grow. For instance, at least for a time, all three countries kept and circulated inventories of immigrants rejected for political reasons, radicals deported, and known Bolsheviks.[86]

The newly centralized state security agencies were also well placed to adopt scientific methods to aid their work. This movement corresponded to a trend in industrial society which had been going on for years and which, through Taylorism – the scientific measurement and control of work – would advance in the twentieth century. Visions of applying technology to the problem of creating a new security method were not new. One American suggested in 1873 that Congress offer 'a reward for the discovery of an invention which would provide a proper way of determining loyalty.'[87] In the 1830s the French police had moved with the changing times to embrace card indexes and the classifications systems of business. Other security agencies followed. The second directive issued by the Royal North-West Mounted Police commissioner after it assumed new security duties in 1918 was to establish a comprehensive system of security records on radical organizations and individuals. One of the innovations introduced to the FBI's radical-hunting division by J. Edgar Hoover was a card index of suspects. By 1919 it contained some 200,000 names.[88] But Hoover's unique gift to security work was the introduction of a scientific tool which initially seemed of greatest value for criminal identification – fingerprinting.

2

The politics of identification: Fingerprinting to 1939

On 22 October 1931, when he ordered the fingerprinting of all members of the Royal Canadian Mounted Police, Commissioner Major-General Sir J.H. MacBrien expected some of the resistance but probably few of the remarkable consequences of his act.[1] Why he issued the directive is not recorded, but the conditions surrounding his decision provide some clues. A war hero who brought considerable political influence with him, MacBrien was a forceful modernizing leader of the force.[2] Then just three months into his tenure as commissioner, MacBrien saw himself as a new broom. The RCMP had been established as a police force with military regulations and strict discipline. MacBrien would maintain that tradition, but he would also sweep the force into the scientific age. It was a curious anomaly that a corps which by 1931 had twenty-five years' experience in fingerprinting, and which prided itself on selecting only the finest, most dedicated young men, did not already make a basic check on the backgrounds of its recruits by comparing their fingerprints to those in the Fingerprint Section at headquarters. MacBrien also had reason to believe that the Communist party was seeking to slip its members into the RCMP.[3] Fingerprinting might help detect these infiltrators. Moreover, the RCMP had only the month before begun regular fingerprinting of new civil service appointees, seeking to bar criminals from 'appointments ... where integrity and trustworthiness are prime essentials.'[4] Why should the men guarding the purity of the civil service not also be scrutinized?

Still, anticipating internal opposition, the commissioner allowed the Mounties to object to the procedure, with explanation. At least four members did so. Among them was Detective Sergeant C.C. Brown of Saskatoon, who wrote: 'The idea of having my finger-prints taken is repugnant to me. Having been closely associated with criminal work for a long period, the fact of being finger-printed is identified in my mind with crime. *I have always felt that a man's personality suffered through the process.*'[5] Brown's belief that fingerprinting was degrading, a humiliation which ought not to be inflicted upon a non-criminal, was seconded by another officer. Corporal R.M. Wood called the process 'an indignity, submission to which would be most repugnant.'[6]

There is higher irony still in the opposition of another Saskatchewan RCMP officer. Sergeant Alexander Drysdale, stationed in Prince Albert, wrote a detailed memo citing five reasons for his objection. 'Fingerprints are associated in my mind, with Crime and Criminals,' he declared. Drysdale did not know it then, but, as the officer in charge of the Intelligence Section from 1941 to 1944, he would help direct a security-screening monolith that would collect some 2 million fingerprint files from his fellow citizens.[7] He may have had some premonition of later events, for in his 1931 memo he placed one caveat on his own rejection of non-criminal fingerprinting: 'I can see no good reason in having such record taken, *except in time of war* ...'[8] A decade later a similar sentiment must have made hundreds of thousands of other Canadians, who shared Drysdale's aversion to the process, place the unique identification marks of their fingertips onto a registration form to be sent to the RCMP.

Commissioner MacBrien's fingerprinting directive produced another shock. Aside from the written dissent of the four officers, objection within the RCMP to fingerprinting also took the form of passive resistance. In March of the next year, the officer in charge of the Fingerprint Section reported a very slow response from several RCMP detachments. The foot-dragging might have been based on more than principle. Among those RCMP officers who had already submitted their fingerprints, two were discovered to have criminal records.[9] Even some members of Canada's premier police force had dubious pasts, pasts relentlessly exposed by the fingerprinting process.

In their objection to fingerprinting and their belief that the process violated them psychologically, these RCMP officers voiced a conviction held by many people of the day. This indignity was for criminals; imposing it upon men and women convicted of serious crime was acceptable, but forcing it on others was intolerable. Attitudes have changed little. Today, fingerprinting is widely regarded as abhorrent because of its criminal connotations.[10] It is seen as an investigatory tool employed by police after a crime has been committed. Its history, however, contradicts its image as a purely forensic practice.

Years before it was used in Canada, fingerprinting was devised and implemented in India. In Britain's most prized colony, nineteenth-century administrators had a pressing problem: how to keep tabs on subject peoples whose allegiance to their European masters remained dubious. Fingerprinting offered a solution – a scientifically grounded, unerring system to identify individuals. In its service to British imperialism, fingerprinting represented the application of scientific knowledge to attain greater political control. Once established, its focus shifted somewhat, so that it became known as a criminal procedure. Nevertheless, it did not entirely lose its political character, and in Canada it became a central element, indeed the very heart, of the RCMP's security-screening system before and during the Second World War. Understanding the security-screening system requires a prior grasp of fingerprinting.

THE HISTORY AND SCIENTIFIC FOUNDATION OF FINGERPRINTING

In the 1850s, India was as much the thorn as the jewel in the crown of the British empire. Open rebellion, seen in the great mutiny of 1857, was merely one problem. Less dramatic but also troublesome was the difficulty of administering a land so populous, so different from Britain and so ethnically and religiously diverse. One of the Raj's great predicaments was how to keep track of the colony's 300 million people. Sir William Herschel, the chief administrator for the Hooghly district of Bengal in the 1850s, was particularly concerned about the effect of personal anonymity in daily commerce. A later commentator described his problem in this way: 'Herschell [sic] found that among the three hundred millions of brown-skinned natives, it was almost impossible to prevent fraud and deception in business matters. *To an European, practically all natives looked alike.* Few of them could sign their names and the commercial affairs of that great land were in dire confusion.'[11] For British imperial officials this inability to distinguish individuals among the Indian masses posed a profound challenge, especially for the day-to-day control necessary to colonial administration.

Seeing the difficulty firsthand, Herschel began to experiment with fingerprints, which held out the promise of being able to place a unique mark on each of those millions of people so faceless to their rulers.[12] In fingerprinting, Herschel was pursuing an identification technique with a lengthy past. For centuries fingerprints had been regarded in India 'as incontrovertible signatures to documents of value.'[13] But Herschel's challenge was to attach scientific authority to fingerprinting. He did that, in part, by demonstrating that a person's fingerprints do not change from birth to death.[14] By the 1870s Herschel had a method sufficiently reliable that he was able to introduce it in several departments of the Hooghly district administration. But his suggestion that it be more widely applied was rejected, possibly because of the lack of an accompanying classification system.[15] From the beginning, Herschel's experimentation was aimed at establishing fingerprinting as a method to deal with an identification problem, not as a forensic investigation tool, which is how we often regard it today.[16]

Sir Francis Galton also made a prolonged study of the subject and published a book about fingerprints in 1892. Galton's demonstration that there was a minimal risk of error in basing identifications on fingerprints was an important contribution to its eventual use. But Galton only partially addressed a significant drawback to the use of fingerprints: the need for a foolproof classification system.[17] This flaw prompted studies by another British administrator in India, Sir Edward Henry.

Although he later gained fame as commissioner of the London Metropolitan Police, Henry spent the first twenty years of his career in the Indian civil service as a magistrate, tax collector, and secretary to the Board of Revenue. In these posts he doubtless encountered the same frustrations that encouraged Herschel to look into fingerprinting. In 1891, when he was appointed inspector general of police in Bengal, Henry assigned two of his Indian employees, K.B. Aziz ul-Haque and R.B.H.C. Bose, the task of perfecting and implementing the fingerprint classification system which today bears Henry's name. In 1897 the Indian government, satisfied by his trials, officially adopted fingerprinting and the Henry classification system as a criminal identification method.[18] In 1901, following the recommendation of a secretary of state's commission of inquiry, fingerprinting was also adopted for the same purpose in England and Wales.[19] The same year, Henry became assistant commissioner of the London Metropolitan Police (Scotland Yard), in charge of the Criminal Investigation Department. Significantly, one of his duties in London was to maintain surveillance of Indian revolutionaries in Britain and on the European continent.[20] In this task his identification expertise from India must have been extremely beneficial. In 1903 he became commissioner, a position he held until the unprecedented London police strike of August 1918 forced his resignation.[21]

Fingerprinting was not the only procedure developed in the nineteenth century which turned science to the interests of identification and social control. Another was the Bertillon system. It was also devised as a way to take identification out of the hands of error-prone humans and place it into the realm of infallible science. Police in the nineteenth century relied on expert personal identifiers, much like the factory recognizers who monitored the workers of Britain's National Filling Factory No. 7 in the First World War. Police identifiers became remarkably proficient at recalling the faces of wanted persons. But it was time-consuming work, which relied greatly on intuition. To replace it, in the 1870s the French anthropologist Alphonse Bertillon began working on an identification system based on a complex variety of measurements of the human body. It was introduced publicly in 1880 and began to be employed by police in northern Europe very quickly.[22] By 1886 it was in use in the United States. The method briefly gained favour there after 1893 when the Chicago police adopted it as a way to identify the criminals who were expected to prey upon people attending the Chicago World's Fair.[23]

For a short time at the end of the nineteenth and the beginning of the twentieth centuries the Bertillon and Henry systems were used simultaneously, each having its advocates. But Bertillon measurements were both difficult to take and complex. Moreover, criminals did not conveniently leave their Bertillon figures at the scene of a crime. The competition between the systems was dramatically resolved in 1903. By a coincidence which astonished police, two prisoners at Leavenworth jail in Kansas were found to have identical Bertillon measurements. The same striking similarity was evident in photographs of the two, Will West and William West. Yet the two men were manifestly not the same person, and they claimed to be unrelated. When the fingerprints of the two were taken and compared, the patterns bore no resemblance. Fingerprinting had been able to distinguish one from the other, while the Bertillon method had not. The Bertillon system never recovered its credibility. Moreover, the case gained a prominent place in police lore about the infallibility of fingerprinting.[24] Within a matter of years, fingerprinting completely replaced the Bertillon method.[25]

The Henry fingerprint classification system, with some modifications and extensions, is still in use today. The system relies on two facts: (1) that it is possible, using a magnifying glass, to distinguish and count the individual identifying points on each fingerprint, mainly the pattern of ridges and other distinguishing points called minutiae; and (2) that all fingerprint patterns can be placed into one of five categories – arches, tented arches, whorls, ulnar loops (a loop slanted towards the ulnar bone, the large bone on the outside of the wrist of that hand) and radial loops (a loop slanted towards the radial bone in the wrist of that hand).

The analysis of each set of fingerprints is a six-step classification process. Each step leads to increasingly detailed categories into which a fingerprint may be placed. For example, one frequently occurring primary classification contains over 25 per cent of the total number of prints. Hence, when a print falls into one such large group it is necessary to complete the classification to greater levels of detail.[26] Numbers and letters are assigned at each of the six classification steps, and the result is an alpha-numeric classification code. A typical Henry description of one person's ten fingerprints might be:

$$\frac{12 \quad M \quad 9 \quad R \quad OIO \quad 11}{S \quad 1 \quad R \quad IOI}$$

The formula resulting from the classification process is usually sufficient to identify a small number of fingerprints with similar characteristics, or even one fingerprint set. In some cases, for an exact identification, detailed study of each individual print is necessary.[27]

In the interwar period, fingerprinting and forensic science were almost synonymous. When police referred to the application of science to their work they frequently spoke of fingerprinting. It was 'one of the most important branches of criminal investigation.'[28] Fingerprinting was featured regularly on the pages of élite scientific journals (such as *Scientific American*, where it was the subject of twenty-five articles and letters between 1910 and 1940, *Science*, and the British-based *Nature*), and in mass-circulation American magazines (such as *Popular Mechanics* and *Popular Science*). After the establishment of the *RCMP Quarterly* in 1933, fingerprinting was the subject of five articles in the first six years of publication, far more than any other forensic method.[29] In the late 1930s, when fingerprinting was linked with the newest and most powerful information technology of the day, electromechanical tabulating equipment, it was seen to be doubly potent. So integral did the words 'science' and 'fingerprinting' become that the latter has taken on a generic meaning, used broadly to describe a range of scientific identification techniques. For example, the modern forensic science of analysing the distinctive DNA in samples of body fluids and hair is called 'genetic fingerprinting.'[30]

Fingerprinting enjoyed such status because it was scientifically based. It traced its credibility to two essential developments. First, experimentation proved that no two people had the same fingerprints. Second, it was bolstered by an alphanumeric classification system which held out the prospect of certain identification. If a person had ever been fingerprinted, an expert could, without fail, match that record with a new set of prints from the same person, or distinguish the prints on record from those of a different person.

Perhaps because of its scientific foundation, fingerprinting became virtually an object of veneration, an icon among police. Clearly it had the capacity to link a person's past to the present. Once fingerprinted, a person could not hope to discard previous misdeeds; the infallible science of identification would always detect an offender. But for the police, fingerprinting also had the capacity to influence the future. Once marked by fingerprinting, a person knew that anything he or she did could be traced. This would tend to ameliorate future behaviour, to force a person to think twice about stepping out of line. The 1912 convention of the Chief Constables' Association of Canada was told that 'the greatest deterrent to the commission of crime is the knowledge of the existence of the metric and finger print methods in the hands of the police.'[31]

As Richard Ericson and Clifford Shearing point out, science is an important ideological prop for the police. Science holds 'special powers of construing the truth which reduce complexity to statements of authoritative certainty.'[32] It also lessens unpredictability. Certainty is much sought after in police practice since the endeavour is plagued by mystery, unresolved crimes, conflicting stories, and dubious witnesses. Security intelligence agencies face similar difficulties and therefore would also have great use for a tool which promises to enhance their certainty and authority. Science also helps the police to legitimize their authority by making them appear to be 'technical agents of scientific rationality rather than instruments of particular interests and a morality reflecting those interests.'[33] As the foremost police science during the inter-war era, fingerprinting played a vital part in lending authority to the police.[34]

DEVELOPMENT OF FINGERPRINTING

Once it gained a cachet of scientific authority through perfections in its classification system and by demonstrating its superiority over rival identification methods, fingerprinting rapidly spread among police forces in Britain, the United States, and Canada. Under Sir Edward Henry, Scotland Yard established the world's first central fingerprint repository, the Finger Print Bureau.[35] Scotland Yard was more than willing to share its knowledge of such a valuable police instrument. The first overseas student to receive instruction in fingerprinting there was a lieutenant in the New York City police department.[36]

Despite this early interest among U.S. policemen, Canada created the first central fingerprint repository in North America. The founding spirit of the Canadian Criminal Identification Bureau (CCIB) was Edward Foster, who went on to become an inspector in the RCMP and the head of its Fingerprint Section. Foster was an enthusiast, a tireless promoter of fingerprinting. By a stroke of good fortune he attended the first lecture on fingerprinting given in North America. A Scotland Yard expert, Sergeant John Ferrier, presented a paper on the subject to the International Association of Chiefs of Police in St Louis, Missouri, in 1904. At the same time, Foster, then a constable in the Dominion Police, was helping to guard a Canadian display of gold at the St Louis World's Fair. Infected by Ferrier's passion, Foster became an avid fingerprint student and advocate.[37] He spent his off-duty hours in St Louis immersed in the intricacies of the process. When he returned to Ottawa, Foster pressed for the establishment of both a national bureau and a chief constables' association, which would provide the organizational foundation for a national fingerprinting effort. Foster's zeal coincided with social conditions that encouraged increased use of fingerprinting. Governments and police were growing concerned with vagrants and criminality, and senior police officers were captivated by professionalization and scientifically based identification techniques, which were seen as an integral part of it. Greg Marquis's study of the Chief Constables' Association of Canada (CCAC) directly connects fingerprinting and the CCAC: 'The need to scientifically collect, store, and disseminate information on the 'criminal class' – convicted offenders – led to the fingerprint movement, which helped spark the creation of the Chief Constables' Association.'[38] Foster, along with his superior officer, the commissioner of the Dominion Police, Sir Percy Sherwood, and Henry J. Grasett, chief of the Toronto police, were instrumental in inaugurating the CCAC in 1905, the very year after Foster returned from St Louis. Lobbied by the CCAC, the Canadian government approved an order in council in 1911 creating what would be the country's permanent fingerprint repository, the CCIB.[39]

Thanks to his own preparatory work Foster had a collection of 2042 fingerprints, mostly of federal prison inmates, at the bureau's founding.[40] Police departments in large Canadian cities began to contribute fingerprints, and by 1919 there were 69,622 sets in the bureau. Exchanges of fingerprints with British and American authorities also began. In 1915, 29 prints were received from the United States, rising to 952 sets in 1919.[41] Although the Federal Bureau of Investigation's Identification Division was not established until 1924, by the 1930s the exchange of fingerprints between the two countries, even those of minor offenders, had become routine.[42] Regular exchanges of fingerprints between Canada and Britain occurred by the early 1920s, with the RCMP providing fingerprints and photographs of people deported from Canada as criminals.[43]

When the Dominion Police was absorbed by the RCMP in 1920, the bureau and its collection of thousands of sets of fingerprints went with it, and Inspector Foster remained as officer in command until he retired in 1932. It was known as the Fingerprint Section (FPS) throughout the 1930s and well into the Second World War. During this time it was within the Criminal Investigation Branch, along with sections like Firearms, Modus Operandi, and the RCMP *Gazette*, a bulletin disseminated only among police forces. In 1944 an internal reorganization spawned a new Identification Branch incorporating fingerprinting and other aspects of criminal identification.[44]

The RCMP worked constantly to improve its fingerprinting techniques, and often did so in consultation with local and foreign police forces. In the 1920s, for instance, Inspector Foster pioneered a method of sending fingerprint information by wire. This innovation helped disseminate awareness of fingerprint procedures, improved the communication between police forces in western Canada and the CCIB in Ottawa, and linked local police forces more closely to the RCMP.[45] News about equipment was also circulated among police forces in several countries.[46] Fingerprinting's status as 'the one [identification] method common to all countries' made it a singular part of international police cooperation, RCMP Commissioner Wood told an International Association for Identification conference in Washington in September 1937.[47] By the eve of the Second World War, the RCMP had built up a considerable bank of knowledge and lore about fingerprinting.[48]

The development of this new identification technique and its adoption by police were quickly followed by its legislative recognition. In Canada a 1908 order in council added a regulation to the 1898 Identification of Criminals Act giving police the power to fingerprint.[49] Aside from similar subsequent orders in council changing regulations associated with the 1898 act, the Identification of Criminals Act has not been changed to the present day.[50]

The CCAC also directed its attention to provincial governments, urging the various attorneys general to cooperate by allowing the fingerprinting of prisoners in provincial correctional institutions. Between 1912 and 1914 fingerprinting was endorsed by Saskatchewan and New Brunswick and introduced in several Manitoba jails. Private police agencies, many from large industrial corporations, were also members of the CCAC, and at least one of them began to contribute fingerprints to the national repository.[51]

The quick and legal sanction given to fingerprinting, however, yielded longterm frustration for the police. The act allowed police to fingerprint people, but only in severely limited circumstances.

A person could be fingerprinted only if he or she were charged with or convicted of an indictable offence. An indictable offence, more serious than a petty crime (a summary offence), is one that is punishable by two or more years in prison. Being associated with serious crime gave fingerprinting a stigma of criminality. The popular distaste for the procedure which emerged persists to today.[52]

AUTHORITIES' AMBITIONS FOR FINGERPRINTING

Police in Britain, Canada, and the United States came to hold fingerprinting in high esteem and eagerly promoted it. After Ferrier spoke enthusiastically about it at the St Louis World's Fair in 1904, it swiftly swept the United States, as it had Canada. Within a decade fingerprinting became an internationally accepted identification technology. The rapid spread of information about it also led to a common attitude towards its potential and the need for public acceptance of it. Organizations such as the International Association for Identification, formed in 1915, and the International Association of Chiefs of Police preached the virtues of fingerprinting, urging all police forces to adopt it, to exchange both fingerprints and details about its use, and to proselytize it among the public.

By the 1920s police forces in different countries were beginning to chafe at the disparity between fingerprinting's potential and the legal constraints on its use. Police officials were convinced that nothing but good could result from fingerprinting much more liberally than existing laws allowed, and many of them pressed for compulsory, universal fingerprinting.[53] Some governments moved quickly to seize the opportunity presented by fingerprinting. An international police conference in New York City in May 1925, where universal fingerprinting was promoted, heard that all Argentinians were required to carry an identity book with fingerprints.[54] But in Britain, the United States, and Canada laws remained restrictive.

In Britain and the United States, police became public promoters of wider fingerprinting. Scotland Yard campaigned to gain the right to fingerprint people arrested for virtually any crime.[55] National registration by fingerprints was discussed in Britain during the 1930s, but, in the absence of any 'real and general desire for such a system,' the home secretary rejected it.[56] Indeed, the stigma of fingerprinting was so intense that police officers in Oxford were prepared to be fired, and were, rather than themselves submit to fingerprinting in 1939.[57]

Probably the most zealous fingerprint advocate of all was the head of the FBI, J. Edgar Hoover. After 1924, when the FBI's central fingerprint repository was created, Hoover urged police throughout the country to fingerprint everyone they thought it 'desirable to fingerprint' and send the prints to the FBI.[58] Hoover's efforts to promote mass fingerprinting took on the air of a personal crusade. He travelled the country to spread the word to local policemen, delivering testimonials in the style of 'a Rotary Club business man.' Under him, the FBI sent out instructions to city detectives and town sheriffs alike, telling them how to take proper fingerprints and what equipment they needed. It mailed out millions of eight by eight inch fingerprint cards that became not only the American but also an international standard.[59] Hoover had a belief in the power of fingerprinting that bordered on the mystical: 'A fingerprint flies faster and truer than a loftful of stool pigeons in leading us to the man we want,' he rhapsodized.[60] One sceptical congressman declared that Hoover had aroused such a fingerprint fervour that police throughout the country 'take and file the fingerprints of every man they arrest, whether he is drunk or disorderly, or just fighting.'[61]

Under Hoover, fingerprinting became an overtly political tool. It moved out of the realm of being an adjunct to criminal prosecution and began to be used to record the identities of and monitor people who the FBI believed posed a threat to the government and the established economic order in the United States. An indication of the highly political manner in which fingerprinting came to be used during the interwar years was the FBI's creation of a separate, non-criminal fingerprint collection. The FBI established its Civil Identification Section in November 1933, receiving as a down payment the fingerprints of more than 140,000 U.S. government employees and job applicants.[62] Hoover augmented the collection by urging municipal officials to fingerprint people applying for relief. In the late 1930s his agency received over one million fingerprints of people enrolled in New Deal Works Progress Administration projects and used them to isolate potential troublemakers.[63] By 1939 the FBI's total fingerprint collection numbered 10 million, about half of them non-criminal fingerprints.[64]

American conservatives believed fingerprinting was a potent weapon against political dissidents. In 1922 a spokesman for the United States Chamber of Commerce urged universal civilian fingerprinting as a device to eliminate agitators from the ranks of industrial workers.[65] The campaign for universal civilian fingerprinting intensified during the Depression. A writer in the magazine *Good Housekeeping* described the strands of patriotism, trust in the state, and anti-communism which were woven into the movement's pitch. At FBI headquarters, Vera Connolly was shown the bureau's Civil Identification File. The collection moved her to write: 'To me it was symbolic – that little file of fingerprints of public-spirited Americans with nothing in their pasts to hide; who trusted their Federal law-enforcement officers and were thankfully accepting their protective care. No communism in the minds of these individuals. No red revolution. Simply old-fashioned American faith in American institutions.'[66] Connolly's words illustrate the way in which fingerprinting had changed to become a prop for the existing political order.

The American Civil Liberties Union considered the threat so potent that it issued pamphlets about it in 1936 and 1938. Probing the motivations behind the universal fingerprinting movement, which had 'taken on really formidable proportions,' the ACLU said: 'It is backed primarily by police and crime-prevention agencies, but it is also promoted by employers, obviously with a view to better control of labour activities.'[67] Large business organizations, like the National Manufacturers Association and the Hearst newspaper conglomerate, and patriotic leagues, like the Daughters of the American Revolution, actively joined the interwar fingerprinting crusade, according to the civil liberties union.[68] The

ACLU also detected and condemned an attempt by police to apply fingerprinting specifically against left-wing political activists. In 1934 police in Boston passed an order 'under which Communists and "other radically inclined" persons holding street demonstrations are arrested and "brought to police headquarters to be photographed and finger-printed." A special file of suchpersons [sic] is kept in the Bureau of Records for "future reference."'[69] Similarly, in 1936 in Berkeley, California, a mass fingerprinting program was launched, said the chief of police, to 'enable us to follow the movements and activities of Communists, Anarchists and Radicals.'[70]

Advocates of more widespread fingerprinting brought their message from the United States into Canada. In the late 1930s the American Universal Fingerprint Movement spread to Canada.[71] The FBI itself crossed the border to promote compulsory fingerprinting. At the 1939 annual convention of the Chief Constables' Association of Canada, for instance, FBI agent John S. Bugas offered Canadian police advice based on FBI experience. Speaking about strategies to impose universal fingerprinting in Canada, he acknowledged that the FBI's all-out campaign had backfired. Hoover, he implied, had been 'advocating it too strongly.' As a result 'a *very natural stigma* is attached to it.' Bugas advised patience: 'When you advocate universal finger printing, it must be a gradual process, in my mind, and something we must approach slowly.'[72]

Canadian police needed no instruction; on their own they had conducted a long and vehement campaign to extend fingerprinting. One forum that saw frequent appeals for extension of fingerprinting was the Chief Constables' Association annual meeting. Inspector Edward Foster of the RCMP Fingerprint Section told the 1927 and 1928 conventions that everyone should be fingerprinted.[73] The plea was echoed by Canadian municipal police officials and the RCMP throughout the 1920s and 1930s. They repeatedly asked the government to put more teeth into the Identification of Criminals Act so they could fingerprint immigrants and prospective immigrants, anyone in legal custody, and even every citizen.[74]

Police were particularly adamant about fingerprinting vagrants. In 1927, RCMP Commissioner Cortlandt Starnes urged this upon the deputy minister of justice, but no favourable amendments to the legislation were obtained.[75] Acting on requests for it at the 1930 and 1931 annual conventions of the Chief Constables' Association, a high-level delegation of police chiefs, including the RCMP commissioner, approached Justice Minister Hugh Guthrie. But Guthrie's reply was negative. He believed 'there would be strong opposition to the amendment of this Act so far as covering vagrants was concerned.' Indeed, Guthrie suggested that 'the tendency of the day on the part of legislators was to reduce the stringencies of the law.'[76] The police persisted. Again in 1934, RCMP Commissioner MacBrien suggested broadening the act so as to provide the police with the right to fingerprint vagrants. This would please various police forces in the country, 'particularly those operating in the larger cities,' according to Assistant Commissioner G.L. Jennings. Although the deputy minister of justice replied that he would recommend an amendment to the act, no change resulted.[77] Again in 1937 an RCMP officer insisted that a change to the act 'is very urgently desired.'[78] Yet the Identification of Criminals Act remained unchanged.

These police requests were at least partly politically motivated. Vagrancy was a criminal charge that was especially useful to police during the Depression. It was a catch-all charge, which could be applied in a variety of circumstances as a means to regulate social disorder. It allowed police to exert control over public places by arresting unemployed drifters and political dissidents on little pretext. If the arrested men were immigrants, they were often deported.[79] Flouting the law, police often went ahead and fingerprinted vagrants, a transgression acknowledged even by the deputy minister of justice.[80] Nor was vagrancy the only charge they used in this quasi-political manner. In Vancouver, during the turmoil arising from demonstrations of the unemployed in the late 1930s, police routinely fingerprinted men they arrested for the minor offense of soliciting funds on the street.[81] Since these collections were organized by communist-led movements of the unemployed, fingerprinting participants gave the police records on agitators close to the Communist party. Even railroad police invoked minor criminal charges in order to fingerprint men riding the freights.[82] Similarly, the Immigration Department, which began to fingerprint people deported from Canada for criminal offences in 1920, counselled its officers to fingerprint even those deportees 'whom you *believe* to be guilty of some offense.'[83]

As the Depression dragged on and war loomed in Europe, the man who would soon be RCMP commissioner again raised the plea for universal fingerprinting. Speaking as director of criminal investigation to a convention of the International Association for Identification in 1937, S.T. Wood called for all Canadians to be fingerprinted. He admitted, however, that 'fingerprints have been connected in the public mind with criminals and therefore a certain odium is attached thereto.'[84] Once the curtain of war descended, the RCMP was in the forefront of those calling for 'national registration by fingerprints.' In a wartime address to the Chief Constables' Association of Canada, the officer in charge of the RCMP Fingerprint Section, H.R. Butchers, made the oft-repeated pitch and then enlarged upon it. The scrutiny of fingerprinting should fall, he proposed, upon all the living and the dead. 'Many whom we consider substantial citizens have at one time or another committed an indiscretion for which their fingerprints have been registered at the Bureau. After death, a check of their impressions against Bureau files does no harm and permits their fingerprints to be removed from our active collection.'[85]

In advocating national fingerprinting, and in overstepping the law, the police revived fingerprinting's political heart, which had given life to the technology in the nineteenth century. Their public campaign, on the contrary, strived to depoliticize it by insisting that it was benign and indeed beneficial to the public. The association of fingerprinting with criminals should not prevent honest citizens from having their own fingerprints recorded by the police, argued Inspector George Guthrie of the Toronto city police. After all, 'no one objected to their names appearing in city or telephone directories alongside some of those who had broken the law.'[86] In a 1935 article in the *RCMP Quarterly* explaining how national fingerprinting would benefit the public, Sergeant Butchers called on other police officers to build a public campaign to sanitize fingerprinting.[87] But many Canadians remained highly suspicious of fingerprinting and refused to let the police guide their hands to the ink pad. As a result, in April 1939 the RCMP non-criminal fingerprint collection numbered a mere 18,128.[88]

For police on both sides of the border, fingerprinting was not a purely criminal technique. It was also valued as a method to monitor non-criminals and to track political dissidents, and it was extensively used in this manner during the interwar years. When war broke out it was therefore not surprising that police became even more reliant upon fingerprinting and turned to their already extensive fingerprint collections as a means to exert control in a challenging environment.

THE POPULAR IMAGE OF FINGERPRINTING

Like the views of police officials, public opinion about fingerprinting tended to straddle national borders. Indeed, the international antipathy to fingerprinting appeared very early. For example, in 1906, seeking a way 'to hector the [East] Indians out of South Africa,' the government of Transvaal introduced a motion to require every Indian to be registered by fingerprints. Those who failed to register would be deported. When the act was passed, the initiative was seen as 'an unforgivable affront' to the Indian community, equivalent to labelling an entire community as criminal. The ensuing campaign was marked by the emergence of both a new leader and a novel means to resist state action. The rising protest advocate was Mohandas K. Gandhi, and his innovative resistance strategy was civil disobedience. Gandhi and many others declared their readiness to endure prison rather than submit to fingerprinting. The opposition triumphed over the regime's jails, and the hated fingerprinting law was rescinded.[89]

In North America, U.S. magazines and books spread information about the procedure and alerted people to its dangers. There, the anti-fingerprinting mood was particularly vehement, a reaction to the intense zeal of the FBI and other police forces to have people accept fingerprinting as a patriotic duty.[90] The American Civil Liberties Union launched a campaign in 1936 to halt the compulsory fingerprint movement. In doing so it emphasized the political nature of fingerprinting, citing the danger of its being used to compile blacklists, to intimidate employees, and to create a system of national registration.[91]

For their part, Canadians demonstrated no willingness to defer to police authorities' ambitions to fingerprint more people. For all their devotion to the task, police were singularly unsuccessful in convincing various Canadian governments to extend police powers under the Identification of Criminals Act. One reason why the act was not made tougher was the strength of popular opinion against fingerprinting, which senior police officers acknowledged. People persisted in seeing it as a criminal procedure, a violation of civil liberty and a measure to bring citizens under the supervision of the police.[92] Even advocates of wider fingerprinting had to admit that it was an unpopular idea. William Banks, writing in *Saturday Night* in 1928, acknowledged: 'Because it has so long been associated with the battle against crime, the police realize that their finger-printing suggestion [to fingerprint all immigrants and vagrants] will meet with public opposition.'[93] J. Arthur Piers, proposing universal fingerprinting in 1938 in the *Canadian Magazine*, had to concede that 'To the great majority of people, finger-printing is very definitely associated with the criminal, and it has been a difficult matter to alter that attitude.'[94] In the House of Commons, the Progressive member of parliament from Brandon, Robert Forke, condemned the CCAC's proposal to fingerprint immigrants, saying 'I want the house to imagine the feelings of any decent Englishman who may be required to have his finger-print taken before he is allowed to enter the country.'[95] Some of the resistance to fingerprinting clearly related to its capacity to identify people. Debating a motion to introduce identification cards for all immigrants, Liberal Senator George E. Foster put his finger on the public disgust with being labelled: 'A dog on the street is tagged, maybe muzzled; a cow is marked with a slit in the ear or some mark on the horn; but there is something repugnant to that sovereign being, Man, in being tagged and met with a demand for his photograph and identification card ... '[96] Significantly, this proposed bill, while it would have required immigrants to carry identification cards, did not call for fingerprinting, perhaps because of the stigma attached to it.

Fingerprinting was deemed to be particularly odious when the cause of arrest was a quasi-political offence. For example, the detention of unemployed men in Vancouver who were participating in tag days caused a women's support group to object to the men being fingerprinted. It *places the stigma of crime on them,* the group declared to the prime minister. They demanded that the practice end and that the fingerprints already taken be destroyed.[97] Similarly, *The Canadian Congress Journal*, the organ of the Trades and Labor Congress, condemned the Padlock Law in Quebec as an iniquitous act which allowed 'raiding and breaking into homes without warrant and searching, finger printing, photographing and questioning men without any charge being laid against them.'[98]

Even in criminal cases people objected to being fingerprinted. The RCMP in 1934 reported 'considerable trouble in obtaining the fingerprints of persons charged under the Excise Act as it *is being circulated that we have no rights to take their* prints.'[99] In this case the resistance to fingerprinting reached the level of a complaint to the Department of Justice. The complainant was emboldened by criticism of fingerprinting in the House of Commons. Charles Bell, the Conservative member of parliament for Hamilton West, scolded the minister of justice, saying that 'to take the finger prints of any man accused simply because he has been accused ... is an outrage and ought to be condemned by every member of this house.'[100] This notoriety made the RCMP wary of demanding fingerprints.[101] Assistant Commissioner Jennings acknowledged that popular doubts about whether the RCMP had the legal jurisdiction to fingerprint people charged even with indictable offences were causing the force to shy away from taking them.[102]

Fingerprinting was not just an accidental discovery welcomed by those who sought greater social control. It was the product of that desire. Fingerprinting represented the application of science to an age-old state problem – how to identify and monitor an anonymous or potentially troublesome population. It is most accurately seen as the application of science to the attainment of greater social and political control. After it was established, its focus shifted somewhat, so that it became known as a criminal procedure. To this day, despite the best efforts of its enthusiasts, it has never shaken the stigma of criminality it acquired. Yet its political character was not lost, and its potential as a political tool excited both official ambitions and public concern about it in the 1930s. The result was a public conflict between popular fears and police aims for the technique. Fingerprinting's success as a scientific method of social identification combined with popular distaste for it to force governments to limit its legal use. Although it was accepted into law very quickly, in Canada it remained constrained – officially, at least – to use for indictable offenses.

Fingerprinting also contributed considerably to cooperation among police forces in Britain, the United States, and Canada. The exchange began with explanations of the technique, but it soon blossomed into a traffic in fingerprints. In short, this was an early example of criminal and political intelligence communication among the three countries. Just as fingerprinting contributed to the creation of the Chief Constables' Association of Canada, so it also helped improve international police and security intelligence rapport. Indeed, it would become an integral part of the intelligence collaboration between the three North Atlantic countries, a cooperative effort which would improve in the 1930s and become very significant in the Second World War.

3

The birth of state vetting: Security screening in the interwar period

The 1931 appointment of Major-General Sir James H. MacBrien as RCMP commissioner signalled several developments in the force that were noticed by critics and friends alike. One of them was a new attention to political security. The RCMP had languished in the 1920s, reaching a low point in 1926, when it had just 963 men. MacBrien's arrival in 1931 reversed the slide and gave the RCMP the initiative to take on new enterprises. When he came to Ottawa to head the Intelligence Section in 1935, Inspector Charles Rivett-Carnac described the transformation in outlook this way: 'From almost a question mark in 1923 when I had first joined ... it had found a new growth in a changed age of mechanization, its stature greatly increased in Canadian affairs.'[1]

It was no surprise that R.B. Bennett's Conservative government settled on MacBrien as commissioner. He was an outspoken anti-communist and an advocate of an integrated security intelligence system to deal with dissent. As an army commander in 1919, MacBrien had championed the idea of a comprehensive defence plan which, in the immediate postwar era of labour strife, would concentrate on communism and labour unrest.[2] When he became RCMP chief MacBrien paid no less attention to security intelligence.

Not everyone in Canada liked the prospect of having a military man with a taste for tougher security heading the RCMP. Public trepidation about the appointment was expressed in the House of Commons by J.S. Woodsworth, a left-wing member of parliament and civil libertarian. In August 1931 Woodsworth declared that 'I think it is rather a significant fact that recently we have had an increase in the Royal Canadian Mounted Police and have placed at the head of the force a military man.' 'And a good one,' shot back the minister of trade and commerce, Conservative H.H. Stevens. Woodsworth was unimpressed. Using 'military methods' against the unemployed was 'all wrong,' he insisted. In 1932 Woodsworth again took up his criticism of the militarization and strengthening of the federal security police force. Particularly abhorrent was 'the spy system' used by the RCMP against labour. 'I object to labour being considered dangerous in character and to having government officials push their way into trade union or other labour class organizations in order to spy upon them.'[3]

Spying on labour was not the only security intelligence measure the RCMP made use of during the early 1930s. Indeed, infiltration was an old practice. MacBrien introduced another routine which was genuinely innovative – security screening of civil servants. This began in 1931, and by the end of the decade it embraced virtually every new civil servant. During the 1930s the RCMP refined its techniques and developed a standard vetting routine. By the end of the decade the force was well placed to expand into full-scale wartime security screening with minimal confusion.

This new security initiative of vetting did not materialize overnight. To understand its characteristics it is necessary to return to the last months of the First World War and trace a decade of preparation and consolidation of the Canadian state's security intelligence capacity. In May 1918 the government ushered in a troubled postwar era with security legislation of unprecedented ferocity. Prime Minister Robert Borden commissioned a Montreal lawyer, Charles Cahan, to study the radical labour movement in the country. Cahan, who had worked with the British secret service to counter wartime German espionage in the United States, warned that Bolshevism was the major danger to Canadian security. In a September report he proposed strict measures to deal with the perceived threat.[4] Acting on his recommendation, the government later that month issued orders in council which outlawed fourteen socialist and anarchist organizations, stifled the foreign-language press and prohibited strikes and lockouts. These were followed in June 1919 by an amendment to the Immigration Act which allowed for the deportation of any immigrant who was deemed to be a revolutionary and, in July, by a drastic change to the Criminal Code which outlawed any organization whose professed purpose was to make 'governmental, industrial or economic change' by force.[5] These draconian bills were part of the government's all-out assault on the labour ferment that peaked in the Winnipeg General Strike of May-June 1919.

The government also moved to strengthen its security apparatus. Cahan's report had recognized that the state's security enforcement agencies were poorly coordinated, and he recommended the creation of a centralized security service. The result was the Public Safety Branch within the Justice Department, which he himself headed.[6] But when the PSB failed to become the powerful civilian security coordinating body he envisioned, he resigned.[7] By filling the vacuum Cahan identified, the RCMP rose to prominence as the Canadian state's main security vehicle.

For a small paramilitary force whose base was the prairie West and whose forte was wilderness patrolling, this enhanced security role was somewhat unexpected. At war's end in November 1918, still known as the Royal North-West Mounted Police, the force had just 303 members, almost exactly its size at its founding in 1873. In Ottawa, rumours suggested it would be disbanded.[8] However, in December 1918 the government took steps to lift this cloud of doubt. It issued orders to bring RNWMP strength up to 1200. In a reorganization, the RNWMP was given the responsibility of enforcing federal laws and security regulations from the head of the Great Lakes to the Pacific, previously the duties of the older, but smaller, Dominion Police force.[9] The authorized strength was raised again in July 1919, and by September 1919 the RNWMP had 1600 men.

The RNWMP had taken a tentative step into the shadows of intelligence work in 1904, when it hired a handful of detectives.[10] It had also gained valuable security experience in the First World War because many of the enemy aliens and labour radicals who were considered prime threats lived in the West, the jurisdiction of the RNWMP. They had been monitored by a motley collection of government agents, private detective agencies, secret agents paid from Dominion Police funds, and the RNWMP's own regular members.[11] By 1917 the force was using its Regina headquarters as a clearing-house for dossiers on several hundred western Canadian radicals.[12] The government's rising fear that Canada would be seized by revolution was prompted in part by reports it received from the RNWMP.[13]

During the force's postwar expansion its involvement in the surveillance of labour and radical organizations grew. In December 1918 the RNWMP had just eight secret agents and six detectives in its entire operation, but in February 1919 the federal government approved funds to hire twenty more. The force must have had in addition a healthy stable of paid freelance informers, for in January 1919 it undertook the ambitious project of penetrating all the major labour organizations in western Canada.[14] The force was not wandering blindly into this assignment. Commissioner A.B. Perry showed a firm grasp of the objective of his force's political intelligence when he insisted: 'It must be borne in mind that the only information which is of any value in connection with Bolshevism is the valuable and first hand information of what is going to happen before it occurs in sufficient time to permit arrangements being made to offset any intended disturbance.'[15] The commissioner's goal was clearly related to security intelligence rather than policing, since, in Gregory Kealey's assessment, 'Perry made it clear that he preferred implantation to prosecution.'[16] This in itself was a sign of the RNWMP's developing professionalism in security intelligence. By April 1919 the RNWMP had succeeded in organizing a covert intelligence operation in western Canada. Secret agents or detectives had managed to penetrate every important radical organization, and some of them occupied executive positions. Agents of the force had also slipped in among the Winnipeg General Strike organizers.[17]

Even as it sank the roots of its informer network into the labour milieu, the RNWMP was also improving its capacity to gather and analyse the information from its agents. The Criminal Investigation Branch, founded early in February 1919, gave the RNWMP a central division which coordinated intelligence, correspondence, and instructions on security and criminal matters between headquarters and the field.[18] Intelligence reports were carefully scrutinized and distilled at the CIB office, and from there went to the commissioner and to political authorities.[19] Until it was reorganized in 1946, the CIB housed both the Intelligence Section and the Fingerprint Section, which were destined to work together closely in security matters. It is significant that the RCMP's security intelligence office was headquartered within an ostensibly criminal branch. In part this helped to disguise the operation, which had no statutory authority and which was not even acknowledged in the House of Commons until 1934.[20] Equally important, it revealed the mutual interdependence of political and criminal intelligence, both in method and in the minds of RCMP personnel.[21]

The RCMP's growing facility with security matters made it by 1919 the logical force to assume those duties throughout the country. In July, the same month it passed the draconian Criminal Code Section 98 outlawing revolutionary organizations, the Borden government opted for a centralized security force. It made the RNWMP both the federal police and the security intelligence force across the country. The Dominion Police, comprised of 150 members, was merged into the larger force, and the reorganized whole was renamed the Royal Canadian Mounted Police, formally inaugurated in 1920.[22] Working out of a new headquarters in Ottawa, the RCMP was provided with sufficient staff to meet political policing demands without having to resort to local police or private detective agencies.[23]

One vital accoutrement which went with the RCMP to Ottawa was its records. During the labour crisis of 1919, Commissioner Perry had ordered that a system of security files be created. One category of files dealt with suspected subversive organizations, the other with individuals. In 1920 this file system was moved to Ottawa. Central Registry, the department assigned to maintain the files, was within the Criminal Investigation Branch, but security and intelligence files were kept as 'a distinct group which required special attention.'[24] As 'the key to any successful intelligence system,' these records made up the core of what would become by the end of the 1920s a registry incorporating thousands of files and millions of pages.[25] It also formed the heart of the RCMP's security-screening system as it evolved in the interwar decades.

By 1920, the period of intense confrontation between an aroused labour movement and the Canadian state had drawn to an end. The result was, on the one hand, a temporarily quiescent labour force, and, on the other, a single centralized federal security force with a widespread network of informers and agents among labour radicals. That infrastructure proved highly useful to the RCMP within a year. In 1921 the revolutionary stream within the labour movement united to found the Communist Party of Canada, which the RCMP was to regard as its mortal enemy and the main threat to the security of Canada for the next forty years. So well placed were RCMP agents that one of them was among the twenty-two delegates present at the party's inception.[26] RCMP infiltration of the Communist party represents one of the major successes of its early years as a watchdog on political dissent. Through the Depression of the 1930s, as Communist party membership rose from 4000 in 1931 to 16,000 in 1939, the RCMP's constant objective remained monitoring communist leaders and activists.[27]

The Canadian state's interwar security effort was based upon the belief that agitators and communists were mostly foreigners and the conviction that such troublemakers should either be prevented from entering or be deported back to whence they came.[28] Towards that end the state went to great pains to provide a firm legal foundation. The effort began just before the First World War descended. In May 1914 the Borden government passed the British Nationality, Naturalization, and Aliens Act. It dramatically altered Canadian naturalization practice and gave police considerably more justification to inquire into the background of people of foreign birth. The act changed the main naturalization requirements from three years' to five years' residence and adequate knowledge of French or English. More importantly, the applicant had to be 'of good character.' The act gave the Secretary of State the power to deny naturalization according to what was deemed to be 'the public good,' and there was no appeal of this decision.[29] What constituted 'good character' or 'the public good' was not defined in the act, and this gave the police considerable leeway. An adverse police report, therefore, could block an immigrant's bid for citizenship. Parliament's 1919 changes to the Immigration Act gave the RNWMP (later the RCMP) significant added influence in the granting of naturalization, since that agency was the essential intelligence source for the Immigration Department.[30] The vetting of potential citizens became one of the RCMP's undertakings. RCMP records show that in 1926 applicants for naturalization were being fingerprinted and the results compared to the RCMP's criminal records.[31] In 1933–4 the RCMP checked an average of 1200 naturalization fingerprints each month. By 1935 this had risen to about 2200 per month.[32] At the beginning of the Second World War the RCMP was systematically investigating the character and background of all naturalization applicants, based on a long-standing arrangement between the force and the Secretary of State.[33]

Naturalization intelligence was shared between the RCMP, the Immigration Department and police authorities in Britain. The RCMP forwarded to Scotland Yard fingerprints of British deportees from Canada who were suspected of having criminal records in their home country.[34] And MI5 sent lists of undesirable immigrants and known communists from London to Ottawa.[35] In addition, criminal charges were often laid against communists and other radicals; once arrested, deportation was frequently their fate.[36] This screening of potential immigrants illustrates one way in which criminal and political intelligence became merged.

Try as it might, however, the Canadian state could not exclude everyone it regarded as an agitator. For example, the Immigration Department's 1924 attempt to deport Sam Scarlett, a member of the Industrial Workers of the World (IWW), failed, to the department's acute embarrassment. The fiasco effectively demonstrated that the state would have to live with this and other thorns in its side.[37] Harsh laws and increasingly sophisticated deportation procedures notwithstanding, the state could not deport a movement. Faced with that reality, keeping dissidents from positions of power within the state gained new importance.

Until well into the twentieth century, civil service appointments were based upon the political affiliation of the candidates. The Civil Service Act of 1918, amended in 1919, was touted as a measure to eliminate this partisanship. A guiding principle of the act was to enshrine merit as the method of selecting civil servants. Merit was to be ensured by requiring that appointments be made only through open competitions, decided by examinations.[38] By 1921 the commission had created an Examination Branch, which enforced competitive exams for all appointments.[39] Establishing an objective civil service selection process is usually seen as heralding the creation of a modern society in which career advancement comes by merit rather than by class or political connections. But a society with a relatively insignificant 'old boys' network, which was casting out political patronage – and patronage, it should be pointed out, is a form of vetting through politicians and local party organizations – could be expected to institute a new form of screening.[40] The fact that freedom from any taint of radical politics became a major, if not the primary, criterion for acceptance reflects the highly polarized political environment of the years after 1917.

Security screening was the new political filter designed to maintain the purity of the civil service. Beginning in 1931 Civil Service Commission (CSC) appointees and applicants were subjected to fingerprinting and security screening, and this was stepped up towards the end of the decade. The commission initiated fingerprinting after it was embarrassed by a bribery scandal in which outsiders paid cash to be admitted to low-level jobs in the civil service even though they had failed the civil service exams. The resulting criminal prosecutions went to trial in April 1931 but ended in acquittals.[41] The case prompted the commission to experiment with fingerprinting as a means to ensure that the applicant, exam writer, and appointee were one and the same person. In March 1931 the CSC approached the RCMP to obtain the benefit of the force's expertise in comparing fingerprints. The commission asked the RCMP to undertake the work of finger-printing applicants and appointees, a task the RCMP agreed to do.[42]

What began as a response to a criminal problem, however, soon assumed security applications. In September 1931, after a three-month trial of a straightforward fingerprint comparison, William Foran, the commission's secretary, suggested that the RCMP step up its involvement. He requested aid in 'ascertaining in appointments ... where integrity and trustworthiness are prime essentials, whether or not the persons being appointed have had previous criminal records.' What the commission deemed to be sensitive positions, however, covered a very broad spectrum, from newly hired prison guards to appointments to the Post Office and the customs, immigration, and finance departments. (Employees of the Canadian Broadcasting Corporation, unlike their colleagues in Britain, were not vetted.[43]) RCMP Commissioner MacBrien agreed to perform the screening and said nothing about the possible civil liberties consequences of such an act – if indeed they occurred to him.[44] But this fingerprinting was more than an affront to civil rights. It was illegal. According to the Identification of Criminals Act, fingerprinting was authorized only for people convicted of an indictable offense. Nor did any legislation exist to authorize the fingerprinting of naturalization applicants.[45] The Civil Service Commission appeared to believe that it did not need to obtain the permission of the government or cabinet for this new security initiative, or indeed even to inform its political masters about it. No record has come to light which shows that elected authorities approved or knew about security screening of civil servants.[46]

In the first year of civil service screening, 233 fingerprint searches were conducted by the RCMP Fingerprint Section. The number of civil servants being investigated increased markedly after that. In the eighteen months from 1 October 1932 to 31 March 1934, 1231 non-criminal fingerprint checks were made by the RCMP; 336 of them were of recruits to the force. The remainder were of federal and Quebec civil servants and applicants for weapon permits. The 1936 RCMP *Annual Report* recorded 2417 security-related fingerprint searches, including new RCMP members (347), federal civil servants, 'applicants for positions of trust in the province' of Quebec (222), and recruits to several provincial and municipal police forces. The number rose to 2501 civilian fingerprint searches in 1936–7, 4422 in 1937–8, and 4991 in 1938–9.[47] The absolute numbers may appear small, but they represented a significant proportion of all CSC appointments. In 1938 there were only 843 permanent and 5563 temporary federal civil servants hired.[48] In 1939 the director of the Canadian Immigration Branch declared that all civil servants were fingerprinted. His assertion is probably exaggerated; he likely meant all new appointees to the civil service. Nevertheless, it is clear that a concerted campaign to check the backgrounds of civil servants was under way before the Second World War began.[49]

The inquiries into civil servants were not limited to fingerprint searches. By 1938 the RCMP had expanded its screening of CSC appointees to a level that is not usually believed to have been invoked until the post–Second World War years.[50] A 1938 RCMP memo called for very detailed checks, and pointed out: 'In investigations of this nature, instructions are issued to the N.C.O or Constable detailed to the inquiry, that whenever possible, information concerning the character of the applicant must be obtained from others than those who have already submitted testimonials.'[51] In other words, security screening of civil servants in 1938 involved both record checks of RCMP indexes and field checks in which the force sought information from people beyond the applicant's listed references. This is 'positive vetting' of the kind which was not officially practised until after 1945.

It should also be kept in mind that the RCMP had been accumulating experience in conducting field checks for naturalization applications since the 1920s. The procedure described in 1932 was remarkably similar to a civil service field inquiry for vetting purposes: 'The Naturalization Branch ... supplies us with the names of applicants; these are borne to the divisions concerned; and an investigation is made into the character of the applicants. On the report being forwarded to headquarters it is transmitted to the naturalization authorities, and all decisions rest with them.'[52] The

1932 RCMP *Annual Report* mentions the force making 7500 naturalization investigations in that year alone.[53] This reveals the extent of the Canadian state's screening system in the interwar period. It was also a potent expression of the state's fear of the foreign-born.

The force's vast Central Registry was an indispensable part of screening. The essence of the screening operation was a matching exercise, drawing upon information from two categories. All applicants for or incumbents of government positions were checked against records of criminals and suspected subversives. The matching was performed by hand in Canada. In the United States, the FBI used International Business Machines electro-mechanical sorters to search its fingerprint database beginning in 1934.[54] The machinery speeded the search, but matching as a technique was used before equipment came along to assist it.[55] Indeed, the first condition for such a method is the possession of an index arranged in some logical way. Having a Central Registry organized into several categories, as the RCMP one was, allowed for a variety of matching options.[56]

Its very existence is not the only remarkable aspect of this intensive security screening. What motivated it is also significant. It was a response to the economic crisis of the Depression and the political challenge to the status quo represented by the Communist Party of Canada. The RCMP's fear of and distaste for communism grew more and more tangible in the 1930s. The interwar editions of the RCMP *Annual Report* are a testament to the rising concern about agitation which it believed originated in the Soviet Union. Although mention of the Communist party was rare in reports throughout the 1920s, after 1933 a section of the *Annual Report* was regularly devoted to accounts of industrial disturbances in which communists featured prominently. Such dissent was 'the execution of plans conceived outside the country, and furnished to and imposed upon our agitators from abroad.'[57] The communists, too, saw themselves as agents of the Comintern. But the conditions which gave rise to strikes, demonstrations, and confrontations, were home-grown, not imported.

Like its security police, the federal government of R.B. Bennett was also seized by a fear of communism. Echoing the RCMP commissioner's own anxiety in 1933, Justice Minister Hugh Guthrie called political conditions 'not at all satisfactory ... I regret to say that ... the communist party ... is perhaps more active and dangerous to-day then it has been at any time in recent years.' Senators were also preoccupied with the problem. Speaking on a 1931 bill to force immigrants to carry identification cards, Conservative Senator C.P. Beaubien called the measure 'useful and timely' because 'Communistic activites throughout the land have lately become intensified.'[58]

Late in the decade suspicion of communist activity among workers and preparations for possible war prompted the RCMP to initiate a scheme to vet people employed in munitions plants, a system that would be greatly expanded during the Second World War. In the spring of 1939 the RCMP formed a Civil Security Branch within the Intelligence and Liaison Section and initiated consultation with owners and managers of plants with munitions contracts. The branch had already written the booklet *Notes on Industrial Security,* telling managers what security measures they should take in their plants, and was then awaiting Department of National Defence approval for it. A screening plan was also afoot to identify 'foreign elements' in the 'important plants,' with the understanding that 'these individuals can then be checked with our subversive files so that full particulars will be available respecting the personnel employed.'[59] The procedures would be beneficial in peacetime or in a wartime emergency, the intelligence section believed. Indeed, as part of the national survey of vulnerable points, the commanding officer of 'E' Division, British Columbia, proposed a plan to check the employees of major industries, such as Boeing Aircraft and Imperial Oil, and provincial power plants. He wrote to the RCMP commissioner suggesting that 'these firms should be requested, in addition to furnishing us with a list of their employees at this time, to notify us immediately [of] the names of new hands.' The lists would also help to select loyal long-term employees who could 'be used as part-time agents in supplying information to this Office regarding the activities of their fellow-workers.'[60] By 1938 the military also believed that the primary threat of industrial sabotage came from disaffected employees rather than outsiders.[61]

Communist infiltration of another part of the state, the military, had long been a concern of the RCMP. In 1919 the force seized revolutionary literature at the Esquimalt dockyards, Canada's main West coast naval station.[62] Then, in 1930, authorities at the base were alarmed at the appearance of a pamphlet addressed 'To all Soldiers and Sailors.' The leaflet was the work of a former member of the Canadian Permanent Force, R.C.C. Stewart, who had become a Communist party leader in nearby Victoria. Stewart was arrested and convicted of incitement to mutiny and sentenced to two years in jail.[63]

In March 1931 military intelligence warned General Andrew McNaughton, the chief of the general staff, about increased communist infiltration and subversion of the military. Military intelligence was basing its belief on a study of Communist party propaganda, which signalled a move against the armed forces. McNaughton called for screening of new recruits to both the regular force and the militia. The screening must also have been directed against those already in the forces, because in July 1934 the adjutant general reported that at least thirteen and up to seventeen communists had been identified in the army. He asked that all new recruits be put under observation and that reports be made about their habits, associates, and spare-time activities. Naturally, this surveillance was coordinated with the RCMP, which retained a monopoly on state information about subversion. One soldier in the Princess Patricia's Canadian Light Infantry didn't bother to use official channels to chastise a communist in his own unit. When the communist asked the PPCLI member to steal rifles for the party, the soldier said: 'There was no responsible person or policeman in the neighborhood, so I knocked him down and left him laying there.' Military men who joined the Mackenzie-Papineau Battalion to fight for the republican government in the Spanish Civil War also caused concern. The army wanted to know who was going, and, at the conclusion of the war in 1938, who might be returning and seeking to rejoin the militia.[64]

Fear of communists influencing the military probably contributed to RCMP attempts to convince the Department of National Defence to fingerprint all recruits. The suggestion had first been made in 1917 by Percy Sherwood, the chief commissioner of the Dominion Police, but it was rebuffed.[65] In October 1938, just seven months after becoming commissioner of the RCMP, S.T. Wood repeated the plea for military adoption of fingerprinting, as the American military had done in 1906 and 1907. As evidence of one benefit Commissioner Wood cited a United States Navy report that its fingerprint bureau had 'prevented undesirables from entering the service under assumed names.' However, the defence department again rejected the proposal, on the oft-cited grounds that it would deter new personnel.[66]

The political discord resulting from the Depression brought on several other security and intelligence developments within the RCMP. One of them was that training within the force became more overtly directed towards ideology, especially after Wood became commissioner in 1938. This trend was noted by C.W. Harvison, a detective sergeant in the force in the late 1930s. He observed that in 1938 instructional sessions offered by the Mounted Police began for the first time to include lectures on communism and, secondarily, fascism.[67] Although ideological schooling was new in the RCMP, a marked political orientation was not. Anti-communism had been a mainstay of the force for some time. Indeed, Wood was following the lead of Commissioner MacBrien, who launched a public campaign against the far left after he became commissioner in 1931. Not content to speak publicly against communism, MacBrien founded the *RCMP Quarterly* in 1933 to warn Canadians about its threat.[68] Beginning in 1935 the *RCMP Quarterly* regularly attacked communism, a tirade that indelibly marked the force ideologically.[69]

Harvison observed a second security-related development in the late 1930s. The force began to expand its security and intelligence capacity and improve its international contacts. He recalled that

special branch sections across Canada were increased; administrative and coordinating staffs at headquarters were strengthened; contacts and liaisons were established with intelligence agencies in the United Kingdom and the United States; training courses were set up in Canada; and selected members were sent abroad for specialized training.[70]

This cooperation between intelligence agencies had begun years before. British and Canadian security authorities had exchanged intelligence during the First World War, and for the RCMP this British connection remained primary throughout the 1920s. Scotland Yard and the Intelligence Service of the War Department supplied information on the Comintern and about the movements of Canadian communists visiting Britain.[71] The RNWMP began to receive British security intelligence materials on a regular basis in May 1919, and had commenced routine reporting to Britain at least by October 1920.[72] British and Canadian intelligence agencies strengthened this liaison as the Second World War approached and concerns about sabotage came to the fore.[73] The RCMP's decision to publish a security guide for plant managers and to screen workers followed recommendations from Guy Liddell of MI5, who had been invited by the RCMP to visit Canada in 1938 to advise on British security precautions and to suggest ways for Canada to improve its security.[74] The British handbook on plant security helped Canadian security officials lay down the rule that military contractors were to be responsible for their own plant's protection. The police and military were to confine themselves to ensuring protection against attack from the outside. The British handbook was very likely the model for the RCMP booklet *Notes on Industrial Security* which was printed in the spring of 1939 and which served as the state's security guide for munitions manufacturers for the first year of the Second World War.[75] In addition, the Canadian government as a whole looked to the British government for guidance on security matters. For example, O.D. Skelton, undersecretary of state for external affairs, in arguing for a wait-and-see attitude towards action against the Communist party in December 1939, suggested using British regulations as a guide.[76]

The American connection, tenuous at first, grew to eclipse the British link by 1945. In 1919 the RCMP liaison and intelligence officer, Colonel C.F. Hamilton, had inaugurated official intelligence cooperation with American police officials by visiting Washington. But the exchange stagnated until 1924, when J. Edgar Hoover became director of the FBI.[77] During the Depression informal contacts between the FBI and RCMP grew in importance until November 1936 when RCMP Commissioner MacBrien wrote directly to Hoover to resolve the problem of how to obtain information on the movements of Canadian communists who visited the United States. MacBrien followed up this inquiry by visiting Hoover in Washington in 1937.[78] In October 1938, after preparations for industrial sabotage were uncovered in the United States, Commissioner Wood became alarmed at the possibility of similar attacks in Canada. As a result, RCMP Intelligence Officer Rivett-Carnac met with an American counterpart to discuss ways to prevent sabotage and espionage.[79] These intelligence coordination meetings would lead to three western hemisphere intelligence conferences and to permanent liaison officers during the Second World War.[80]

Although it remained tiny, the RCMP's intelligence organization was centralized and strengthened throughout the 1930s. A distinct Intelligence Section was created within the Criminal Investigation Branch in 1936 and the number of personnel increased to six from four in 1934. In addition to Inspector Rivett-Carnac and Sergeant John Leopold, the section was made up of a stenographer, a translator, and two other officers, one in charge of the all-important registry and one handling agents. Moreover, intelligence sections also existed in some of the divisions.[81] And S.T. Wood, who had headed the division in politically volatile Saskatchewan, gave security intelligence a greater priority when he became commissioner in 1938.[82]

As for supervision by elected politicians, security screening was overlooked. The RCMP's surveillance and infiltration of radical groups became controversial after 1920 and remained so throughout the interwar period.[83] But no voice was raised against security screening. The dubious legality of fingerprinting civil servants was not a subject of public debate. The propriety of inquiring into the backgrounds of people who applied for Canadian citizenship or who wished public service appointments was not discussed in the House of Commons or in newspaper editorials. No Canadian government brought it to the public's attention, let alone sanctioned it by legislation. Its secrecy doubtless helped shield it from criticism. In the Depression, becoming a citizen or gaining a job in the civil service was such a sought-after plum that applicants were probably loath to complain about being finger-printed and scrutinized. Although there was no public criticism of security screening, the fact that the state felt compelled to check civil service applicants for possible criminal records and to inquire into their background marked a new level of surveillance and supervision within Canadian society.

British and American security intelligence agencies also insti-tuted security screening during the interwar period. In both cases their systems were consistent with the Canadian methods. In Brit-ain, vetting emerged in the late 1930s, and appears to have begun with the inauguration of a special department within MI5, the internal security agency. The section responsible for vetting was 'C' Division.[84] By 1937 it had instituted a security-screening sys-tem covering people in key government sectors like the military and the BBC.[85] It took its toll on civil servants. In February 1939 the National Council for Civil Liberties reported civil liberties vio-lations such as the interrogation of Post Office workers. In addi-tion, the political views of civil service clerks who were active in unions were probed.[86]

MI5 was also immersed in vetting industrial workers before the Second World War. Little is known about this, but Hinsley and Simkins' official history of British intelligence cryptically observes: 'The weekly average of vetting submissions rose from 2,300 in January 1939 to 6,800 in September and to over 8,000 in June 1940 when the vetting of many industrial grades was aban-doned to ease the load.'[87] One look at these figures confirms the scale of MI5's security-screening operation. In the eight months prior to the war, the service vetted at least 75,000 people. Another 100,000 were checked in the first four months of the war. Clearly a functional screening system was in place months before the war began.

This does not mean that British vetting was complete or adequate. At least five Soviet agents found their way into British security intelligence agencies and the Foreign Office during the 1930s. Most of them were in the civil service before vetting was introduced. But the vetting in effect before 1948 would still probably not have caught these traitors. This was a transition period in the system in which class bias competed with the demands of security. As Bernard Porter points out, the British upper middle class, which dominated the secret and diplomatic services, looked for recruits from among men they knew personally and those like themselves. Since it would insult a gentleman to apply intrusive vetting practices to him, selecting people mainly from their class was their form of screening.[88] Of course they had no objection to vetting their social inferiors. As Peter Wright observed, even in the 1950s, suspicion about the cause of leaks from British government offices usually fell upon clerks, cleaners, and secretaries.[89] From this perspective, screening the help only made good sense, and it was begun in the 1930s.

As in Canada, technique was an important part of the screening operation. The core of MI5's system was its extensive card index of suspected subversives, which grew considerably during the interwar period. Using this indispensable intelligence repository, MI5 was able, with some assurance, to check the names of all new employees in sensitive sections of the government and military, and thousands in industry as well. By early 1939 this vetting had already proven its worth by detecting a communist within the British Territorial Army.[90]

In the United States, formal and systematic security screening began by 1921, carried out by the FBI for the Civil Service Commission.[91] By 1936 the *FBI Manual* included a detailed outline of the requirements for investigating applicants for civil service postings, including the proper way to glean information about 'organizations of a quasi-political nature.'[92] Obtaining reliable information about the political affiliation of civil servants was obviously an important part of the FBI's vetting process. What the instructions describe is a positive vetting process, involving both a record check and background investigations and interviews.

As in Canada, the FBI's vast fingerprint records were central to its vetting operation. Its Civil Identification Section was founded in 1933, but even before it existed, in 1929, the Civil Service Commission began to send the fingerprints of its applicants to the FBI.[93] The manner in which fingerprinting was conducted during the 1930s demonstrates how important fingerprinting was to security screening in the United States. J. Edgar Hoover himself viewed them as inextricably linked. In January 1940, still twenty-two months before the United States entered the war, he told the House Appropriation Committee that many industrial employers were fingerprinting their employees, and that the fingerprints were 'being transmitted to the Bureau for check to ascertain whether any of these individuals have been engaged either in criminal or *subversive* activities.'[94]

Anxiety about political developments in the interwar years was accompanied by security screening of citizenship applicants, civil servants, and people in 'positions of trust.' By 1939 the RCMP had accumulated a wealth of security-screening experience through more than a decade of practice. The result was a security-screening system that had been well tested in a small-scale but authentic environment. Citizenship applicants were screened from the 1920s, and in the late 1930s the RCMP conducted at least a rudimentary security screening – fingerprinting and a check of records – of every newly hired permanent civil servant. In addition, the RCMP conducted full field inquiries into some civil service applicants' backgrounds.

Security screening was launched well after the First World War and well before the Second. Thus it cannot be seen as a response to a wartime emergency. It is true that in the late 1930s the imminence of a second confrontation with Germany hastened vetting, but it had begun long before 1939. At no point did the RCMP or the Civil Service Commission oblige historians by setting out for the record exactly why they introduced civil service screening. All we can discern is that the process began in a decade marked by political volatility, economic depression, international tension, the perfecting of fingerprinting and a grasp of its political use, the advance of police organization and preparation, and the existence of a growing bureaucracy freed from the constraints of patronage appointment. The political climate of the 1930s was thick with fear of economic malaise and revolution. In retrospect, we can see that Western security officials and politicians of all stripes, left and right, exaggerated the threat from Bolshevism and the world communist parties it nurtured. But this is hindsight. For contemporary participants, the fear – to some, the hope – of the Bolshevik Revolution was as pure as the colour red. In the absence of a single cause for the commencement of security screening, these factors must suffice to describe the pressures that encouraged its birth.

Although we cannot specify a single cause for the creation of the security-screening system, we can identify an outcome. Because of its years of security intelligence development, the RCMP was well prepared to deal with internal dissent when war loomed in the late summer of 1939. Accustomed to operating a complete, if small-scale, vetting system, the RCMP was able to use that experience to good advantage in the hectic early months of the war. The system was in place; the RCMP had only to extend the number of people caught up in it. The existence of this integrated machine also gave the RCMP a certain momentum by September 1939, so it had less difficulty reaching full speed during the war itself.

4

The infernal machine: Security screening during the Second World War

Saturday, 8 March 1941, was a momentous day in the Second World War. The United States Senate approved the Lend-Lease Bill, putting the industrial might of that officially neutral giant at the service of a beleaguered Britain. Italian forces were in retreat before a Greek offensive in Albania; an agitated Hitler darkly threatened a Balkan invasion. With so many pressing world events to report, it was little wonder that a matter-of-fact announcement about new controls on workers in Canadian war factories did not make page one of the *Globe and Mail*. The *Globe*'s article was meagre in the extreme – just six sentences long. It was also curiously vague – no dateline indicated where and when it had originated. It was, moreover, almost the antithesis of news, stating what seemed to be established practice:

Workers in factories engaged in war work are being fingerprinted as a measure of precaution ...

Finger-printing already is under way at factories with war contracts. Plans for this system were made toward the end of last year.

The Federal Government issued orders direct to the companies working on war work stating that finger-printing was necessary for the protection of all concerned.[1]

Brevity was not the only peculiarity about the article. Even its placement was odd. This measure, which would see 1 million Canadian workers subjected to a procedure that Canadian law applied only to serious crimes, and which the public abhorred, was not even consigned to a news page. The article was placed on page 25, the *Globe*'s funnies page. 'They'll Do It Every Time,' 'Life's Like That,' and 'Little Annie Rooney' competed for the reader's attention.

Two months earlier, the Royal Canadian Mounted Police had announced that industrial workers would soon be subject to screening which would require them to give 'particulars as to birth, naturalization and domestic affairs together with character references.'[2] But fingerprinting had not been mentioned. The cryptic *Globe and Mail* article and a similar story the same day in the *Toronto Star* were the first public announcements of the largest fingerprint registration in Canadian history.

The fingerprinting of war plant workers was a program initiated and implemented by the federal Department of Munitions and Supply (DMS) and the RCMP. It was an essential element in a huge security-screening program and, in the RCMP's view, 'an important cog in the machinery of internal protection.'[3] In the course of the war the RCMP received fingerprints from some 500 companies which had munitions contracts with the Canadian or British governments, as well as from public utilities, oil refineries, distilleries, and even a few corporations without war contracts. Each day over 500,000 people laboured in those plants.[4] By 1945 1 million Canadian workers had found themselves under the scrutiny of the RCMP.[5]

Wartime security screening did not stop there. The RCMP was also the final authority in the vetting of all applicants for the three armed forces. This involved fingerprinting and checking approximately another 1 million Canadians.[6] In addition, merchant seamen were fingerprinted, and many civil servants were screened.[7] In sum, the fingerprints of some 2.3 million civilians and military personnel were taken by the RCMP and military identification services during the war years.[8] The size of the group under surveillance is significant. In 1941 Canada's population was 11.5 million. So one Canadian in five was subjected to some form of security inquiry during the Second World War.

The scope and importance of this dramatic expansion of state security activity has been overlooked by all historians. For instance, writing about the Gouzenko case, Robert Bothwell and J.L. Granatstein argue that the vetting which went on in the Second World War was at best cursory. This claim, they say, is 'proven by the [1946 Kellock-Taschereau] Royal Commission's evidence that demonstrated that active communists held positions of trust. [During the war] vetting only rarely looked at ideological questions.'[9] In fact, the Second World War security-screening system was meticulously organized, extensive, and explicitly ideological. Its targets were several, but communists remained its primary focus. In other words, its most important purpose was overtly political, to monitor and control left-wing radicals.

This system was the most formidable inquiry into the lives and beliefs of Canadians ever seen in this country. In order to understand its features, how it worked, who it incorporated, what it did, and when and where it was implemented, we must first look at the conditions in which it was created.

THE WAR BRINGS NEW CONDITIONS

Just days before conflict on the Polish-German border flung the world into a six-year cataclysm, the *Globe and Mail* commented editorially that Canada's lack of air raid protection 'serves to remind us of how utterly unprepared we are for the catastrophe [of war].'[10] But, as Reg Whitaker has pointed out, Canada was ready for war in one regard – 'internal surveillance and control.'[11] Secret precautions to enforce internal security had already been taken. In 1936 the threat of a European conflict prompted the government to consider some of the internal security consequences of modern warfare.[12] More consistent efforts to strengthen Canada's internal security for the possibility of war began in 1938. One of the most important of these was the creation, in March 1938, of an interdepartmental committee to draft emergency legislation. The committee issued sixty-four proposals which became the core of the Defence of Canada Regulations (DOCR). Proclaimed under the War Measures Act on 3 September 1939, these regulations supplied the cabinet with the authority to rule by fiat throughout the war.[13] In the assessment of distinguished historian C.P. Stacey, the power thus conferred upon the cabinet and the prime minister was enormous.[14]

Canada's declaration of war on Germany in September 1939 created a new situation in the country; major changes would be necessary. By enacting the DOCR the government made it clear that peacetime freedoms would be severely curtailed. To reach a war footing Canada had to transform itself, mobilize en masse, vastly increase its production of war material, impose censorship and rationing, and take a host of other tough measures. No citizen would be spared from sacrifice and even hardship. Drastic changes to the prewar status quo were imperative. One of them would be a grand security-screening operation.

In such extraordinary circumstances, the Canadian labour movement was of particular importance. The two major labour centres, the Trades and Labor Congress (TLC) and the All-Canadian Congress of Labour (ACCL; after September 1940 the Canadian Congress of Labour, or CCL) both backed the government's war campaign. The TLC annual convention in September 1939 pledged its unwavering support to the Canadian and British governments.[15] In 1940 it also voted overwhelmingly to support the Defence of Canada Regulations, explaining that in war everyone had to be prepared to 'sacrifice personal liberty to some degree as the price to be paid for national security.'[16] In the same vein, the ACCL executive board declared in September 1939 that it had no hesitation 'in assuring the Government of its support in this period of crisis.'[17]

But while labour unions were prepared to make extraordinary sacrifices they were not ready to do so without qualification. Their loyalty came with conditions; one was that the full force of strict regulations should not fall only upon labour. Moreover, they wanted the state and employers to cooperate fully with labour and to recognize traditional union rights – to organize, to bargain collectively, and to strike. The *Canadian Congress Journal*, for instance, warned against the adoption of an extreme stand against labour such as was taken by the *Montreal Gazette*, which said that 'there should be no strikes in war industries anymore than there should be desertions from the Army.' 'The war will not be won by making the industrial workers of this country into industrial slaves,' admonished the *Journal*.[18] In addition, labour wanted to be taken into the government's confidence and properly consulted about wartime policies. In September 1939, after assuring the government that it supported the war, the *Canadian Unionist* quickly added that it endorsed Prime Minister Mackenzie King's own proposal for 'a National Advisory Council, on which Labour shall be represented ... for the purpose of co-ordinating all activities of the nation ... in the struggle in which the country is now engaged.'[19] Urging that union representatives be invited to join state war coordinating committees was a theme frequently, sometimes plaintively, reiterated throughout the war by these two influential labour journals. 'The workers want to co-operate in the war-effort; they can co-operate only through their unions. Wouldn't it be a good idea if they were allowed to co-operate?' editorialized the *Canadian Unionist* in April 1941.[20]

The foremost enemy of such cooperation within the labour movement, and the most feared national security threat, was the communists. By 1939 conservative and social democratic labour officials could look back on almost two decades of strife with communists over the direction of the labour movement.[21] The communist response to the war generated further distrust. The party had been vociferously anti-nazi for years before September 1939. But with the Soviet-German Non-Aggression Treaty of 23 August 1939 and the Comintern's opposition to the war, the Canadian Communist party made an awkward half-turn twist. Its policy spun from support for the Canadian war in early September to condemnation in October, to follow the Comintern line.[22] 'Stop the Imperialist War!' was the communists' major slogan for the March 1940 federal election.[23] After the Soviet-German pact, opined the *Canadian Congress Journal*, 'as far as the Communists were concerned, Naziism was no longer to be feared or fought.'[24]

The leadership of both the TLC and the CCL abhorred the communists and other subversives within unions and strove ceaselessly to purge them. Delegates at the fall 1940 conventions of the

TLC and the CCL took very similar stands in simultaneously linking and condemning nazis, fascists, and communists and urging
member unions to oust anyone who was known to espouse such
views. The *Canadian Unionist* avowed that workers 'will give
short shrift to "fifth columnists" and their dupes; they have no
sympathy with "fellow travellers" and the stupid or ignorant who
swallow their poisoned dope.'[25] In some cases communists were
barred; for example, Communist party members were cast out of
the Toronto District Labour Council.[26] But it was no easy task to
eradicate all communists, since they were key figures in many
unions, especially those affiliated with the Committee for Industrial Organization.[27] Banishing the communists was tightly bound
to the goal of attaining peace within the labour movement, which
would allow all-out participation in the government's war drive.
A.R. Mosher, president of the CCL, expressed the connection succinctly in March 1941 when he declared: 'When the workers are
adequately organized, *under proper leadership*, they will remedy
the evils which now cause discontent.'[28]

DEFINING THE ENEMY

In the public mind, aliens constituted a grave threat to Canada's
security. In the first year of the war people of German and Italian
origin were particularly targeted.[29] But the official view of people
of foreign birth was quite different. The Interdepartmental Committee on Emergency Legislation, created in 1938, had established
a special subcommittee to study the problem of immigrants and
subversion. It believed that most immigrants in Canada would be
loyal to the state in case of war. For that reason it recommended
that non-citizens of enemy origin should not be arrested or
detained en masse. They would be required to register with the
local Registrars of Enemy Aliens, but no further action would be
taken against them unless there were reasons to suspect an individual of disloyalty.[30] Once the war began, this internment plan
was carried out, and the number of interned enemy aliens was
surprisingly small. Prewar plans, for instance, called for just 814
people to be detained.[31] By war's end some 1100 enemy aliens had

been interned, compared to 8600 in the First World War.[32] This was not a mass roundup of immigrants but a selective seizure limited to specific targets.[33]

During the war the RCMP held a judicious attitude towards people of foreign extraction. The federal police were careful to contradict the notion that a foreigner equalled an enemy agent. Commissioner S.T. Wood, for instance, publicly proclaimed in early 1941 that it was not the alien but the communist who was the country's greatest adversary: 'Whereas the enemy alien is usually recognizable and easily rendered innocuous by clear-cut laws applicable to his case, your "Red" has the protection of citizenship, his foreign master is not officially an enemy and, unless he blunders into the open and provides proof of his guilt, he is much more difficult to suppress.'[34] Wood's declaration was important for more than the fact that it refuted the public fear of enemy aliens. It signalled a far-reaching transformation in security policy. Foreigners as a group were no longer considered to be the primary security problem. Wood's complaint about 'your "Red"' was that he was a *citizen* and invisible in the Canadian population. Within that population the enemy hid, and extraordinary security measures were going to be needed to detect him. This change in the target of the state's security police constituted an important shift in security and intelligence thinking in the first half of the twentieth century. Although as late as the 1930s police still saw 'dangerous foreigners' as the state's greatest adversary,[35] that perception faded in the early years of the Second World War.

One internal enemy was nazi sympathizers. Canada had its share of them, some directly connected to Hitler's regime.[36] Nazi-inspired agitators were the targets of raids by the RCMP beginning on 4 September 1939, six days before Canada was officially at war. This swift effort to intern 200 pro-German leaders effectively broke the movement's back.[37] Clifford Harvison, an RCMP intelligence officer during the war, later recalled that the raids 'completely wrecked' the nazi apparatus in Canada.[38] Thereafter the RCMP discounted the nazi threat. After September 1939, in its secret intelligence bulletins to the government and in public statements, the RCMP consistently maintained that nazis posed a secondary security threat.[39] This attitude was the cause of criticism from an official in the prime minister's office early in the war. In November 1939 Jack Pickersgill wrote a scathing memo which berated the RCMP's tendency to focus on the communists as the state's main enemy. Analysing the 30 October 1939 RCMP *Intelligence Bulletin*, Pickersgill detected an 'anti-Red complex' and 'an almost exclusive pre-occupation with so-called subversive organizations, and ... very little information about Nazis or Fascists.'[40]

Communism was a virtual obsession for the RCMP. As a target, the Communist party rose to prominence shortly after the end of the First World War, and it maintained that status in the RCMP's eyes throughout the interwar years.[41] Its warnings about the threat posed by the party intensified as the Second World War opened. Thus, in a 25 August 1939 letter to Justice Minister Ernest Lapointe in which he outlined a number of preventive actions in case war broke out, Wood called for 'a more rigid and extended surveillance of Communist Agitators, particularly those active among industrial workers.'[42] According to the RCMP, the party was especially dangerous because it 'has cells in practically every industry.'[43] In November 1939 the police revealed to the prime minister papers and copies of letters which showed, King wrote, 'efforts of communists to create dissatisfaction and sabotage.'[44] Throughout the Second World War, then, the federal police force devoted most of its attention to the internal adversary which had emerged at the end of the First World War.

Fear of communism was not confined to the RCMP. As with labour leaders, popular and élite opinion was strongly suspicious of the communists. Many people doubted the communists' loyalty to the country and feared that they were as dangerous as the nazis in their potential to sabotage the Canadian war effort. The *Vancouver Sun* expressed the suspicion that the nazis and communists had in fact united in May 1940 when it editorialized that 'Communism and Nazism are as alike as two peas. The fact that they go under different names is all the more reason for alertness.'[45] *Saturday Night* reiterated this view in asserting that Canadian communists were agents of Soviet policy, which was 'to aid Germany, up to a certain point, by hampering the war effort of the

Allies.'[46] The RCMP held a similar view. In April 1940 the *Intelligence Bulletin* editorialized against a 'Sickle-Swastika' alliance.[47]

The *Intelligence Bulletin* also drew a link between communists and industrial disruption. 'Better wages and working conditions ... are now seen only as a "legitimate" excuse for enlisting mass demonstrations calculated to retard our war efforts,' it argued in April 1940.[48] The RCMP claim appeared to be confirmed when a strike organized by the Canadian Seamen's Union, which was led by communists, tied up shipping for six days on the Great Lakes in April 1940. Some people, Ontario Fire Marshal William J. Scott among them, saw the strike as an act of sabotage.[49]

The Communist party's actual campaign against the war effort relied mostly upon propaganda and agitation.[50] Indeed an underground communist paper, the *Toronto Clarion*, dismissed the use of violence, saying that communists' duty 'to work night and day for the defeat of their "own" bourgeoisie ... does not mean foolish, anarchistic acts of violence, as the bourgeois press says.'[51] Peter Hunter, a long-time Communist party activist, dismissed out of hand the idea that party members would have obeyed the party's exhortations to turn the imperialist war into civil war. He has recalled that 'very few Party members I knew would have even considered such a policy. Many remained inactive.'[52] Historian Ivan Avakumovic declares that the party's political peregrinations caused members to leave in droves.[53] If the communists had been responsible for any sabotage the RCMP *Intelligence Bulletins* would have been sure to announce it, and the bulletins from 1939 right through to 1945 report no violent sabotage perpetrated by them.[54]

Canadian communists' oppositional phase ended abruptly on 22 June 1941, when German forces invaded the Soviet Union and the party reversed its stand on the war one more time. The Communist party's transformed position on the war was announced in a striking banner headline in the *Canadian Tribune* on 28 June 1941: 'World Fascism is Doomed!' An imperialist war had been transformed into a just war, according to party leader Tim Buck, because 'a fundamental change has taken place in the character of the war and the international situation.' The new conflict 'cuts across class lines,' declared Buck, and he called for all members and supporters of the party 'to exert all efforts to defeat Hitler.'[55] For the duration of the war the Canadian Communist party devoted itself to the Canadian government's policy of all-out war. The RCMP, however, refused to believe the transformation was genuine, and communists headed its list of security risks for the remainder of the war.[56]

CANADA'S FIFTH COLUMN CRISIS

With its vision of the internal enemy thus skewed, the RCMP was able to take advantage of a panic which engulfed the country in the early months of the war – the fear of sabotage. It was a singular and especially useful phobia. Sabotage emerged in the nineteenth century as a purely domestic threat, involving destruction of machinery by workers. But in the twentieth century, the enemy within was linked to an external antagonist. Saboteurs came to be seen as people who were trained to perpetrate violence against their own citizens to aid a foreign power. This connection to an outside enemy was an important development for security intelligence, because it denied the suspected saboteur protection from state surveillance or harassment.[57]

Sabotage was practised and feared during the First World War, but it took on a somber aura of terror during the 1930s. Anxiety about it was a staple of popular literature, like Richard Rowan's apocalyptic sagas, *Spies and the Next War*, *The Story of Secret Service*, and *Secret Agents against America*. Alfred Hitchcock, the film master whose finger was never far from the public pulse, directed four films on the subject in three years – *The Man Who Knew Too Much* (1934), *The Thirty Nine Steps* (1935), *The Secret Agent* (1936), and *Sabotage* (1936).[58] By 1939 sabotage had also become a potential threat familiar to Canadian business leaders. A Toronto firm, which specialized in procuring industrial spies, declared in a 29 March 1939 promotional letter that 'A recent survey indicates that manufacturers and business men in general, are alive to the necessity of protecting their business and their employees from sabotage.'[59]

Sabotage was a potent label outside of the capitalist world, too. 'Saboteurs' and 'wreckers' were the favourite charges used to purge thousands of Communist party members in Stalin's Soviet Union. As in the West, it signalled fear of the undetected enemy within, the traitor whose public face gave no cause for alarm. More vividly than any other word, it signalled the collusion between a foreign power and innocent-appearing citizens. Ironically, Canadian communists contributed to the fear of sabotage in this country through articles warning about nazi spies in the *Daily Clarion* during the late 1930s.[60]

In Canada action to combat sabotage began even before the war. By April 1939 plants of the Hydro-Electric Power Commission of Ontario were already guarded. The next month the commission's chief engineer rejected requests to photograph its Leaside power site because of 'our present concern about possible sabotage.'[61] And the RCMP used the threat of sabotage to justify the arrest of pro-nazi agitators in the early days of September 1939.[62]

If talk of sabotage was a current before the war, it swelled to a flood with the outbreak of war and became a raging torrent in the spring of 1940. Denmark, Norway, Luxembourg, Belgium, and Holland all toppled before the German *blitzkrieg*. Ruinous as they were, those defeats were dwarfed by the unimaginably swift collapse of France in June 1940. These catastrophes forced the Canadian state and people to recognize the dire situation they were in. Britain itself was in grave difficulty. If it fell, Canada, as its major ally, could face the full force of German military might. On 12 June Justice Minister Lapointe warned Canadians that they 'could no longer rely upon the Allied armies and the British fleet for protection against invasion.'[63] Prime Minister Mackenzie King declared before a solemn House of Commons on 18 June: 'The plain facts are that the defeat of France has brought the war much nearer home to Canada ... It is now wholly apparent that additional measures both for the assistance of Britain and for the defence of Canada are essential.'[64]

The crisis aroused a public alarm in the country, the centre of which was the fear of internal saboteurs and fifth columnists. The

Germans' lightning conquest of the western European countries provoked concern and speculation. What else could explain the victories but the presence of enemy agents inside the target nations?[65] Mass meetings throughout Canada in May and June called for sweeping action against enemy aliens and suspected fifth columnists. In Vancouver rallies of 7000 on 26 May and 5000 on 28 May demanded that the federal government organize veterans to assist the police in fighting 'espionage or sabotage, whether of word or deed, or in any other role,' and urged the government to bar 'aliens of enemy birth ... from employment in any government or municipal service or in key industries, and discharge those at present employed.'[66] In Calgary a crowd of 7000 demanded internment of Germans and other measures to combat the threat of fifth columnists. Fear of possible rioting there led Police Chief David Ritchie to close the Ukrainian Labor-Farmer Temple Association office and the Russian Workers and Farmers Club.[67] In Windsor an assembly of 3000 ex-servicemen called for protective measures, such as the registration of every person in Canada and internment of all enemy aliens.[68] In Toronto 50,000 ex-servicemen rallied on 9 June to demand that the federal government act decisively to put the country on a total war footing. The most effective fifth columnists in Canada, Major the Reverend H.F. Woodcock told the crowd, 'are those in positions of authority who have adopted half-hearted purposes, thus bringing only a fraction of our power to bear on the problem of winning a war.'[69] In Montreal a gathering of 7000 at Atwater Market on 27 May heard Colonel J.J. Creelman declare that the peacetime maxim of allowing 100 guilty persons to go free rather than jailing a single innocent must be abandoned. In wartime, all suspects must be arrested, he asserted.[70]

This fear of the fifth column and the demand for internment, national registration, and, most importantly, active prosecution of the war, were also voiced in the House of Commons, by public officials, and on the pages of daily newspapers. Waterloo South MP Karl Homuth told the House on 27 May that 'there is a real fear on the part of people. There are a great many of these enemies at large in Canada.' He called for the internment of suspects who,

he said, could later be given an opportunity to prove their innocence. He also reiterated a popular belief that registration of all
citizens would help ease public concern by allowing for a check
on subversives.[71] Vancouver East MP Angus MacInnis presented
a communication from the mayor of Vancouver reporting 'considerable feeling ... against enemy aliens and enemy sympathizers.'
The mayor added that 'unless there is an assurance from the federal government that adequate measures are being taken to cope
with subversive activities of such people, citizens may organize
for that purpose.'[72]

Among the leading figures who seized the sabotage issue, none
was more driven than Ontario Fire Marshal William J. Scott.
Scott's position kept him in close communication with the director and assistant director of the Federal Bureau of Investigation in
the United States, J. Edgar Hoover and Edward Tamm respec-
tively. The FBI heads directed a stream of advice, news, and
inquiries to him. Scott's prestige as fire marshal in the province
with the greatest concentration of wartime industry made him a
useful ally north of the border. Scott reciprocated by feeding the
FBI information about developments in Canada. His connection
and ideological affinity with Hoover and Tamm helped him to
bask in their reflected prestige, adding considerably to his own
influence. It also fuelled him with delectable secrets about 'incendiary bombs and other infernal machines' which he divulged in a
torrid round of sermons to police forces, civic leaders, civilian
protection committees, and public service groups in the first years
of the war. As visual aids the FBI provided models of incendiary
devices disguised as pencils and cigars, while Scott repaid the
debt by sending south medals awarded to Canadian communists
who excelled at signing up members or newspaper subscribers.[73]

As a conduit of sabotage tales and lore between the United
States and Canada, Scott helped to generalize experience from
one country to the other. His purpose in speaking and writing
about sabotage was not just to alert Canadians to its possibility.
He also spoke frequently in the United States and sought to put a
scare into Americans by distributing 'some Canadian war propaganda along the lines of what the Germans did to them last time

when they were at peace [1914–1917], and what they can expect the Germans, and probably the Communists, also to do now.'[74] Scott was also a persistent advocate of security screening, beginning his campaign in an October 1939 War Emergency Bulletin, which he issued to thousands of corporations, government departments, and police forces in Canada, the United States, and Britain.[75]

The rising tide of fifth column fear is revealed through a day-by-day reading of the *Globe and Mail* and the *Toronto Star* in the months of September 1939 and June 1940. In September 1939 the *Globe* published 26 articles about sabotage, spies, and the fifth column. On the same subject there were four editorials but no letters or photos. The *Star* published 103 articles, three letters, one editorial and two photos about the fifth column. In June 1940 the *Globe* published 116 articles, ten editorials, four letters, and four photos on the subject. In the same month the *Star* published 164 articles, one editorial, seven letters, and three photos about the issue.[76]

The public's intolerance for dissent in the gloomy days of May and June 1940 was revealed after the Canadian Civil Liberties Union (CCLU) brought together in Montreal some 500 people in a national conference dealing with civil liberties in wartime. RCMP Superintendent H.A.R. Gagnon, commanding the Quebec division, reported that 'this Office has since been deluged with complaints from various individuals and many of prominents [*sic*] in connection with permitting this organization to function.' The public yen for vengeance seemed even to cause the RCMP some jitters. Gagnon told the RCMP commissioner that 'it is time that some drastic action be taken before we are confronted with demonstrations by the complaining organizations.'[77] On 5 June 1940 the police got their wish: the government banned sixteen groups, including the Communist party and organizations affiliated with it (although not the CCLU).

The RCMP was anxious not to let public frenzy get out of hand. There was 'no room for sixth columns,' the force warned in the pages of its *Intelligence Bulletin*. 'Police forces are swamped with a flood of complaints regarding alleged subversive activities. Switch-boards are jammed with messages to the same effect. A well meaning but ill-informed public, particularly veterans and their organizations, are letting their imagination run riot. Old incidents, second-hand gossip, a German-sounding name, a Teutonic haircut, almost anything now assumes a sinister aspect.'[78] By late May the RCMP was so overwhelmed by telephone reports of fifth columnists that it appealed to people to write letters detailing their complaints rather than calling the police.[79] In Montreal the RCMP urged citizens to stop denouncing aliens as fifth columnists in public and in their homes.[80]

Federal politicians also tried to calm the collective fear. Three days after the RCMP issued the above warning in its *Intelligence Bulletin*, Justice Minister Ernest Lapointe repeated the statement word for word to a House of Commons committee examining the Defence of Canada Regulations. Apprehension about the fifth column 'had reached a stage bordering on hysteria,' he was reported to have said.[81] Like the RCMP, Lapointe wanted Canadians to leave anti-subversive work to the police. 'They know better; they are trained.'[82] Lapointe and Air Minister C.G. Power publicly chastised Ontario Premier Mitchell Hepburn as 'reckless and impetuous' for alarming the public by claiming that nazi sympathizers in the United States were preparing to invade Ontario. Even the *Globe and Mail*, which throughout June 1940 insisted that authorities deal with the sabotage threat, labelled the premier's story 'hysteria.'[83]

In June the tumult peaked; thereafter, it began to decline. Two bold steps by the federal government that month seemed to calm citizens by acting on at least some of their demands. On 5 June it banned nazi and communist organizations and on 18 June, just two days after France capitulated to Germany, it announced national registration. The National Resources Mobilization Act which imposed registration was passed swiftly in parliament, and in August 1940 the registration was accomplished.[84] The King government finally appeared to be taking the decisive measures required for total war.

By March 1941, when the RCMP's industrial vetting program was significantly expanded, the popular fixation upon the fifth column had almost dissipated. The issue was disappearing from the pages of daily newspapers. In March 1941 the number of articles in the *Globe* on sabotage and the fifth column was only twenty, and three of these dealt with sabotage perpetrated by the nascent resistance movements in occupied Europe. No editorials and just one letter and photo each were published on the subject. The change was equally dramatic in the *Star*. In March 1941 that newspaper published just thirty-three articles, two letters, one photo and no editorials on the subject. One signal of the calmer atmosphere in March 1941 was the fact that the *Globe and Mail*, which had frequently criticized the government for complacency in the spring of 1940, was now complaining about an overreaction. On 12 June 1940 the *Globe and Mail* had editorialized that 'there is a potential danger in this country which the Federal Government is treating with tragic complacency.' Articles and editorials with the same thrust were common throughout the months of April, May, and June 1940. The *Globe*'s language was frequently less than judicious, and one must ask whether the newspaper itself did not contribute to public concern: 'Spies used to work in twos and threes, but it is now seen in Denmark and Norway they may invade a country by battalions. They seek to sabotage the national war effort ... They are highly organized and dangerous. They are everywhere.' Nine months later, however, the same paper declared: 'Those who had been complacent went to the other extreme and became arbitrary and autocratic, throwing hundreds of innocent people into internment camps without a hearing of any sort. British justice was flouted.'[85] This relative serenity in newspaper rhetoric by March 1941 suggests that, while public fears of sabotage played a role in introducing security-screening, that factor was reduced by the time the program began to work in earnest.

Less agitated than the public, federal government agencies and departments like the RCMP and Munitions and Supply were nonetheless determined to ensure that no fifth column undermined the Canadian war effort. RCMP officials consistently cited sabotage in explaining the need for security screening.[86] This threat was the official justification for the full-scale program of security screening which began in January 1941. A dramatic *Tor-*

onto Star article summed up this view. In March 1940, just seven months after the war began and a full year before the security-screening program was publicly announced, the newspaper printed an article based on an interview with Superintendent E.W. Bavin, head of the RCMP Intelligence Section. The headline issued an ominous warning: 'R.C.M.P. Intelligence Dept. Ready to Jump on "Trusted" Industrial Workers.' Clearly intended to calm public dread of sabotage by showing the RCMP to be on top of the problem, the article gave no specifics about the program that was being devised. But Bavin revealed how wide-ranging the RCMP inquiry would be when he confided that the saboteur 'may be a trusted, or at least unsuspected, employee who has wormed his way into the confidence of his employers.'[87] Given this type of propaganda it should not have surprised the RCMP at all that employers began asking the force to conduct background checks on people who had worked for them for as long as twenty years.[88] Even those who were apparently most loyal were now under suspicion.[89]

What constituted sabotage was broadly interpreted. For public authorities, sabotage became a term of convenience, a handy catch-all that could be used to condemn many types of dissenters. In the House of Commons, it was thrown back and forth by the government and the opposition. According to Liberal Hughes Cleaver, anyone who 'attempts to undermine or weaken confidence in the government's prosecution of the war is positively guilty of sabotage of the nation's war effort.'[90] From the opposition side, Victor Quelch issued the accusation: 'For five years [before 1940] the government deliberately sabotaged the life of this country' by failing to create the industrial capacity needed for the war.[91]

The RCMP also had a broad, amorphous understanding of the meaning of sabotage. In the pages of the wartime *Intelligence Bulletin*, sabotage was used to describe a variety of actions. Since violent sabotage was virtually non-existent, the bulletins devoted attention to other forms. The most important of these were strikes, almost always fomented by communists.[92] The RCMP appeared to have no faith that workers were capable of resisting communist machinations in the workplace. A handful of communists – as few as five in a plant – constituted a threat to normal production.[93] Moreover, according to RCMP thinking, workers could be manipulated by communists into acting as unwitting saboteurs. Communist union officials could push production costs 'so high that Management will refuse to pay them and the Workers will walk out thus sabotaging our defence of democracy.'[94] The bulletins also applied the term sabotage to misinformation about Canada given to potential tourists from the United States and to the purchase by two American firms of the entire Canadian supply of calves' bellies (necessary to the production of rennet, an ingredient in cheese).[95] In 1942, RCMP Inspector Joseph Howe warned that the most dangerous form of sabotage was 'extremely slow work.'[96] And the same year, when he acknowledged that 'no organized system of sabotage exists in Canada,' Assistant Commissioner R.R. Tait asserted that the 'most insidious types of sabotage' were those involving 'carelessness, error of judgment, or oversight.'[97] These concepts of sabotage were not necessarily invalid. Pierre Dubois's study indicates that sabotage takes many forms.[98] Nevertheless, it is important to recognize that the meaning of sabotage was so ambiguous that it could be stretched to cover potential political and economic acts by a variety of dissidents, union members and workers. The fact that the word remained amorphous was useful to the RCMP. It meant that security screening could be invoked and justified as an effective measure against several types of problems and foes.

Public fear of an ill-defined threat, then, was a vital part of the context in which security screening was inaugurated. More importantly, the fear was useful to the RCMP, which often invoked the spectre of sabotage in justifying the need to delve into people's pasts. Such a rationale seemed entirely supportable, but it was an argument that played more to public anxiety than to the RCMP's genuine concern. This is not to suggest that the RCMP used the threat cynically. Certainly the force was not above referring to it as a reality, even though it believed that it had forestalled sabotage through its timely arrests of nazi sympathizers in September 1939.[99] Its own internal assessments, issued throughout the war, stressed that there was no organized sabotage in Canada.[100] But the RCMP was never as swept up in the alarm as was the public. Indeed, it strove to calm the winds of hysteria in the spring of 1940.

In short, what we observe is a difference between the public's view of the threat of sabotage and the assessment of the Canadian state's security intelligence agency and federal government officials. The public mood was very agitated, even hysterical. The RCMP's statements, to the public and privately to the government, stressed that the situation was under control. It believed that it had nipped the problem in the bud by interning opponents, guarding vulnerable points, and instituting industrial protection measures, and it held to this view before and after the fifth column crisis of May–June 1940.[101] Nonetheless, the RCMP cited the fear of sabotage as a justification for industrial vetting. How much this was genuine and how much it was a concession to the public mood is impossible to say. In any case, even the public mood seemed to shift after the disastrous days of spring 1940. By January 1941, when the full-scale screening program was introduced in industry, Canadians' preoccupation with sabotage was largely spent.

THE SECURITY-SCREENING SYSTEM AND HOW IT WORKED

The vetting of many people, including civil servants and some industrial workers, proceeded smoothly as Europe slid from apprehended to actual war. Early in 1939 the RCMP had worked out a scheme to vet people employed in munitions plants. The program was aimed at identifying 'foreign elements' who would be registered in the subversive files of the RCMP.[102] The system was immediately applicable once Germany invaded Poland and Canada found itself at war. In the ensuing years of conflict, the system improved organizationally, and it engulfed more and more Canadians.

By May 1940 established practice was that civil servants hired into the Department of National Defence were checked for 'subversive tendencies, etc.' The RCMP advised the Civil Service

Commission that fingerprint records for these civil servants could also be searched, and it set out the vital prerequisites for such a search: (1) voluntary agreement by the employee to an RCMP check of the prints (by law, only people committing indictable offenses could be fingerprinted); and (2) proper training for CSC staff in how to take fingerprints, which the RCMP offered to impart.[103]

Fingerprinting of civil servants was recommended as a security measure in a 1 August 1940 report of the Interdepartmental Committee for Co-ordination of Intelligence for War Purposes. The committee made the proposal because it saw Ottawa as the place with the greatest potential to harbour espionage, even though it contended that leaks were more likely to occur through civil servants talking shop outside the office than through agents working their way into the government.[104] The Interdepartmental Committee had earlier in 1940 assisted in establishing an efficient system to channel intelligence about civil servants to the RCMP.[105]

By February 1940 the RCMP had begun to recommend fingerprinting to twelve private companies. For example, the Force urged Ottawa Car and Aircraft Ltd to fingerprint applicants and employees alike, company president Redmond Quain reported to Ontario Fire Marshal Scott.[106] The twelve probably owed their special status to the fact that they supplied munitions to Britain.[107] A vetting program was confined to those twelve companies until January 1941. In place for more than a year before the formal announcement of screening, this system was an early version of the much grander operation that began in 1941. Before this full-scale screening system was launched, the RCMP produced a new industrial security manual, *The Protection of Industry in Time of War*, replacing the booklet *Notes on Industrial Security* it had written in spring 1939. Complete by November 1940, *The Protection of Industry in Time of War* addressed itself to corporations filling contracts for the Canadian Department of Munitions and Supply (DMS) and the British Supply Board. In it industrialists were 'strongly advised to have all present and prospective employees fingerprinted.'[108]

The Department of Munitions and Supply (DMS) was a driving

force behind the vetting proposal. Its historian's description of the department as 'the centre from which all war production radiated' distills into a phrase its innumerable tasks.[109] One of those assignments was coordinating industrial security among the hundreds of corporations with munitions-supply contracts. Industrial security was a concern of the department virtually from its inception in April 1940. At first the Legal Branch of the DMS was responsible for security, but the duty soon became sufficiently onerous that a separate branch, the Industrial Security Branch, was established in July 1941.[110] In November 1940 the DMS appointed a security officer, R.L. Anderson, to carry out security efforts and coordinate them with the RCMP. One of Anderson's first actions was to send a letter to companies with DMS contracts advising them to screen their employees, to fingerprint them, and to submit the fingerprints to the RCMP. The 21 January 1941 package, largely prepared by the RCMP, contained a sample employee application/registration form (appendix 1), the RCMP's fingerprint identification form (appendix 2) and the RCMP's industrial security booklet, numbered and marked 'Secret.'[111]

Before the war began the RCMP undertook an ambitious national survey of vulnerable points.[112] When war was declared, among the first people to be fingerprinted and screened were the 1100 special constables hired by the RCMP to guard some eighty-five vulnerable points across the country. Since the RCMP expected immediate sabotage attempts, it quickly took on a great number of guards, most of them ex-servicemen. Only then were they fingerprinted. They were no angels, as Inspector Harvison foresaw in July 1939: 'a certain percentage of the returned men have grown long on the drinking and short on the discipline and would be about as hard a gang to handle as imaginable.'[113] Checks of their fingerprints revealed many to have criminal records. By the end of November 1939 in Montreal alone seventy-eight guards had been discharged because of past crimes.[114] However, the screening of the home guards was not perfect. Among the guards at the Kananaskis internment camp in Alberta was Jimmy Wilson, who fought in the Mackenzie-Papineau Battalion during the Spanish Civil War.[115] This record should have marked him as a sympathizer, if not a member, of the Communist party, but Wilson was put to work guarding interned communists.

The number of people swept into the system grew apace. In the first year of the war the RCMP screened several thousand civil servants and industrial workers. The exact number is unknown, since there are no detailed figures from the RCMP Fingerprint Section's Civilian Identification Collection. However, by December 1943 the collection numbered three-quarters of a million.[116] In 1943–4, 310 organizations forwarded a further 362,545 sets of fingerprints to the RCMP, and in the 1944–5, 233,000 sets were submitted, bringing the total to over one million.[117]

Security screening and its concomitant fingerprinting did not stop there. The DMS fingerprinted all of its employees, eventually numbering almost 5000.[118] The 1941 annual report of the RCMP Intelligence and Liaison Section listed a number of other government departments and branches of the armed forces whose members were being screened by the section. For example, persons assigned by the Civil Service Commission to employment in the departments of National Defence, Naval Service, Militia Service, and Air Service, as well as personnel in the Department of Transport and the Inspection Board of the United Kingdom and Canada, all had their names checked against RCMP subversive and general records. Personnel in the Royal Air Force Ferry Command were checked against the RCMP subversive records.[119] By 1941, according to the RCMP *Annual Report*, the force vetted 'practically all departments of the Government.'[120]

Personnel in the National Research Council and those in associated institutions like McGill University who were working on NRC projects were checked against the RCMP subversive records.[121] Screening of NRC personnel began as an effort to prevent any 'leakage of information.'[122] In October 1940 the RCMP intelligence officer, Superintendent E.W. Bavin, approached NRC president C.J. Mackenzie about vetting his employees. Having talked with Mackenzie about the top-secret experimental work going on at the council, Bavin urged immediate action: 'It seems necessary that the most extensive enquiries should be instituted with regard to the reliability of the personnel employed in these laboratories and also of the clerical staff who deal with the correspondence ... Mr Mackenzie is very anxious for this to be done, as he says he and other members of the Council spend many sleepless nights wondering how safe this important information is being kept.'[123] Commissioner Wood assigned a trained intelligence investigator, Detective Sergeant T.G. Scrogg, to the NRC, and informed Mackenzie that within days 'we will commence extensive inquiries, first of all to establish the reliability of all employees.'[124] Detective Sergeant Scrogg reported early in 1941 that questionnaires had been received from NRC employees. The investigation process he set out had two prongs: 'Those employees belonging to the Secret Radio Division and of Chemical Warfare will be investigated individually as to their antecedents. The remainder of the employees will be checked with our files.'[125] In 1945 this screening was still going on. And the end of the war in Europe did not conclude the RCMP's security inquiries into NRC employees. In July 1945 Intelligence Officer C.E. Rivett-Carnac reported that the RCMP would still check its files on employees. 'In any special cases where extra secret work, etc. is concerned a specific request will be made for more detailed investigation.'[126] The particulars of this screening system are unknown, so it is not clear how people like Dr Raymond Boyer and David Shugar, who were identified by the 1946 Kellock-Taschereau Royal Commission as members of the Soviet espionage ring, slipped through the investigation.[127] While it is evident that the system was not flawless, system there was.

The 1941 Intelligence and Liaison Section report also noted that 'Applicants for employment on work of a secret and confidential nature and applicants of foreign origin have also been investigated for the Navy, Army, and Air Force, as well as for the Chief Postal Censor, the Air Service Department, Canadian Pacific Railway. These latter employees being engaged in ferrying aircraft from Canada to the United Kingdom.' In addition, names of personnel of the Royal Canadian Air Force were checked against subversive and criminal records, as were those in 'certain private industries employed on Government contracts.'[128]

The 1945 report of the same section remarked that the force's duties included vetting of all applicants for the three armed forces and

security investigation of persons in the employ of Canadian and Allied governments; enquiries on behalf of the U.S. Consular Offices in connection with persons of foreign extraction desiring entry into the United States. Enquiries made at the request of the U.S. United Services operating in the North West Territories on the Alaska Military Highway and the Canol project covering employees on both operations involved a great deal of investigation and correspondence.

This report added that three other groups underwent security screening: Canadians recruited to work for the United Nations Relief and Rehabilitation Administration, Canadians interned in Europe who sought to return to Canada, and Jewish refugees from Europe.[129] This shows how far security screening extended late in the war. The people returning to Canada were citizens, so the inquiry was not justified by naturalization application. And they were not applying for civil service work. They were being investigated because they had lived in a region defined to be infected ideologically – by both nazi and communist thinking. And the screening was conducted in depth – to the extent of field investigations 'where there was a question of identity.'[130]

All three branches of the Canadian military also relied on fingerprinting as part of their security-screening system, and their security routines were coordinated with the RCMP. The RCAF inaugurated its identification bureau in 1940, requiring of its personnel both fingerprints and photographs. Each member was also issued with an identity card. By 1944 an IBM card index system had been completed for virtually every Air Force member, some 250,000 in total. Each card contained the name and fingerprint classification of a recruit or civilian member.[131] Occasionally the RCAF asked for special screening, such as that for 2500 men who were being given secret training at fifteen Canadian universities.[132]

The Canadian Army Identification Bureau was established on 1 September 1942 under an order authorizing the fingerprinting and photographing of all military and civilian personnel in the Department of National Defence. A progress report of 10 July 1943 noted that almost 314,000 military and 16,000 civilian personnel had been fingerprinted to that point, with some 223,000 identification cards having been issued. Later in the war army and navy identification records were merged into the Canadian Bureau of Identification. By the end of March 1945 it had fingerprinted and photographed some 837,000 army and navy personnel.[133]

Enemy aliens were required to be fingerprinted when they registered, which, according to the director of the Immigration Branch, 'should not cause any uneasiness as the same method is followed in connection with persons entering the Dominion Civil Service.'[134] In addition, an order in council in June 1940 provided for the photographing and fingerprinting of anyone detained or convicted under the Defence of Canada Regulations.[135]

An overview of the security-screening system will demonstrate how it worked. Since before the outbreak of the war, the government had insisted that primary responsibility for the safety of a private corporation rested with the company's owners. At least in theory, the RCMP and the DMS strictly applied this principle to security screening. The 21 January 1941 letter sent by the DMS to industrial plants insisted that plant security officers conduct the first check on any employee 'concerning whose bona fides there is any doubt.' If, after that process was completed, doubts still existed about the employee, the security officer was urged to ask the RCMP to check its subversive records. The RCMP declared itself willing to 'check any number of employees when the above conditions are complied with, but WILL NOT check mere lists of names as this is largely a waste of time.'[136] The same process was applied later in the war to the military.[137]

Several steps were involved in comparing the names and fingerprints of war plant workers and others with the Force's subversive and criminal records.

1/At the Criminal Investigation Branch (Fingerprint Section), RCMP headquarters:
a A name comparison was made between war-plant lists and

criminal records. Some people were immediately identified as having committed offenses; most were not. (After the system was in place for a time the RCMP asked companies to submit the names of employees in key positions on special lists, so that the Fingerprint Section could check them first.[138])

b Fingerprints for each person were classified and given an alphanumeric identification following the Henry system.

c The Henry code for each employee's fingerprint was compared – sometimes manually but sometimes with the assistance of IBM tabulating equipment – with fingerprint codes in the RCMP's files. For those identified as having criminal records, the nature of the offense was recorded and the application set aside.

d The fingerprint forms for war plant employees were filed in the civilian identification section of the RCMP Fingerprint Section. Those for government employees were returned to the department in which they worked.[139]

2/ At the Intelligence and Liaison Section, RCMP headquarters:

a Each name on the lists submitted by employers, the Civil Service Commission, and military intelligence was sent to the appropriate divisional office in each province and compared to the index of known and suspected subversives and associates.

b If no subversive record was found at the divisional level, a check of the subversive records at RCMP headquarters was undertaken.[140]

c When full character investigations were carried out, the procedure involved a check of (1) RCMP criminal records; (2) Enemy Alien Office records (where applicable); (3) RCMP Intelligence Branch files (subversive records); (4) fingerprint records (when fingerprints were provided); (5) referees and associates of the person.[141]

3/ Results of the checks of subversive and criminal records were forwarded to divisional headquarters (for war plant workers), where a civil security liaison officer would contact the security officer at each company to relay information about those deemed to be security risks. For civil servants, the subversive or criminal records were sent directly to the employee's department; for armed forces personnel, to the appropriate military identification or intelligence bureau.[142]

Conducting security screening on this scale severely taxed the RCMP's personnel resources. The size of the total RCMP organization increased considerably during the war, rising from 2540 in 1939 to its wartime peak of 4928 in 1943. But it was the Intelligence Section and the Fingerprint Section which shouldered the main burden of wartime screening. Each grew enormously in the war years. On the eve of the Second World War the Intelligence Section at headquarters numbered just 6, and the senior intelligence officer, Charles Rivett-Carnac, doubled as the editor of the *RCMP Quarterly.* By 1943 the group at headquarters involved in intelligence numbered 98, with at least 48 others in the country's three major cities.[143] The RCMP's entire headquarters staff in 1943 was 203, so the Intelligence Section constituted almost half of that group.[144] As for the Fingerprint Section, in 1937 the staff numbered 25, all of them regular RCMP officers. By 1943 the FPS staff, including regular officers and civilian women, totalled just over 100.[145] Although the wartime growth of these security-related sections was remarkable, even at the peak their absolute size was small, and we know, for instance, that the FPS was greatly overburdened.[146]

The RCMP, however, was not alone in gathering, filtering, and processing intelligence about workers. The federal police strongly advised plant owners to create an internal security service to take the first step in weeding out subversives. *The Protection of Industry in Time of War* warned: 'The most elaborate and costly system of guarding and other external protective measures are rendered completely worthless if no effort is made to seek out the saboteur who nonchalantly passes the guards and punches a time clock at the employees' entrance.' While the RCMP discouraged the use of private detective agencies in industrial plants, it highly recommended that plant security officers secretly organize 'old and trusted employees' into a corps of 'Security Watchers intent on performing a patriotic duty by maintaining one hundred per cent production.'[147] In some plants this must have been hard to do, and the management had to resort to more blatant methods to accumulate security data. Workers at DeHavilland Aircraft in Toronto, for instance, were instructed by notices hung throughout the plant that 'it is your patriotic duty to report subversive or un-British talk to your Charge Hand or to the Security Officer.'[148]

In addition, many security officers, some of whom doubled as personnel officers, were former RCMP officers.[149] For example, the plant security officer at the Marine Industries factory at Sorel, Quebec, was a special agent who provided the RCMP with information over the course of four years.[150] Developing undercover agents in factories was considered by the RCMP to be a high priority and an effective anti-sabotage tactic.[151] Intelligence gleaned from the security officers was fed into the RCMP and DMS network.[152] By using the plant security officers and their loyal employees as informants, the RCMP increased the state's intelligence network within the private sector. It is difficult to determine how widespread or effective this practice was, since no official records on it have been found. But its scope might be gauged by one claim. In March 1941 the *Toronto Clarion* – as the Communist party's main underground paper admittedly not an unbiased source – reported that RCMP agents were rife in factories. These 'stool pigeons, strikebreakers and *agents provocateurs*' were performing their mischief in eighty-five companies, it alleged.[153]

Even this extensive screening system was at times not enough for employers. In early 1941 corporations plotted other strategies to trace and even blacklist workers, with the assistance of the state. At the February 1941 meeting of the Ontario Co-ordinating Committee for Security, senior corporate executives and police officers frankly discussed establishing, in the words of Ontario Provincial Police Inspector A.S. Wilson, 'a clearing house in the Dominion of Canada through which firms engaged in war production could be supplied with information regarding employees discharged for subversive activity, suspicion of sabotage or disloyalty, etc., where the evidence has not been sufficient for prosecution.' Ontario Fire Marshal Scott, a lawyer by training, warned about possible libel suits if such information accidently became public. Still, he expressed enthusiasm for a blacklist of the names of every worker who resigned, 'even if the man had apparently left the position for an honest reason.' That view was seconded by C.I. Scott, the National Steel Car Aircraft Division director of personnel and security. He also dismissed concerns about potential violations of civil liberties by asserting that 'we in Canada were sticking too close to the fine points in this time of war.' In the end the committee members were mollified by the information that new federal regulations penalized a company which enticed employees from another, thereby discouraging workers from changing employers. The committee also passed a motion to have Ottawa order companies to both fingerprint and photograph all employees and to notify the RCMP 'of any act, or suspected act, of subversive activity or sabotage on the part of any of their employees.'[154]

THE EFFECTIVENESS OF SECURITY SCREENING

The security-screening system in Canada during the Second World War represented an exercise in vigilance by the Canadian state in which considerable care was devoted to details. This belies Bothwell and Granatstein's description of it as cursory. Yet there has so far been no answer to the question raised by Bothwell and Granatstein: if a vetting system was in place, how was it possible for communists to penetrate the Canadian state?

Entrance to the state was not an open door. Although we will never know how many dissidents were kept out of the civil service by security screening, we know of at least one case. A Montreal woman who applied to perform temporary editorial work for the Nationalities Branch of the Department of National War Services was ruled out because an RCMP security report concluded that she was a subscriber to the *Canadian Tribune* and secretary of the local branch of the Writers, Artists and Broadcasters War Council, an organization 'the Communists are taking some interest in.'[155] In any case, as the Security Panel concluded in 1947, it was doubtful that any of the people named as spies by the

Kellock-Taschereau Commission 'would have been discovered by any conceivable system of "screening."'[156]

Still, it is true that communists worked in the state. Herbert Norman was one. His is perhaps the most renowned instance of a communist or former communist joining the Canadian government in the early war years. Norman was one of the bright young men attracted to communism during his student days at the University of Toronto in the early 1930s. He pursued his studies – and his infatuation with communism – at Cambridge University at a time when it was the breeding ground for Soviet spies like Kim Philby, Donald Maclean, Guy Burgess, and Anthony Blunt. Norman completed his PhD at Harvard University in 1940, writing a landmark study of the formation of the Japanese state. By the time he began his career in the Department of External Affairs at the Canadian legation in Tokyo in May 1940, his interest in communism appeared to be strictly academic, and in his subsequent career in External Affairs he devoted his brilliance to serving Canada. During the Second World War, his wealth of knowledge about Japan and his familiarity with the Japanese language made Norman invaluable. It was not surprising, then, that in 1942, upon his return to Canada from internment in Japan, Norman became head of the Special Research Section of the Examination Unit, a top-secret signals intelligence branch which was administered by the National Research Council but which reported to the Department of External Affairs, Norman's own department. Norman's section analysed the data obtained from monitored Japanese telecommunications signals. This put Norman in one of the most sensitive intelligence posts in the Canadian government. Because of the Examination Unit's liaison with code-breaking organizations in Britain and the United States, Norman was also privy to details about one of the Allies' most formidable secret weapons, the cryptanalysis which came to be known by the code name ULTRA.[157] After the war, Norman went on to become a prominent diplomat before committing suicide in 1957, depressed by a cloud of suspicion and McCarthyist persecution concerning his past. The fact that a man who had been a communist could hold such senior and sensitive government posts verifies that the screening system had its faults.

Setting aside the simple but erroneous assertion that no screening system existed, there are plausible reasons why Norman was undetected. First, missing Norman might have been merely fortuitous. The RCMP's ongoing investigation of communists did come close to homing in on him. In February 1940, before Norman entered the foreign service, the RCMP had learned from an agent that a Professor Norman of McMaster University in Hamilton was a communist. The RCMP went to the trouble of checking on professors at McMaster and even contacting families in Hamilton with the surname Norman. As it happened, the report was just incorrect enough that Norman escaped detection at the time. (Norman's wife's family lived in Hamilton; he had taught at Upper Canada College in Toronto, but was at Harvard University until May 1940.) The depth of the RCMP investigation – on the strength of a simple report that a Professor Norman was a communist – indicates that the RCMP search for communists was vigorous, even if it was not flawless.[158]

Secondly, not all government departments were screened. Ironically, it was two of the most sensitive ones – the Prime Minister's Office (PMO) and the Department of External Affairs – which fell outside the RCMP's protective purview. H.S. Ferns, a Canadian who, like Norman, was an intellectual Marxist in the 1930s and 1940s, is proof positive that neither department was vetted by the RCMP. Ferns worked in the PMO from April 1940 to the spring of 1943 and then carried on in External Affairs until November 1944. His reminiscences of the period mention no security screening of any kind.[159] What scrutiny existed was a British form of appraisal by a circle of friends and acquaintances. According to a Department of External Affairs historian, Don Page, new officers 'were known by their friends, or by an old-boy network when they came into the department.' Even clerks and secretaries at the department were not vetted.[160]

This serious security lapse appears to be the fault of the departments themselves. Their belief that they did not have to be subjected to screening arose partly from their disrespect for the RCMP's competence in security intelligence. The senior civil servant in the Department of External Affairs, Undersecretary of

State Norman Robertson, disparaged the RCMP's security intelligence capacity, and this was mirrored by lower-level bureaucrats.[161] Ferns, for example, wrote that the RCMP's political intelligence was 'characterized by boneheaded stupidity,' and he dismissed them as 'simply "dumb cops,"' ill-educated and of limited knowledge and mental capacity.' According to Ferns, Jack Pickersgill, who worked in the Prime Minister's Office, displayed outright contempt for the RCMP *Intelligence Bulletin*. This attitude of superiority might have arisen from class prejudice. Compared to RCMP officers, civil servants like Herbert Norman and Lester Pearson tended to be extremely well educated and to come from élite, if not rich, families; T.A. (Tommy) Stone, the security specialist in External Affairs from 1942 to the end of the war, was rich.[162] But lack of cooperation in security intelligence could equally have been a result of the fact that External Affairs' ongoing interest in security intelligence matters made it an active rival of the RCMP. It is possible that these departments simply did not deign to submit their employees' names to the RCMP. Hence the presence in the bureaucracy of communists like Herbert Norman should not automatically be attributed to the lack of a screening system. External Affairs and the Prime Minister's Office were probably responsible for the fact that their staff was not vetted.

In any case, Ferns acknowledged that even had the RCMP been 'honours graduates of the University of Toronto' they would probably not have spotted the communists in the civil service who Gouzenko unveiled. Few people except of those who had direct experience with it understood the tyrannical nature of the Soviet regime and its determination to infiltrate Western governments, Ferns believed.[163]

Even when civil servants were closely identified with the Communist party, they did not automatically lose their jobs. Claire Eglin, for instance, became the subject of a screening check on 18 November 1942 when the secretary of the Civil Service Commission asked the RCMP to investigate her 'character and habits.' Then twenty-four, Eglin was living in Victoria with Garry Culhane, who had been interned briefly in late 1941 because of his Communist party activities. The CSC report was requested because Eglin had applied to work as a clerk in the Treasury Department at the Esquimalt, B.C., naval dockyard – scarcely a site where a security risk would be expected to be employed. Just two days after the requested check, the RCMP Finger Print Section reported that Eglin had no criminal record. But at 'C' Division headquarters in Montreal, where Eglin was born and lived until 1942, a record existed of Eglin's activities with the Communist party and the Canadian Civil Liberties Union dating back at least to March 1940. A 28 November 1942 RCMP report observed that 'it is evident that Claire Eglin was very active in the radical movement whilst she stayed in Montreal.' This information was conveyed to the Civil Service Commission on 2 December 1942, just two weeks to the day after its initial request for an assessment. Despite the adverse security assessment, on 29 December 1942 she was reported to be still working at the dockyard, and it did not cause her to lose that job. Assistant Commissioner C.H. Hill, commanding 'E' Division (British Columbia), noted on 6 January 1943 that Eglin 'will be kept under supervision'; this continued throughout the war and beyond.[164]

Clearly, communists were not always fired. But neither was their presence in the state always undetected. The screening system largely did the first of its tasks – identifying the contagion. Yet for several reasons it did not always complete the assignment of purging the infection. This is not necessarily a flaw in the screening process. According to the operating principles of many security-screening systems, resolving the fate of a security risk is not in fact the responsibility of the agency performing the security-screening. Deciding whether or not to oust a perceived security risk is an administrative matter, not the jurisdiction of the security agency. That was the procedure in the Canadian state. During the war there was no government security-screening policy to guide the RCMP. Nonetheless, the procedure was utterly clear about what consequences would follow an adverse security report: the RCMP was not to be involved in any decision to retain or dismiss a person it considered a risk. It was the responsibility of the organization receiving the security evaluation to decide whether or not the confidential information justified the rejection of an applicant or the firing of an employee. Within the government, each department followed its own course. The potential for inconsistency was clearly high, and adding more uncertainty were interdepartmental rivalries, especially involving antagonism between the RCMP and other agencies.[165]

Probably because of this practice, a negative security report from the RCMP did not always lead to an employee's losing his or her job. For instance, in December 1940 Commissioner Wood criticized industrial firms who continued to retain the services of employees in spite of criminal records or connection with what the force considered to be subversive organizations. Wood claimed to know of 'numerous cases' of this kind, adding that 'this renders the investigation futile.'[166] In addition, labour unions were able to free some employees caught in the security-screening net. The plant manager at Fairchild Aircraft in Longueuil, Quebec, for example, found that his agreement with the International Association of Machinists required him to justify any firing, making it difficult for him to dismiss two employees whom the RCMP had reported to be security risks.[167]

After June 1941, when the USSR joined the allies, communists might have been able to take jobs in the state because of a more relaxed attitude towards them. Although the RCMP maintained its hostility toward communists, it appears that it may have been pressured to let down its guard. In 1942, for instance, the prime minister's principal secretary, W.J. Turnbull, complained about the RCMP's fixation on communists: 'a change of policy might well be indicated to them, with Russia a valiant ally.'[168] The effect of this tolerance can be seen in the case of one communist. Ruth McEwen was a member of the Communist party before it was banned in 1940, and later of the Labour Progressive party. In February 1942 she volunteered and was accepted for service with the Canadian Women's Army Corps. The Directorate of Military Intelligence was aware of her record, but, as it later explained, she was inducted on the grounds that 'co-operation by the Communist Party was complete' in 1942. Similarly, the RCMP acknowledged that, 'while she was active in the Party, there had never been anything definitely against her.' On the strength of her service as a CWAC lieutenant and an honourable discharge, in September 1946 she was hired, through the Civil Service Commission, as a clerk in the Prime Minister's Office. She remained there for four months before resigning. A year later the issue was raised in the House of Commons by a member of parliament who claimed that a communist worked in the PMO. This charge also tended to reinforce the faulty belief that no security-screening system operated.[169]

Many months before the outbreak of the Second World War the Canadian state began to develop methods to deal with the internal opposition it expect to encounter in case of war. The RCMP was particularly well prepared, and even before war was declared it had acted swiftly to neutralize nazi sympathizers. Its precautions to deal with industrial security were also well rehearsed. By September 1939 vulnerable points had been surveyed and an industrial security manual was in preparation. Security screening of workers in twelve companies supplying munitions to Britain and Canada began soon after the war erupted.

Thus a small-scale screening system, complete with fingerprinting, was in place by the spring of 1940, when the country was shaken out of its lassitude by the German Wehrmacht's sweep through western Europe. By June 1940 the Canadian public was highly agitated by fear that the country harboured a fifth column serving foreign masters. This panic put considerable pressure upon the Canadian state to act, and the government responded by imposing national registration and banning sixteen organizations. But there is no evidence that the RCMP implemented security-screening as a result of this public fear. The program had begun before the crisis and it continued after public fear dissolved. By 1941 it had evolved into an extensive state security-screening system. This system included all the features of the screening system implemented after 1945 – the criminal and subversive records checks and fingerprint checks which are called 'negative vetting' and the background investigation which is known as 'positive vetting.' Not everyone was given the complete treatment, and we know of several people who received no screening. But the fact remains that a modern security-screening machine was in place early in the Second World War.

5

Reds under the khaki: Screening the military and merchant marine

One year after Germany's attack on the Soviet Union made Canadian communists ardent allies in the struggle against fascism, they were still being shunned by the Canadian military. One of them was John McNeil of Winnipeg. His effort to enlist and the response to it illustrate some of the trends in military security screening during the Second World War.

In June 1942 McNeil decided to join the navy to do his part to demolish fascism. An experienced machinist with twenty-one years' service at the Canadian Pacific Railway (CPR), the forty-one-year-old McNeil responded to advertisements imploring skilled workers to assist the naval effort. His reference from the CPR declared that his work there had been 'entirely satisfactory.' But the letter also added that he had been interned from July 1941 to March 1942. A Winnipeg judge had acquitted him of the charge of 'continuing to be a member of the Communist Party,' after it was formally banned in June 1940, but the RCMP still considered him an active communist and interned him under the Defence of Canada Regulations. He was released nine months later, after his case had been reviewed by an advisory board.

The word internment rang alarm bells in the Winnipeg naval headquarters. When he completed his application, McNeil was told he would get a reply in two to three weeks. Just two days later he got a rejection letter. 'I was curtly told,' McNeil recalled, 'that the Navy does not need experienced machinists.' The letter added that 'there is no suitable appointment in ... the Canadian

Naval Forces, which can be offered to you.' Incensed, McNeil fired off a caustic protest letter to Prime Minister Mackenzie King, asking 'Are we fighting this war to crush Hitlerism or is it a game of tag for some people?'[1]

McNeil was convinced that the RCMP was behind his rebuff, but the true picture was more complex. The day after McNeil first walked into the recruiting centre, the naval recruiting officer in Winnipeg telephoned the local RCMP office to ask if the prospective recruit was the same person as the John McNeil who had been interned. The RCMP advised him that he was and that McNeil was still reporting periodically to the RCMP office as a condition of his release. Commander E.T.C. Orde at Winnipeg naval headquarters also contacted the CPR about McNeil. Learning of his political activities, Orde decreed that McNeil 'was not a desirable type to recruit for the Navy.'[2]

The McNeil case illustrates the methods and practice of security screening in the Canadian military during the Second World War. The navy made the final decision to accept, or in this case reject, a potential recruit, but it did so after consulting both the RCMP and a private employer. The military put considerable stock in the political views and practices of the applicant. Communists were considered suspect and rejected outright, preferably before they could join. Late in 1942, the military policy of shunning communists was reversed, so Spanish Civil War veterans like Jules Paivio and Fred Kostyk and interned communists like Ben Swankey could sign up.[3] Still, once in uniform they were kept under close surveillance to determine what threat they posed. Discharge was swift for those deemed to be a continued risk.

The challenge that faced the Canadian military brass in September 1939 made security screening seem absolutely imperative. Arrayed against the German war juggernaut, Canada had a puny military – 4500 full-time soldiers and an additional 1800 naval and 3100 air force professionals. From this minute core would grow a force that by 1945 would incorporate 1.1 million Canadians.[4] The prospect of carrying out an expansion of this order must have caused acute apprehension within the senior staff. How could they know who was being admitted? Were the new recruits to be the thousands of blanketstiffs who for a decade had been riding the rods, chased hither and yon by Mounties, city cops, and railway bulls? Were they the same vagabonds who had been mobilized by the Communist party in the fractious strikes, treks, and protests of the 1930s? If so, the military was in for trouble. Security screening was the response to the greatest challenge that the Canadian military had faced: how to raise the largest military force in Canadian history, to do it virtually overnight, and to keep it free of contagion.

Suspicion of soldiers first loomed in 1931, when both the RCMP commissioner, James MacBrien, and the chief of the general staff, Andrew McNaughton, were warned about communist infiltration of the forces. That revelation caused the army to begin to screen both new recruits and serving personnel; a handful of suspected communists were ferreted out.[5] Until the war, however, all branches of the military resisted the RCMP's call to fingerprint the forces. During the war, fingerprinting became the first line of defence within the military security-screening system. The police had initially attempted to convince the military to adopt fingerprinting in 1917. Percy Sherwood, the chief commissioner of the Dominion Police, urged the Canadian military to fingerprint its recruits, as the U.S. Army did at the time. The adjutant-general of the Canadian militia rejected the proposal on the grounds that 'so many people, rightly or wrongly, connect the taking of fingerprints with criminals and prisons that to authorize it at the present time ... would, I think, add to the already difficult task of recruiting.'[6] In 1938 the then adjutant-general used a virtually identical argument to reject fingerprinting. In the intervening two decades fingerprinting had become no more popular, and he contended that its notoriety would 'raise unfavourable comment.' The senior air officer of the RCAF curtly spurned the fingerprinting suggestion as 'derogatory.' Only three months later RCMP Commissioner S.T. Wood made another appeal, citing the value of fingerprinting to the American military, where it had prevented the enlistment of undesirables, reduced impersonation, and allowed the identification of deserters and unknown dead. This proposal also fell upon deaf ears.[7] Germany's invasion of Poland was only six days old, and Canada not yet officially at war, when Wood renewed his call for fingerprinting in the military. This time the adjutant-general was sympathetic, yet he still thought finger-printing would be 'undesirable ... under a system of voluntary service such as ours.'[8]

When fingerprinting was introduced to the military as a means to screen recruits, the RCMP's long-standing fear of communism was a central cause. Weeks after hostilities opened, the force warned that a plan was afoot for Communist Party members to 'gain admission into "key" industries and Defence Forces, in order to sabotage and cause disruption at an opportune time.' The exposé featured prominently in the RCMP Intelligence Bulletin circulated to members of the cabinet and senior bureaucrats.[9] With the war begun, the RCMP's effort to alert senior military commanders and politicians to the danger of communist infiltration started to take effect. In November 1939 General McNaughton, the commander of the First Canadian Infantry Division, confided to the prime minister that the regular army was 'an uncertain quantity, largely dissatisfied men with Communistic tendencies.'[10] By December 1939, 'Communists of the more virulent type' had already slipped into the air force, causing the chief of the air staff to alert its Montreal recruiting officer to take the necessary steps to 'avoid further enlistments from members of the Communist Party or any other such radical group.'[11] In February 1940 the minister of justice, Ernest Lapointe, publicly repeated the Mounties' claim that subversive organizations had instructed their members to join the army and to get employment in munitions plants in order to find an opportunity to undermine Canada's war effort.[12] The RCMP's campaign appeared to be having the desired effect.

Declared illegal in June 1940, the Communist party maintained active underground cells, some of them engaged in distributing anti-war leaflets to military training camps. In October 1940 communist literature was found at Camp Valcartier and turned over to the RCMP, resulting in arrests and convictions. By February 1941 an estimated 100 communists were in the army. Communists were especially effective agitators because they rarely came into direct conflict with authority, worked hard, and gave the appearance of being good soldiers. Nazi sympathizers also made 'model soldiers and rapidly assumed the confidence of their officers.'[13] Although an insignificant number of soldiers – only 123 – cast votes for communists during the March 1940 election, the RCMP was fearful enough of communist influence in the armed forces that it monitored how many soldiers' votes had gone to the communists and for which candidates they had been cast.[14]

The Communist party's decision to come in out of the cold and join the war effort in June 1941 did not sway the RCMP. Several months later the force was still convinced that the communists were distributing 'subversive literature' to members of the armed forces. And the force was no more reassured by the Communist party's February 1942 call for 'democratic conscription to build up ten divisions for action on a Second European front ...,' including ten thousand army enlistments from among its own members and supporters.[15] Even in June 1942, a full year after the Communist party's about-face on the war, the RCMP clung to its claim that the party was subverting the Canadian armed forces.[16]

Mass fingerprinting was designed to catch communists. It was first announced to industrial leaders in Ontario, where half of the country's war production went on, in a secret meeting of the Ontario Provincial Police – sponsored Co-ordinating Committee for Security. At the 17 December 1940 meeting, the dominion security officer of the Department of Munitions and Supply, R.L. Anderson, revealed the details of the fingerprinting program. What he called 'communistic chaps' were the target, and identifying their movements through industrial plants was the purpose of the program. As the committee members waxed enthusiastic, it became obvious that the same purpose motivated the army's adoption of fingerprinting. Captain R. Adamson, intelligence officer in Military District Number 2, explained that the fingerprint program did not yet include the armed forces, adding that 'I do not see why it should not ... It would save us a lot of trouble and it would have saved us a lot of trouble if it had been done before because it would have made the tracing of subversive elements in the army that much easier.'[17] Indeed, communists were already in the military, according to Toronto Police Inspector Bill Nursey, a veteran member of the city's Red Squad. Nursey pointed out to Captain Adamson that his office had recently sent a photograph of a communist soldier to the army headquarters at Kingston. As for dealing with such dissidents, Nursey's long-time partner on the Toronto Red Squad, Detective Daniel Mann, seemed to think the police were most effective. He asked, rhetorically, 'The question arises as to whether or not they can take care of them [communists] as well in the army as we can if they are left outside.'[18] Just what he might have had in mind was graphically described by Communist party leader Tim Buck, who in his memoirs recalled being hauled away from a rally to the Toronto City Hall jail: 'Bill Nursey walked behind, treading carefully on my heels, taking all the skin off the back of my legs down to the top of my shoes ... Nursey was really a brute, and he enjoyed it.'[19]

For several reasons, by late 1940 the military had swung in favour of fingerprinting, although its negative image remained a barrier. To deal with this, Lieutenant-Colonel W.E.L. Coleman proposed 'an early education of the Public regarding the value of Finger-printing as a means of protection for the honest citizen.'[20] The government had already proposed that the military fingerprint its recruits. In August 1940 a subcommittee of the Interdepartmental Committee for Co-ordination of Intelligence for War Purposes recommended that the three armed forces consider implementing 'the system of fingerprinting now utilized in ... the Civil Service and ... the R.C.M. Police.' Fingerprinting would help prevent 'enemy infiltration.'[21]

Even before fingerprinting was launched, there was already close liaison between the intelligence directorates of all three branches of the military and the RCMP. The police passed on information about 'undesirable personnel,' paying particular attention to 'subversive or espionage elements' within the ranks. However, the intelligence coordination subcommittee was anxious to see the armed forces adopt a more systematic method to ensure the efficient 'collection and canalization of information ... into Mounted Police hands,' like that already in place for civil servants.[22]

The air force was the first Canadian armed force, and indeed the first in the British Empire, to implement fingerprinting. It began in December 1940, and was authorized by Organizational Order No. 94 of 16 January 1941.[23] Proclaiming the value of finger-printing, the flight officer in charge listed eleven benefits. Although identifying the battle dead and wounded was listed, security reasons were uppermost in his mind. Weeding out 'unde-sirables, criminals and subversive elements,' apprehending deserters, preventing discharged personnel or deserters from re-enlisting under aliases, and investigating crimes at air force bases were all cited to prove the need for fingerprinting.[24] The air force regarded several types of applicants to be undesirable. These included enemy aliens, people with criminal records and 'radi-cals,' including '"subversive elements";[and] those suspected of "subversive sympathies."'[25] It should be noted that not everyone with a criminal record was automatically dismissed. The air force argued that 'many airmen who have lived in a poor environment are capable of rehabilitation in the better surroundings that the Air Force provides.' By July 1941, of the 165 people found to have criminal records, 99 had been deemed fit to remain with the air force, while 28 were discharged outright.[26]

By April 1944 virtually all the 250,000 members of the air force, including service personnel and civilians, had been fingerprinted. Although the employees of civilian contractors working for the air force were not supposed to be fingerprinted, in fact some were.[27] Once the fingerprints were taken, the RCAF used Holler-ith (International Business Machines) electromechanical tabulat-ing equipment to help sort them.[28] They were also submitted to the RCMP for a check against criminal records. As part of security screening, the police also reviewed their subversive indices, a practice that began before fingerprinting.[29] During the three years up to March 1943 the RCMP checked almost 104,000 air force per-sonnel. Five hundred and thirty-nine of them had some history of subversive activity. Because of the pressure of wartime duties, universal screening was then replaced by a system in which only those people performing secret or top secret work were checked.[30]

The army launched the fingerprinting part of security screen-ing later than did the air force, but its intelligence section did not wait for the establishment of an identification bureau to begin screening; it was actively checking the backgrounds of soldiers from early in the war. Although fingerprinting began in October 1941, the Canadian Army Identification Bureau was not formally founded until 1 September 1942, under an order authorizing the fingerprinting and photographing of all military and civilian personnel in the Department of National Defence.[31] A progress report of 10 July 1943 noted that almost 314,000 military and 16,000 civilian personnel had been fingerprinted to that point. Yet only a small proportion of the fingerprints had been submitted to the RCMP to be checked against its records. Army intelligence was following the practice of submitting to the RCMP the fingerprints of only those who were considered to be suspicious.[32]

The army intelligence group, Military Intelligence Section 3 (MI3), appeared to be more suspicious of civilian employees than of recruits. Only 4 per cent of army recruits' fingerprints, compared with 15 per cent of civilian fingerprints, were passed on to the RCMP. Yet the number of criminal records revealed within each group does not appear to have justified the extra caution. Among civilian applicants, 132, or 5.5 per cent, had criminal records; among military recruits the corresponding figure was 641, or 4.9 per cent. This seems to confirm a 1941 joint-services judgment: 'The number of undesirables who are brought to light by means of fingerprinting is comparatively small ...' Nonetheless, fingerprinting was believed to reveal other recruitment aberrations, including desertion and multiple enlistments.[33]

MI3, responsible for loyalty screening, was part of the Directorate of Military Intelligence (DMI). Established at National Defence Headquarters in November 1940, MI3 was itself divided into three sections. Section A was responsible for security of personnel. With this mandate, it devoted a considerable amount of attention to soldiers who were suspected of harbouring any one of a variety of subversive sympathies: communist, nazi, fascist, or Irish republican. At any one moment during the war some 400 to 500 soldiers were under active observation, at least some of these inquiries launched by RCMP information that a suspected subversive had enlisted.[34]

MI3's work was also swelled by character investigations for the Intelligence Directorate and other branches of the army. In each month of 1943 it conducted more than 125 character investigations of people doing secret duties. As the war went on, the number of military positions requiring screening grew apace, so that by January 1945 people in fifteen separate categories required clearance. Investigators also began to look out for more than subversion; suitability and discretion were also taken into account. By January 1945 MI3 was conducting 500 in-depth field checks per month.[35]

Monitoring of suspected subversives was intense. Over a three month probationary term, a report was made out on each one of them every second week. District intelligence officers were instructed to comment on the person's character. Was he a '"Barrack Room Lawyer," given to grousing,' did he have any influence over fellow soldiers, had he been 'engaging in subversive propaganda amongst his fellow soldiers?' If a suspect was granted leave of more than forty-eight hours the RCMP was informed so that it could tail the person.[36]

Although soldiers who were associated with the Communist party had engaged in no subversive activity up to November 1941, Major Eric Acland, head of MI3, counselled keeping tabs on them 'in order that effective action could be taken in the future should such be warranted.' No soldier under suspicion was posted overseas without a thorough review of his case. Some were judged to be so dangerous that keeping them under surveillance was not enough. By November 1941, the end of the first year of MI3's operation, 103 recruits deemed subversive had been discharged.[37]

In the course of the war thousands of soldiers were put under active investigation. By March 1943 over 3000 cases had been dealt with. Inevitably, some of them were accused out of spite, excess zeal, or ignorance of a person's ethnic, social, or political background.[38] And as the war progressed ideological loyalty became more, not less, important. With the military taking on sensitive duties such as signals intelligence and using increasingly sophisticated equipment, deviance became unacceptable.[39] Moreover, these highly technical projects were often joint efforts with the United States and Britain, which imposed additional pressure to ensure the loyalty of anyone working in them.[40] Despite this intense surveillance, investigations had to be handled carefully, 'without engaging in a "witch-hunt,"' Acland cautioned.[41]

Acland's intensive study of the state of army intelligence in 1941 contained a suggestion that MI3 be expanded so that it could conduct its own field investigations, without relying on the RCMP. Having the RCMP delving into the activities of soldiers was dangerous because the Mounties were clearly outsiders. A police officer asking questions at a military barracks 'only serves to put the suspect on his guard.' It could also lead to 'rumours and gossip follow[ing] the officer or man originally under suspicion with disastrous [sic] results to his reputation and character,' Acland warned. He also noted that RCMP and British security coordination officers had 'expressed surprise that the Canadian Army is not in a position to keep its personnel under close observation.'[42]

In July 1942 RCMP Commissioner Wood suggested that the army conduct its own security investigations, which was gradually done. But still in 1943 the RCMP was conducting so many investigations for the army that the force had to amend its normal routine. 'For the sake of expediency and to facilitate the handling of local character investigations,' RCMP divisional commanding officers were instructed to forward the results of their inquiries directly to the intelligence officer of the local army district rather than back to RCMP headquarters. To assist the RCMP's work the army provided its own instructions for character investigations. They suggested ways to discover a person's character and associations before he or she enlisted. The secret form advised investigators to be aware that making such forays into civilian life was 'a departure from the usual procedure in the Canadian Army.' Discretion was imperative: 'The subject must not become aware that an investigation is in progress ...'[43]

By 1945 the RCMP was still carrying out investigations of army personnel and sometimes going to extraordinary lengths to do so. In February 1945 a Mountie ventured out to a front-line Canadian army dugout during the assault upon the German's last line of defence, the Siegfried Line, looking for Bill Walsh. Walsh had been interned as a communist earlier in the war but by then was a veteran of several battles in the Canadian army. The Mountie, wearing a uniform with the brass buttons that were shunned at the front, asked for the intelligence officer of the batallion. It was Walsh. When he learned that he was the object of the investigation, Walsh took the Mountie to the batallion's colonel. Walsh explained that

I'm in the complete confidence of my Colonel, who knows all about my background ... And he [the RCMP officer] wants to know from the Colonel whether I'm reliable, what sort of leadership qualities I have, and if I have leadership qualities, is there any danger of me leading the Canadian troops over to join the Russians, and all sorts of stuff like that.[44]

Walsh's experience reveals the extent of the RCMP's security probes, even within the front-line army late in the war.

The dubious legality of using fingerprints to assist in screening was always apparent to the military. This was an important reason why each service established its own identification bureau to take fingerprints and retain them after they were checked by the RCMP.[45] It allowed each force to contend that fingerprinting was for internal purposes only. The fingerprinting of civilian personnel was especially contentious, and military authorities feared 'suits and claims of forcible fingerprinting' from them. Indeed, civilian fingerprinting went forward only after the introduction of special forms, like those used for industrial personnel, on which the individual agreed to be fingerprinted. Civil Service Commission approval was also required before a fingerprint identification system was applied to civilian employees.[46]

Once the legal objection was bypassed, however, fingerprinting went on apace. By April 1945, 30,721 civilians in the army and 25,739 civilians in the navy had been fingerprinted and photographed. More than 682,000 army recruits and 98,000 navy recruits had also undergone the process. And the war's conclusion did not end screening and fingerprinting. In 1945–6 almost 11,000 civilians working in the army and navy and 31,100 recruits to the two services were fingerprinted and photographed.[47]

Legal and moral qualms about fingerprinting were not, however, dismissed by everyone. In January 1941 the RCAF invited the Royal Air Force (RAF) and the Royal New Zealand Air Force, and later the Royal Australian Air Force, to have its personnel serving in Canada included in the screening system. While the New Zealand and Australian officials accepted the proposal, the British Air Ministry refused it because fingerprinting was associated with criminal convictions. The British Army, likewise, declined to fingerprint its recruits.[48] The British were also unwilling to fingerprint prisoners of war, since it might violate the spirit of the Geneva Convention on treatment of prisoners of war.[49]

Early in 1942 the Canadian Naval Service began to fingerprint civilian personnel and asked the RCMP to conduct fingerprint and subversive record checks.[50] In doing so, the navy was aiming to identify 'undesirables' who might wish to enlist or work as civilians with the navy.[51] Fingerprinting helped the RCMP to discover the criminal records of at least some civil servants and to report these to the navy.[52] But it did not always operate smoothly. In 1944 the Civil Service Commission rebuked the deputy minister for naval services for repeatedly failing to forward to the RCMP the fingerprints of people in responsible positions.[53]

It was not, however, failure to fingerprint that allowed Claire Eglin to work at the Esquimalt naval dockyard from 1942 to 1944. As explained in chapter 4, Eglin was known to the RCMP as a communist supporter, and it reported this fact to the Civil Service Commission. This should have excluded her. In the words of the intelligence staff officer at the Pacific coast naval headquarters in Vancouver, 'a very thorough check of civilians is made by the Security Intelligence Officer before they are hired and chances of undesirables being employed in the Dockyard are reduced to a minimum.'[54] Yet even as this report was written, Eglin was working as a civilian clerk in the Treasury Department at Esquimalt, and she remained there until she resigned to move to Vancouver two months later. Squaring this contradictory information is not easy. Perhaps her position was not considered sensitive, or the Communist party's manifest commitment to the war effort was a convincing argument to retain her.

One of the landmark security developments of the war was the founding of the Joint Intelligence Committee (JIC) in November 1942. The committee brought together the intelligence directors of the three military branches and representatives of the Department of External Affairs and the RCMP. It yielded immediate benefits by helping to smother the occasional flare-ups between army and RCMP intelligence officers caused by the frictions of war. One was the complaint by RCMP division commanding officers that army intelligence investigators strayed beyond personnel inquiries into the realm of subversion and sabotage, which was RCMP jurisdiction. In addition to the forum it provided to relieve such minor conflicts, the JIC had long-lasting significance because it set a precedent; interdepartmental intelligence coordination would be a feature of the postwar era.[55] Although it was useful as a coordinating body, the JIC was not a security executive panel of the type that the British government established in the Second World War and that the Canadian government created in 1946. So it did not provide effective government supervision of the security-screening system.

SCREENING OF MERCHANT SEAMEN

Canada's registration and security investigation of merchant seamen was instigated by an unexpected agent – the government of the United States. In June 1940, still eighteen months away from war, the Roosevelt administration issued an executive order requiring every seaman who went ashore on American territory to carry an identification card with both his photograph and fingerprints on it. The executive order on seamen was part of a much broader initiative to impose fingerprint registration on Americans. The law that significantly advanced this was the Alien Registration Act (Smith Act), a bill which compelled foreigners resident in or visiting the United States to be fingerprinted.[56] By

January 1941 almost 5 million American residents had been fingerprinted under the statute, among them 48,000 seamen.[57] The Canadian chargé d'affaires in Washington saw the Smith Act as a measure that would encourage advocates of universal fingerprinting.[58] But, although Canadian external affairs representatives like Hugh Keenleyside stressed that there was a stigma attached to compulsory fingerprinting, Canadian authorities fell into line with the Americans on fingerprinting seamen. The result was the Merchant Seamen's Identity Certificate, an identity card which had spaces for fingerprints. Copies of the fingerprints were sent, with photographs, to the Department of Transport's Central Index Register of Seamen.[59] In November 1941 an order in council, citing unspecified 'reasons of security,' made it compulsory to carry the card, although including fingerprints on it was not mandatory.[60] But officials let it be known that seamen could expect to encounter 'serious inconvenience in foreign ports' without a fingerprint identification card.[61]

There was particular concern about the loyalty of merchant seamen because their union, the Canadian Seamen's Union (CSU), was led by communists. Beginning with the declaration of war, the RCMP placed the CSU leadership under surveillance. Through its agents in the CSU, the RCMP learned that the Communist party planned to use Great Lakes seamen to smuggle banned literature from the United States. Seamen who were party members were also asked to relay shipping timetable, destination, and cargo information to the party, which indicated a potential for sabotage or espionage. This fear seemed to be confirmed by a week-long CSU strike at the opening of the shipping season in April 1940, which the RCMP Intelligence Section watched closely. The strike caused enough alarm that the Department of Labour declared it illegal.[62]

The deep sea merchant fleet was also rife with communists, who were 'above average at organizing mischief,' according to Fredrick B. Watt, who was in charge of the Canadian navy's merchant ship inspection service in Halifax from its launch until demobilization.[63] By the end of 1943 Canadian ships' delegates and union representatives in the Atlantic ports were predominantly communist or influenced by communists, he estimated. As a result, the reputation for crew trouble in the ships they served had become worldwide.'[64]

The U.S. executive order, plus security fears about communist-influenced seamen, helped set the identification wheels in motion. In October 1940 the RCMP organized a conference of senior bureaucrats to discuss ways to prevent sabotage on the Great Lakes. The session pondered the problem of selecting crew members for Great Lakes vessels and issuing identification cards to them. The cards would 'make it easy to check up on seamen,' according to one representative at the secret meeting.[65] The Department of Transport indicated that it was already coordinating the project. It had only to inform the shipping companies, most of whom had previously agreed to register the seamen and issue the cards.[66]

The department's draft instructions to the shipping companies, however, met opposition from M.H. Wershof of the Department of External Affairs. The guidelines declared that every seaman must carry a card with his fingerprints on it. Wershof pointed out: 'I do not think that there is, at present, legal justification for such a command.'[67] Because of its illegality, fingerprinting remained formally voluntary, although obviously favoured. The British Ministry of Shipping also ordered seamen to carry identification cards and likewise made fingerprinting voluntary. British instructions regarding the cards, in fact, served as the model for the Canadian Department of Transport's instructions.[68]

Security was not the only reason why the authorities kept such a close watch on merchant seamen. Seamen constituted an indispensable labour force, especially during the early years of the war, when Britain's very survival was in doubt. Not only that, seamen were known to be tough and independent. Control over this labouring population was thus absolutely essential.

An epidemic of desertion in 1940 and 1941 must have speeded the registration drive. Watt noticed that desertion peaked in the first half of 1941, the bleakest period of the battle of the Atlantic. There was, as a British Admiralty communique admitted, 'considerable suspicion among Allied crews that we are using their ships for our own ends.' The seamen knew that non-British ships were being sent through the U-boat–infested North Atlantic far more often than British ships.[69] The consequence was dire for Canadian merchant sailors. Of the 7700 men who sailed in dangerous waters, over 1100 were killed, a higher death rate than in any other service.[70] The devastation of merchant ships and seamen, coupled with harsh working conditions on board, led many sailors to jump ship. When they did, the United States was 'the haven of choice.' Watt noted: 'The suborning there of disgruntled crews was constant. A steady stream of alleged welfare workers, clergymen, charitably-minded citizens and compassionate "ladies" visited Allied seamen and caused scores of them to disappear ... The missing men had not only been encouraged to remain ashore; many had been spirited away to jobs in places where they were unlikely to be discovered and brought back.' Greek crews, who suffered an across-the-board wage cut in 1940, were particularly likely to desert. An underground network was created in the Montreal Greek community to smuggle fugitives into the United States. The desertion problem was so acute that later that year the head of the British security intelligence operation in North America, William Stephenson, would begin to direct agents of his British Security Co-ordination in New York to the task of stemming the flow.[71]

The desertion crisis precipitated the creation of a new interdepartmental committee in Ottawa to deal with the problem of seamen. At its inaugural meeting in January 1941, Captain E.S. Brand of the navy reported that many foreign sailors in Halifax were refusing to sail. One of them was Pieter Stroonbants, a Belgian who 'states he has lost his nerve completely, although report of medical officer indicates that he is a strong, robust man and is fit and able to go to sea.' Belgian and Dutch seamen were particularly suspicious of British strategy in the Atlantic.[72] Brand pointed to the need for stronger legal compulsions for seamen, especially Britons and Canadians.[73] The cabinet had already provided some coercive power over non-Canadians in order in council PC 4751 of 12 September 1940, which provided for detention of alien seamen who refused to sail. Under it, from September 1940 to January

1941, 290 men were arrested and many of them sent to jail. Still, there was danger of dissident seamen sailing but spreading discontent once on board.[74]

Seen in the light of the desertion crisis of 1940 and 1941, the fingerprinting of merchant seamen, beginning in 1940 in the United States and in 1941 in Britain and Canada, takes on more significance as a measure of labour control. Fingerprinting was an excellent device to track deserters or dissidents and to know if a sailor seeking a place on an American ship had previously deserted from an Allied ship. How better to make it more difficult for deserting seamen to move to jobs elsewhere in the United States?

The effort to control and discipline merchant seamen took another turn in May 1941, when the cabinet passed an order in council setting out a policy to avoid delays in departure of merchant vessels from Canadian ports. The Merchant Seamen Order created investigatory committees which could board ships and remove and detain any seaman who was 'likely to delay sailing.' The committees were composed primarily of RCMP officers. The order was passed because of incidents in which seamen refused to sail or were suspected of carrying on subversive activities either on board ship or ashore.[75]

The way the Merchant Seamen Order was used during the balance of the war makes it clear that labour discipline was a far more vexing problem than was subversion. In October 1945 the military judge advocate general reported the causes of disciplinary action under the Merchant Seamen Order. Of the 2553 cases handled under the order, only nine, or about 0.03 per cent, involved a seaman engaging in subversive activities on board. More than 46 per cent of the cases arose from desertion. In 17 per cent of the 2553 cases a seaman had refused to sail; in 19 per cent seamen refused to perform regular duties on a ship; 15 per cent involved seamen causing delay in the departure of a ship.[76] In short, while the Merchant Seamen Order was invoked to deal with subversion, it was used in practice to force seamen to perform their duties. The state recognized that the work of seamen was as important to the war effort as that of munitions workers.[77]

Keeping such vital workers on the job – by compulsion, monitoring, and surveillance, if necessary – was imperative.

Surveillance took on yet another form, in addition to identification cards and fingerprinting. It was also a central task of the Naval Boarding Service (NBS). The service was established out of fear that German agents would sabotage the essential convoys of war *matériel* to Britain by placing bombs in ships' cargoes. However, Frederick Watt, who was in charge of the NBS, recalls that his boarding parties 'found no bombs, but they were quick to detect explosive attitudes among members of the ships' crews.' During the war 'significant numbers of cargo carriers were paralyzed in harbour by something called, in wartime euphemism, "crew trouble." The term covered all manner of disturbances and delays, from sitdown strikes, to damaging of engines, to desertions ... The convoys faced a threat potentially even greater than that of enemy raiders on the high seas: they faced inner collapse.' In the course of inspecting every merchant ship entering and leaving Halifax harbour, the officers of the boarding service, who were themselves peacetime merchant seamen, became familiar with the signs of labour trouble. As Watt explained, 'this made them valuable intelligence sources to the senior officers wrestling with the crisis.'[78] Operating in nine Canadian ports by war's end, the Naval Boarding Service earned praise from the British navy as an alternative security service. In 1942 the Admiralty's director of trade division, Captain B.B. Schofield, wrote Ottawa: 'I feel that nothing is done over here to bolster the morale of our Allied seamen – or even our own – and that MI5 provide the wrong sort of security officers. They aren't sailors and the masters resent them. Your Naval Boarding Service is a much better show altogether.'[79] The British also sought to create facilities in Halifax to look after seamen's welfare. This would contribute to 'counteracting subversive activities by positive measures.'[80]

These measures had combined by 1943 to create an efficient surveillance system, which was directly connected to a black list of seamen maintained by the Halifax port security office. RCMP security control special constables in Halifax were instructed: 'All crew members will be checked against the Security Control Black List and any member of the crew found to be identical with a suspect on the Black List will be reported immediately to the Asst. to the S.C.O. [Security Control Operative].'[81] MI5 had also developed from the spring of 1941 a pool of 'useful contacts' among seamen to help monitor them.[82]

Hence, a combination of security and labour control concerns led to identification and screening of merchant seamen. Merchant seamen were thrown onto the front lines in the battle of the Atlantic not as combatants but as labourers. Controlling this working population meant monitoring it, preventing desertion, and weeding out subversives and other potential causes of discord. The Allies resorted to fingerprinting, surveillance, and black lists in an attempt to exert the control that survival demanded. The fact that the United States, dependent upon Atlantic trade but not yet at war, forced Canada and Britain to begin to fingerprint seamen shows the interdependence of security and social control issues among the three allies.

Systematic security screening was introduced into the Canadian military remarkably quickly. As late as 1939, the military still had not adopted one basic element of a screening system, fingerprinting. But after spurning it for more than two decades, the senior staff embraced it almost overnight when faced with a war crisis. What forced its hand was fear of subversion. Although military authorities were attracted by fingerprinting's value as a means to identify battle dead, criminals, and deserters, they were mostly won over to fingerprinting because it could help them screen out undesirables, mainly communists.

The fact that fingerprinting alone could not keep dissidents out of the military forced further developments in the military's security apparatus. By the end of the war, the army intelligence section, MI3, had developed a comprehensive security-screening system. It included basic criminal and subversive checks of new recruits – what is now called negative vetting – and, for personnel in more sensitive positions, full-scale positive vetting. Long before the cabinet formally authorized such intensive screening, army intelligence and RCMP officers had developed a considerable security-screening system.

The merchant marine fingerprinting program had a more complex purpose. Merchant seamen were notoriously wilful, unfettered by regulations, and, perhaps most dangerous to the Canadian state, led by a communist union, the Canadian Seamen's Union. Fingerprinting was one way to keep track of the men who performed dangerous but necessary work on the Atlantic and the Great Lakes. It was just one part of a comprehensive surveillance and black list system which endeavoured to discipline and control merchant seamen.

6

'Gathering information regarding communistic chaps': The system's political rationale

The reasons why the federal government never blessed the wartime security-screening program remain a great enigma. The RCMP acutely felt the danger inherent in the lack of any legal sanction to fingerprint and screen hundreds of thousands of industrial workers. Yet the government did not rescue the RCMP by legalizing the most contentious aspect of screening – fingerprinting – or by approving the security-screening program.[1]

It would have been easy to do. After his election victory in March 1940, Prime Minister King had a reliable parliamentary majority, which could have passed the required legislation. Had he wished to avoid a potentially messy debate in the House, King had the ready option of acting through the Defence of Canada Regulations. Under the DOCR, only the agreement of his cabinet colleagues was needed to pass an order in council which had the force of law. Cabinet invoked the DOCR thousands of times during the war for matters as mundane as prohibiting the export of clothes-pins or as momentous as interning citizens of Japanese origin. Yet the government never authorized non-criminal fingerprinting; it remained illegal throughout the war and a potential source of embarrassment to the RCMP and the government. Similarly, security screening itself was never approved by elected politicians.

Fingerprinting did come close to being officially condoned. In March 1943, more than three years after the fingerprinting of thousands of industrial workers began, a proposal to amend the

DOCR to provide for it was forwarded to cabinet. It came on the initiative of the Department of Munitions and Supply, and was endorsed by the ministers of justice and labour, Louis St Laurent and Humphrey Mitchell. The proposal did not arise out of any political discussion in the government but came instead after a director of the Industrial Security Branch of the DMS learned that industrial plants in the United States had been ordered to fingerprint their personnel.[2] Industrial security officers and DMS personnel believed that the American approval added weight to arguments for stricter rules in Canada.[3]

But the bid to authorize fingerprinting and searching of war plant workers suffered a reversal at the March 1943 cabinet meeting. The cabinet was not convinced that the measure was necessary. C.D. Howe, the minister of munitions and supply, argued that 'existing security regulations were adequate.'[4] Only in November 1943, after a rash of thefts in munitions plants, did Howe declared himself ready to subject workers to searches. But he declined to sanction their fingerprinting, and it was not approved.[5] There is no hint of what might have held Howe back from conceding what his own security branch wanted. If his motive was reluctance to abridge workers' rights, it was an uncharacteristic act. Howe is better known as a proponent of big government and a right-wing influence within the cabinet than as a civil libertarian.[6] And the previous year he had supported a proposal to add a clause on fingerprinting to the DOCR.[7] Perhaps the popular stigma attached to fingerprinting stayed his hand. Ultimately, politicians' qualms were of little consequence. Fingerprinting of munitions workers went on, unauthorized.

Aside from that tantalizingly brief record of the abortive bid to authorize fingerprinting, no documentary evidence exists showing political input into the program. No minutes were kept of cabinet meetings, so we know nothing directly about discussions there concerning fingerprinting. There are minutes of the meetings of the cabinet War Committee, which was the key directing committee of the government during the war.[8] Yet those minutes reveal no record of any discussion about fingerprinting or security screening.

Remarkably, even some highly placed Canadian political authorities seemed ignorant of the scale of vetting that was going on in the country. This is confirmed by a memo from a civil servant who was the single most influential voice in security matters during the war years. Norman A. Robertson assumed the post of under secretary of state for external affairs in January 1941, becoming almost overnight the prime minister's closest and most trusted adviser. In September 1939 and again in May 1940, as German armies stormed through Europe, he pored over RCMP intelligence reports deciding which communist, nazi and fascist adherent should be interned.[9] Central though he was, Robertson seemed to have no inkling of the extent of the fingerprinting done for security screening. In December 1943 he expressed his concerns about a Department of National Defence decision to fingerprint Allied aliens who sought to enter the armed forces. Robertson, who has gained a reputation as a civil libertarian, contended that Allied governments might object to the procedure, and opined that it would be 'rather doubtful whether it would be desirable to have fingerprinting ... as a matter of course.'[10] Yet his own military already required fingerprints of Canadian citizens entering the armed forces, and the police fingerprinted applicants for jobs in much of the private sector. It is truly astonishing that Robertson did not seem to know the scope of fingerprinting in Canada. His ignorance, however, must be put in a political perspective. It is a telling statement about how quietly the program was implemented. Moreover, it implies that fingerprinting in Canada was invoked by administrative fiat, not by a high-level decision coming from elected politicians.

A police request that the government authorize civilian fingerprinting had earlier been presented to Justice Minister Ernest Lapointe. But its origin and timing indicate that the RCMP had a relaxed attitude towards the need to obtain political authority to fingerprint war plant workers. On 15 July 1941 Commissioner Wood wrote to Lapointe asking that 'the Federal Government *order* that the finger prints be taken of all persons engaged in any industry classed as an "Essential Service" by the Defence of Canada Regulations.'[11] The request did not originate with the RCMP.

Wood was merely passing on a resolution to that effect which had been approved by the Co-ordinating Committee for Security, a high-level group of police officers and manufacturers in Ontario who were concerned about industrial security. The timing of Wood's letter was also significant. By July 1941 the RCMP had already been processing fingerprints of industrial workers for well over eighteen months, and the program had been significantly expanded four months before. Yet the federal police had not seen fit to ask for authorization to fingerprint before that time.

The lack of political input into the security-screening program was confirmed by a March 1947 memo from an RCMP constable, which summed up the thinking behind the fingerprinting of war plant employees. Constable W.N. Wilson's five-paragraph memo was a testament to the astonishingly informal way in which Canadian security policy was established. In the memo, Wilson explained that 'a study of the file relating to Cooperation with Industry ... reveals that the policy of fingerprinting employees employed in munitions plants came into being quite naturally as a result of numerous discussions between this Force and officials of the Department of Munitions and Supply.'[12] Wilson's review of security policy contained no reference to the political authority for the mass fingerprinting aspect of security screening. The program had been implemented by civil servants and the federal police force; involvement by politicians was non-existent.

It was not even widely promoted among bureaucrats. Two months after fingerprinting was introduced in hundreds of munitions plants, the Department of Labour still did not know about it. When the program encountered loud opposition from an International Association of Machinists local at Fairchild Aircraft, the assistant deputy minister of labour rebuked the RCMP and DMS for not discussing it with his department before instituting it. The DMS director of labour relations did not know of the fingerprinting program's existence before it was implemented, and even the minister of labour was not aware of it until a Co-operative Commonwealth Federation (CCF) member of parliament raised the matter in the House of Commons.[13]

But the quiet way it was introduced does not entirely explain how it was possible for the RCMP and the DMS to carry out a major vetting program without political authority. Another contributory factor was the extraordinary temper of the times. The exigencies of war permitted many expansions of bureaucratic influence to go unchecked. Although he was not speaking specifically about security screening, political scientist J.J. Deutsch offered a useful explanation of how wartime attitudes might have allowed such an operation to spring to life without authorization. Deutsch noted that, during the war

It became necessary over a very short period to mobilize the entire resources of the country under the direction of a highly centralized administrative machine. On the basis off this overriding national necessity it was possible to make short cuts, to experiment, to adopt expedients, to undertake on a large scale programmes that had never been tried before.[14]

Nothing illustrates this better than the fact that Canadian military leaders launched and worked on a chemical and biological warfare program that continued from 1937 to 1947 without consulting either the government or parliament.[15]

It was no accident that politicians failed to direct the security-screening system, according to RCMP historians Carl Betke and S.W. Horrall. In 1978 they produced an internal history of the RCMP Security Service from 1864 to 1966. In it they contend that from 1920 to the 1960s governments refused to give the RCMP any 'guidelines or directives with which to operate and determine its intelligence role.' Ignorance of the RCMP's security intelligence activities does not explain the hands-off attitude, they assert. In fact, the government had ample contact with the federal police. The minister of justice met frequently with the commissioner, and cabinet was informed through regular intelligence reports. Betke and Horrall argue that the absence of guidance was sinister: in appearing to have no hand in security intelligence matters, 'the government made the R.C.M.P. the principle [sic] butt of criticism for those opposed to its intelligence activities.' Issuing no orders allowed various governments to 'shift on to the shoulders of the R.C.M.P. criticism for policies for which they were in the final analysis responsible.'[16] Betke and Horrall's claim that various governments have wilfully turned their eyes from the RCMP's security intelligence activities offers a possible explanation for why the King government never authorized wartime security screening. It was simply following the established practice of Canadian administrations with regard to security matters – the fewer explicit directions, the better.

The evidence shows that when it came to security screening, the security service guided the politicians. Until 1946 security screening existed because the RCMP took its own initiatives, without the formal approval of the government of the day. This development was not unique to Canada. Christopher Andrew and David Dilks's assessment of the relationships between governments and security intelligence agencies in the twentieth century identifies two major trends: 'the gradual and erratic professionalisation of intelligence communities in the West, and the equally gradual and erratic way in which governments have learned to cope with them.'[17] According to these authors, 'creeping bureaucratic growth' accounts for the emergence of much of the security intelligence apparatus in Western countries.[18] This broad pattern appears to hold true for security screening in Canada. After its reorganization in 1920, the RCMP became continually, although erratically, more skilled in security intelligence endeavours. One illustration of this trend is its development of a security-screening system before and during the war. As Andrew and Dilks say occurred elsewhere, the Canadian government coped with this security initiative only gradually, beginning in 1946. As a result, for fifteen years the Canadian security intelligence community developed security screening on its own, without instructions or guidance from elected politicians.

Ironically, according to Betke and Horrall, this lack of political direction had just two exceptions: 'Only during wartime, and with respect to the screening of government employees and applicants as well as applicants for visas and citizenship, has the R.C.M.P. been provided with relatively precise government direction.'[19] The overt rules for security screening, of course, did not emerge until 1946. The oddity is that during the Second World War, precisely at the moment the government offered the RCMP the greatest degree of political direction, one important part of the RCMP's security intelligence procedure was beyond political control. That was the security-screening operation. While other RCMP security activities during the war were closely politically monitored, security screening was not. Moreover, even when the cabinet was made aware that munitions workers were being fingerprinted, it declined to sanction it through the Defence of Canada Regulations.

Although governments failed to set a political bearing for the RCMP, Betke and Horrall insisted that they had 'unearthed no evidence that it [the RCMP Security Service] had ... become an authority unto itself, [or] operated outside the law as a matter of policy.'[20] While their statement may be true in general, in implementing a security screening system throughout the Second World War the RCMP in fact 'operated outside the law as a matter of policy.' Certainly general authorization to protect the country was granted in legislation such as the RCMP Act, the War Measures Act, the Civil Service Act and the Munitions and Supply Act. But nothing in those statutes allowed the RCMP to circumvent the Identification of Criminals Act, which it did throughout the war.

Curiously, neither the RCMP nor the government actively sought to have elected authorities control security screening. On the one hand, the RCMP did not press for political authorization of mass fingerprinting, which it acknowledged was an illegal measure. Moreover, the force showed little interest in keeping the government informed about the extent of its security-screening operation. Beginning in 1942 the RCMP *Annual Report* did tally the total number of civilian fingerprints taken by the force. Nevertheless, in the weekly *Intelligence Bulletin*, the channel through which it informed the government about security developments, the RCMP did not once mention security screening and fingerprinting. Given the significance of the program, and the fact that it entailed breaking the law, this failure to keep the government properly apprised of the full extent of the screening system constitutes irresponsibility at best, malfeasance at worst. For its part, the government showed little interest in actively supervising its political police. When it was given the opportunity to authorize fingerprinting, it declined to do so. And in contrast to the procedure it followed after 1946, it never specifically authorized security screening.

THE POLITICAL MOTIVES BEHIND SCREENING

The absence of political approval did not signify a lack of political content in the security-screening operation. Although the RCMP and DMS had several goals for the program, exerting political control was its central motivation. Woven into its justifications for the security-screening program were unstated and indeed even unconscious concepts about the threat posed by sabotage and subversion.

Potential sabotage of the Canadian war effort was the reason most often cited for implementing security screening. This motive was clearly of paramount concern throughout the war. The Canadian manufacture of vital war *matériel* was one of its single most important contributions to the Allied cause. Anything that could jeopardize the production or delivery of that precious ordnance had to be stamped out. Yet the RCMP never comprehensively explained what connection there was between potential sabotage and security screening, what it understood sabotage to mean, what forms it could take, or who might commit it. Its analysis of the problem seemed sketchy, and it resisted coming to terms with the questions security screening raised. For example, after the war, when the Inter-Departmental Committee of Public Records requested a report on its wartime activities, the RCMP refused to give anything more than a brief outline, citing reasons of national security.[21] But on one occasion in the midst of the war, an RCMP officer who was administering the security and fingerprinting system spoke to the public about the force's mission in launching it. That was an address by RCMP Inspector Joseph Howe, officer in charge of the Civil Security Branch (earlier known as the Anti-Sabotage Branch) in Ontario. Speaking to the Canadian Manufacturers' Association annual meeting in June 1942, Howe asserted that

The German espionage organization select [sic] criminals and other persons of weak character to do their dirty work for them. They will find some person who has a grievance against the state or his fellow men. Blackmail is another method they use to get people to do their bidding. It is therefore necessary for us to be most careful in checking the background of employees in war industries. In Canada we have adopted fingerprinting of employees as an added precaution.[22]

Howe did not, however, provide evidence for his assertion that sabotage was the work of 'criminals and other persons of weak character,' or examples of it occurring.

In fact, screening did not locate many criminals in the war plants. In September 1941 the director of the Criminal Investigation Branch reported that, of 59,728 industrial workers who had been fingerprinted, only eight were wanted criminals.[23] As for those with criminal records, RCMP figures consistently show that they numbered only about 5 per cent of applicants for industrial work.[24] Redmond Quain, president of Ottawa Car and Aircraft, found that only 0.5 per cent of his permanent employees and 5 per cent of new applicants had criminal records.[25]

Nothing in RCMP documents from the era indicates how the RCMP came to the conclusion that politically motivated sabotage was linked to criminals. In the available correspondence and memos discussing the vetting system, the RCMP never referred to First or Second World War cases which had followed such a pattern, either in Canada or abroad. This is not to suggest that the link was invalid. Whatever its accuracy, it remained an ideological cornerstone for the police. In 1943, for instance, it was repeated by the officer in charge of the Fingerprint Section, Inspector H.R. Butchers, to the Chief Constables' Association.[26]

This theory was an early, inchoate version of the view that loyalty and reliability are both criteria to be assessed in security screening. Loyalty meant having no affiliation with a political movement dedicated to overthrowing the state. Reliability referred to character defects that could lead to indiscretion or dishonesty or make a person vulnerable to blackmail or coercion. Although the RCMP appear to have used this as a working guide to the screening system, only after the war did the government's Security Panel set down and explain the principle in greater detail.[27]

RCMP ANTI-COMMUNISM

While the RCMP spoke publicly of using fingerprinting to weed out criminals who might be given to sabotage, it also had a specific target for the program – communists. This fact was divulged at the 17 December 1940 meeting of the Co-ordinating Committee for Security, where DMS Dominion Security Officer R.L. Anderson revealed the details of the fingerprinting program to a group of corporate security officers. In doing so, he directly identified its target:

The R.C.M.P., as you know, over a period of years has been gathering information regarding communistic chaps and they have that all on file at headquarters. Just lately the department in collaberation [sic] with the commissioners have got the R.C.M.P. to agree to check any employees or all their employees, but they tried to stress that it would be confined to employees who are more or less suspicious. They are putting on extra help at headquarters in Ottawa to check fingerprints and photographs.

Toronto detective Daniel Mann, a veteran member of the city's Red Squad, immediately pointed out the plan's obvious flaw: communists are not fingerprinted. Anderson was unfazed. He replied that the RCMP

figure they will have a picture on file. However, the main idea is to check up on those men who are moving from one plant to another. In Quebec we have had a couple of instances just lately of these fellows moving from one plant to another. A name does not mean anything to them but if you are able to get a fingerprint of these fellows once, you have it for all time.[28]

Anderson was expressing a faith that was by then strongly held by police and government officials. His hope that fingerprinting would check the movement of communists was just another manifestation of the belief that fingerprinting, a criminal procedure, could be used against political dissent. J. Edgar Hoover elaborated a related view in 1919, when he introduced a card index to the General Intelligence Division of the United States Department of Justice. He drew a link between transiency and political dissidence: 'one of the main characteristics of the radicals in the United States is found in their migratory nature.'[29]

The RCMP's profound fear of people with left-wing political views was well illustrated by Commissioner Wood's February 1941 *Canadian Spokesman* article. In it Wood labelled communists as the primary wartime threat to Canadian society. He paid particular attention to the covert nature of communism, which works 'under cover of other organizations' with 'innocent titles[s]' and which, when detected, 'simply changes its coat and enters by another door.' He also took the opportunity to chastise the people behind whom the communists hid, those whom he called 'tools for treachery.' He singled out 'criminal and weakminded classes ... dazzled by their [communists'] promises of gain,' as well as civil libertarians, newspaper editors, and even members of parliament, who unjustly criticized the government over its suppression of basic rights.[30]

Wood's skewed conception of Canadian society must have contributed considerably to a belief that security screening was a necessity. How else could the RCMP keep tabs on subversives who were citizens, who worked covertly, and who easily cast off their outward marks of identity? Moreover, the problem was compounded by the ignorance, avarice, and gullibility of ordinary citizens, who not only served as a shroud obscuring communists, but who actually defended the dissidents. Strictly monitoring everyone – subversive and dupe alike – was clearly imperative.

Reg Whitaker has accurately pointed out that communism was an exaggerated threat whose real strength and ability to influence political life the RCMP never did establish reliably.[31] But this obsession had its uses. Having an internal threat to the state which was linked to an external power justified the existence of the RCMP security service and its inquiries into many facets of Canadians' lives. The communists' 'definitional status as "subversive" generally proved adequate for control and surveillance purposes.'[32]

One of the ironies of the RCMP's fixation upon communism throughout the war was that after June 1941 the Communist party became a diligent advocate of total war. With this about-face, RCMP Commissioner Wood later admitted, 'the tension for us was eased considerably.' According to Norman Robertson, the communists 'have even, for tactical reasons, become a restraining rather than a revolutionary influence in trades union organizations.'[33] Nonetheless the RCMP urged the government not to slacken the pressure on the Communist Party of Canada (CPC), and it remained banned.[34] Security screening also continued.

If the focus of security screening was on communists, why didn't the RCMP abandon its security-screening system after June 1941? One reason is that the RCMP had evidence – inconclusive but still troubling – that domestic communists were spying for the Soviet Union.[35] But more important, the RCMP deeply distrusted the CPC and believed that its allegiance to Canada would not last past the end of the war. The communists 'have turned their coats but not their hearts,' the RCMP secret *Intelligence Bulletin* cautioned.[36] In a draft report to the government in 1942 an anonymous RCMP officer candidly parroted the official RCMP line and acknowledged the Communist party's propaganda value to the force. He warned that 'for one to accept at face value an overnight change so contrary to that previously advocated, would be stupid and dangerous ... (Please note the Commissioner wants something along the above lines to appear.)'[37] The RCMP's anti-communist sentiment was undoubtedly heartfelt. But the Communist party also represented a bogeyman, and hence was an enemy too important and useful to let slip away.

In maintaining their surveillance of communists, the RCMP also had their eyes fixed beyond the end of the war. Even in 1942 the force's candid assessment was that after the defeat of fascism 'communism will be the dominant issue to be faced.' The threat was particularly potent because popular opinion was shifting, Assistant Commissioner R.R. Tait told a Western Hemisphere Intelligence Conference in August. Tait feared that 'a substantial portion of the population' was 'in the process of being radicalized and, henceforth, will view the propagation of Communist ideals with considerable sympathy.'[38] When it came to communism, the force was not for turning. In vain did members of the Prime Minister's Office rail against 'men like the notorious Sergeant Leopold, whose jobs would seem to depend on continuing to uncover bolshevik plots.'[39] Communism was the enemy; enemy it would remain. And the foe would be more deadly still immediately at the war's end because Canadians had been gulled into looking on communism with greater favour.

Hence the RCMP had a potent reason to continue screening after June 1941. Keeping the machine well tuned so as to use it after the end of formal hostilities must surely have occurred to the RCMP. The records show that in January 1942 British, American, and Canadian security intelligences agencies discussed the need to thwart communism in the postwar years.[40] Security screening could well have been in their thoughts as they exchanged ideas on dealing with the problem.

DISCIPLINING LABOUR AND EXERTING SOCIAL CONTROL

In implementing security screening, the RCMP, the DMS, and employers also had goals that went beyond tracing and checking communists. They used the system for purposes that could be considered less overtly political. Broadly speaking, these could be described as efforts to exercise social control over workers and citizens in a variety of circumstances, all directed toward maintaining economic stability.[41]

One important subject of social contention was unionization. By the Second World War industrial unionism's time had come. Within eighteen months of the war's start, a large pool of unemployed workers from the 1930s had dried up; the resulting labour shortage created ideal conditions for organizing unions.[42] The

Congress of Industrial Organizations was the most ambitious of the union centres, seeing the war as the opportune moment to expand. Already by November 1939 it had set out a bold plan to double its membership in Canada.[43] Between 1939 and 1945 the total number of organized workers doubled, and the most union-ized and militant sectors were those directly involved in war pro-duction. Almost one-half of the strikes in 1942–3, for instance, were fought in the metal-producing and mining sectors.[44] Strikes to force the recognition of unions were common. Both owners and workers understood the advancing power of industrial unions. If workers and their unions were not to seize the opportunity of the war to sweep the field, owners had to grasp whatever means they could. One of them was cooperating with the state in security screening. That system held out the promise of keeping out union organizers and radicals, but also of inquiring into the private lives and pasts of their employees.

The RCMP and manufacturers shared a compelling fear of communists and their potential to sway labour.[45] In the spring of 1941 the police identified industrial workers as a fertile field for agitators because they provided 'the one really vulnerable point of attack in our political structure.'[46] This vulnerability was tied directly to the communists within unions. Their agitation for improvements in wages and working conditions could lead directly to damaging strikes. To the RCMP, 'such strikes represent *minority rule*. There are only a few Communist agitators in any factory, but these workers ... will take possession of a mass meet-ing and by threats, promises and misrepresentation sway the majority to militant action.'[47]

This is not to suggest that the RCMP was opposed to unions *per se*. On the contrary, the force was careful not to appear to be tak-ing management's side when it came to a dispute with labour.[48] But the federal security police had little faith that workers could prevent themselves from being manipulated by communists in union leadership positions. And the RCMP never abandoned their distrust of the communists, even after June 1941. The result was a contradictory state attitude towards unions. Although the King government passed legislation streamlining the process of union certification, the RCMP remained suspicious of unions, especially when communists were involved.

Employers were even more fearful of organized labour. In May 1941 the Canadian Manufacturers' Association (CMA) warned that 'groups of dangerous men [were] trying to seize control of the key war industries of this country, in order to control the workers ... and to obstruct and restrict the output of munitions which are so sorely needed in the war.'[49] For the CMA, 'dangerous men,' Congress of Industrial Organizations (CIO) organizers, and communists were synonymous.[50] Hence, when it came to keeping tabs on labour the interests of the state and employers corresponded, and they must have welcomed the opportunity to share intelligence on such an immense scale.

When he spoke to the Chief Constables' Association in 1943 Inspector Butchers identified another element to the RCMP's rationale for fingerprinting, this one also being an important reason why employers found the program attractive. This was the problem of the anonymity of mass society, compounded by the mobility of labour that had been promoted by the war itself. Inspector Butchers observed that

In ordinary times the vast majority of persons grow up and live their working days in the community in which they were born and are known to all and sundry, but the concentration of workers in various centres at which war industries are located has resulted in a shifting of population which renders identification, except by a positive and centralized means such as fingerprints, more difficult than is experienced under normal conditions.[51]

The war was the cause of this perceived anonymity. War meant work; with work came social dislocation. Munitions production during the Second World War drew an immense tide of workers across Canada. As manufacturing employment beckoned, 125,000 people flooded east and west from the Prairie provinces. Most of them were drawn to Ontario and Quebec, where the bulk of the factories were located. The war also swelled an existing trend to urbanization. Over 300,000 rural dwellers spilled into cities during the six war years.[52] Unfamiliarity with the crowds who responded to the Help Wanted signs must have worried employers and the state. Busy employers could not be choosy. Yet who knew what flotsom was drifting into the plants on the human wave surging through the front gate?

In such an environment, identification itself became a form of control. Identifying each worker informed him or her that the employer and the state were watching. No heavy-handed surveillance had to take place. The RCMP's standardized industrial application form reminded a worker of the state's close scrutiny. The form asked the applicant to list five previous employers and residences for the past five years. Details of a person's national registration certificate were also requested, along with the birthplace and address of near relatives and information concerning their relatives' employment by the Canadian or foreign governments. Information about all criminal charges was demanded. The final two questions went further still: 'To what organizations (other than Labour Unions) have you belonged at any time during the past ten years?' and 'Are you willing to have your Fingerprints and Photographs taken for record purposes?'[53] (See appendix 1.) These questions sought information which was certainly not relevant to a person's work skills. But they firmly reminded an employee that the state and employer had vital information about him or her. Finally, the factory security officer physically pressed a worker's fingers onto an inked pad and stamped the marked digits upon an official form, which was then sent to RCMP headquarters. (See appendix 2.) There the police would process it using a system promoted as scientifically infallible. Yielding this information to a centralized state system must have intimidated some people. Being channelled through the fingerprint mill would also have reinforced the power of state authority. It is not inconceivable that the system produced an 'identification chill,' which dampened the expression of grievances about the war in general and about fingerprinting and screening in particular.

Labels themselves convey subtle but threatening messages. As in the McCarthy era in the United States, security investigations seemed to be intended to identify, recognize, or tag a person as much as to proscribe a specific behaviour, political attitude, or idea.[54] During the war, as we have seen, public opinion was so highly charged that being called disloyal had serious consequences. Labels like 'communist,' 'fifth columnist,' and 'saboteur' carried a great burden of public blame. The stigma for being identified as a communist was increased by the Communist party's illegality. It is significant that severe punishment, like internment, seemed to be reserved for high-profile labour leaders of the stature of Pat Sullivan and C.S. Jackson. The harshest punishment for most communists fingered by the security-screening system was dismissal. And some who were caught, like Claire Eglin, were not even fired. To the state, identifying perceived troublemakers and thereby keeping track of them was useful in itself.

Inspector Butchers raised another argument which explains why fingerprinting related as much to labour discipline as to national security. He pointed out: 'Naturally, the checking of fingerprints does not solve all problems in averting sabotage, but it does assure the employer that there is no blemish recorded against the applicant's *character*.'[55] Employers' enthusiasm for fingerprinting seemed to stem in part from a desire to know the personal characteristics of those they were hiring and to use this information to resolve traditional labour-management difficulties. Senior executives in the secret Co-ordinating Committee for Security, for example, discussed the salutary impact of fingerprinting on everyday factory problems such as tool thefts. 'Fingerprint them and it will stop tomorrow,' asserted R.M. Foster, security officer for the John Inglis Co. of Toronto.[56] His confidence in fingerprinting was absurdly excessive. The number of workers who routinely and properly would have access to tools in a large manufacturing shop would be enormous. Fingerprints would be myriad. Isolating a tool thief based on fingerprints alone would be impossible. Yet at least in the mind of plant management – and probably equally in the employees' – fingerprinting carried the magical capacity to single out a culprit. This belief is a powerful testament to the disciplining power fingerprinting had by virtue of its place in the popular imagination.

An equivalent justification was offered by the commanding officer at the Goose Bay, Labrador, RCAF station. Writing about civilians employed by the Ferry Command and the Department of Transport who worked at the Goose Bay base, Group Captain E.E. Evans noted that the preventive value of fingerprinting them lay in 'making these people think that we would have some check on them, and with the idea that if they should have wrong intentions, they might not carry them out.'[57] Fingerprinting was a powerful, state-sanctioned technique to keep workers in line.

Another benefit to employers from fingerprinting lay in its capacity to keep track of employees who moved frequently from job to job. The RCMP booklet *The Protection of Industry in Time of War* cautioned plant security officers that

If at any time an employee terminates his employment at the plant under suspicious circumstances, or for no apparent reason, this should be made the subject of a report to the police who will endeavour to discreetly ascertain the reason therefor and take steps to trace the man in question. Precipitant departures of this nature are not infrequent and are sometimes due to a would-be saboteur gaining the impression he is being watched. In instances of this kind the value of fingerprinting and photographing employees is readily apparent and will result in detecting the presence of such an individual upon his attempting to obtain employment in another plant, even though the plant be in another section of the country and the suspect changes his name and uses a fraudulent National Registration Certificate.[58]

This explanation for fingerprinting was phrased so as to emphasize its national security aspect. It is important to recognize, however, how closely meshed were the interests of the RCMP, the DMS and employers. RCMP fingerprinting to suppress sabotage and keep track of workers' movements met employers' concern, in a period of full employment, to acquire stable, compliant workers.

Monitoring and control of labour was also assisted by the DMS collecting data from war plants on labour turnover and absenteeism. According to E.J. Johnson, the DMS director general of industrial security, the main reason he wanted such information 'was to ascertain reasons for large labour turn over & excessive lost time as these usually mean labour unrest & consequently hamper production. (Labour unrest could easily be caused by labour agitators or saboteur.)'[59] The department also maintained a list of war plant employees whose criminal records had been revealed by their fingerprints.[60] In this way the security-screening program delivered information to the state that was of use in identifying broad labour trends as well as in isolating potential troublemakers and dissidents.

Inspector Howe expressed this unity of purpose graphically when he urged continued vigilance upon the captains of industry assembled at the 1942 CMA meeting. He cautioned the executives that it was 'most essential that all industrial plants ... be doubly sure of the integrity of their employees' in order to counteract 'the most dangerous form of sabotage [–] exceedingly slow work.'[61] To people on the production line, slow work would have been a natural reaction to many problems – ill health, conflicts with co-workers or foremen, poor pay, dangerous machinery, or frustrated demands for union recognition. To the state in conditions of war, slow work constituted a security threat.[62] Interpreting sabotage in this way is significant. This meaning was not new; European anarcho-syndicalists proposed sabotage of this type before the First World War.[63] The point, however, is that this was the first time during the Second World War that the RCMP had described sabotage in such terms. It was enunciated just at the moment the RCMP was acknowledging, in secret intelligence meetings, that 'no organized system of sabotage exists in Canada.'[64] Politically based sabotage had been dismissed as a real threat; a definition with stronger economic overtones came to the fore. There is no indication that the RCMP consciously revised its notion of sabotage to justify a program that served the needs of corporations. What happened in practice, however, was that screening proceeded, even though its earlier justification as a means to prevent violent sabotage was accepted as effectively irrelevant.

With the state and employers sharing similar motives, it was not surprising that they worked together so closely on the industrial security-screening system. Although the RCMP and the DMS administered it, employers played an important operational role. Pressure of work forced the RCMP by June of 1940 to place the initial steps of security screening in the hands of the companies which hired labour. Employers were to conduct the first inquiries into people they suspected; if they were not satisfied they were to turn the matter over to the RCMP.[65] In other words, in this state-sponsored screening system, the employer was to be the first line of defence against political contagion.

This link to the state was more than an unprecedented enhancement of the employer's coercive powers. It also represented an expansion of the state's network of political informers. Employers were officially incorporated into the political surveillance system. For corporations, turning informer was particularly attractive, since a plant purged of subversives and undesirables held out the promise of industrial peace and profit. In the words of Ottawa Car and Aircraft president Redmond Quain, finger-printing employees allowed him to isolate those with criminal records, and gave him 'an opportunity of scrutinizing them very carefully, or if necessary dismiss[ing] them.'[66]

Employers were not reluctant to use the threat of an RCMP security investigation to intimidate workers, judging from experience in one General Motors factory. In June 1941 the manager of the unidentified plant upbraided the United Auto Workers' shop committee over an accident at a press which the manager called deliberate:

Don't try to tell me what about it. That thing there was done maliciously ... I think we should fire the both of them ... 2 large machines both out of control in two weeks ... If we put it in the paper we would have every R.C.M.P. down here. We haven't done that. We have tried to protect the workers [by saying] that it was not sabotage.[67]

While this manager claimed that he was protecting the workers, his words contained a veiled threat that no worker could fail to recognize. Trouble on the assembly line could bring down the wrath of the state.

Security screening imposed control in another way as well. One of the crown corporations operated by the DMS was the Allied War Supplies Corporation (AWSC), which supervised and administered the construction of government ammunition, explosives, and chemical plants. When employees there were screened, one of the casualties was a woman whose criminal record had come to light through fingerprinting. She was one of many women hired as 'house mothers' to welcome and supervise the thousands of female workers who lived in dormitories at remote AWSC sites. As John de N. Kennedy delicately recorded in his official history of the DMS, 'one such "mother" was hired, who had an attractive appearance and an even more pleasing manner. Her fingerprints however disclosed that she was a very undesirable character and quite unsuitable for the post.'[68] The woman was one of several house matrons who, according to the DMS director general of industrial security, 'had very shady characters,' and about whom 'the plants have been severely criticized by persons who knew of their character.' The director general asked the RCMP to give the department complete criminal records on DMS employees in order to weed out women who were alleged to have low morals; the RCMP was willing to do so.[69]

What menace the house mother posed to national security is not obvious. More apparent is what the example reveals about one function of security screening – to maintain what the department considered to be proper moral standards and to thwart any public criticism of the department. The system functioned not just to ensure the safety of the state but also to supervise workers, to impose upon them state-prescribed regulations and standards; in short, to discipline.

Another group singled out by security screening was homosexuals. If detected, homosexuality invariably led to a negative security assessment. In this way, national security concerns spilled over into the enforcement of conventional moral standards. According to one RCMP officer homosexuals were regarded as risks during the war because they could be subject to blackmail.[70] But given the RCMP's postwar hatred of and determined campaign against homosexuals, it is difficult to believe that using security screening to identify and fire homosexuals did not also represent a moral crusade.[71]

The way security screening was practised indicates that supervising labour was a strong imperative for it. The program helped give employers leverage at a time when workers were in high demand and many were transient. In other words, security screening was useful to discipline labour, a motivation not strictly related to protection from sabotage. Security screening was also significant because it gave the employer some of the powers of the state. The state was injected into the workplace in a new way, lending authority to the employer. Previously, the struggle for control over conditions in the plant would have pitted worker (or union) against owner or manager. The state would exercise some influence through legislation covering strikes, conciliation, and the like, but this influence would be exerted indirectly, rather than through the direct intervention made possible under the screening program. So the system also gave the state (and especially the policing branch of it) a new involvement in the management of workers. Labour management became, implicitly, part of the function of the state's surveillance system.

No evidence has come to light to suggest that the RCMP and the DMS consciously designed security screening to influence labour-management relations. Instead what seems to have occurred was that, part way through the war, the state realized it could have that effect. This was fortuitous, since the sabotage threat which had been used to justify security screening had not materialized. By then the vetting train was running, and no one ordered it halted.

The wartime security-screening program operated within the context of a total war effort. It was justified by the need to protect the country's industrial production in a war in which Canada's contribution was historically unprecedented. But while the RCMP cited that as its rationale, it devoted far greater attention to another function of the program – imposing political, social, and economic control. Security screening gave the state and employers a method to identify and weed out communists, who, not incidentally, were also active union organizers. As the war went on this motive lost its use as a public rationale, and the immediate, partisan goal of snaring communists declined in importance. Nevertheless, the RCMP could hardly have failed to grasp the value of maintaining the system for its political capacity, since already by January 1942 the force was secretly girding itself for a postwar confrontation with communism. Once the communists became temporary allies, in June 1941, exerting social and economic control came to the fore as a reason to keep the system in place. Disciplining labour was essential to this. It involved identifying workers, monitoring their movements, and curbing their behaviour, all of which served the economic interests of the state and employers. Although the police and political authorities never set out an elaborate theoretical justification for the system, in practice its function was to enforce political conformity and to exert social and economic control.

7

Engineers of conduct: The system's technical rationale

In December 1942, with its security-screening program labouring under a burden of uncompleted fingerprint checks, the RCMP brought specially adapted International Business Machines tabulating equipment into its Fingerprint Section. The force hoped the machinery would dig into the accumulated mountain of unclassified civilian fingerprint forms. Inspector H.R. Butchers, the officer in charge of the Fingerprint Section, probably anticipated some difficulty in adapting the machine to his unique situation. But he might not have expected one fault that plagued the equipment from the moment it arrived. The Justice Building, the stone monolith that enveloped RCMP headquarters, did not meet the electrical standard required for modern office equipment. In the chronically overcrowded building, the Fingerprint Section's IBM sorter was consigned to a room near the elevator. Soon the machine was churning through fingerprint cards at the rate of 400 per minute. Top speed, however, could not be sustained for long. Each time someone used the building's elevator, the electrical circuit overloaded and the sorter ceased functioning.[1]

Irritating as it was, electrical failure was but a minor technical problem in the RCMP's system. Major ones also existed. Several of them arose from the RCMP's technological fixation, which was an important motivating force behind the program. If politics and economics were central to the public rationale of the fingerprint-based security-screening program, using the latest scientific aids headed the RCMP's internal rationale.

Believing that the war would create a critical security problem, the RCMP introduced security screening, at first on a limited scale. That act precipitated its own unanticipated consequence, too many fingerprints to process. That, in turn, required the force to adopt another expedient, acquiring more fingerprint classifiers. Events tumbled on in this way, and at each new challenge the RCMP turned to technological measures. In certain cases these manoeuvres themselves presented a new problem to the force. To step off the technological treadmill, the RCMP reverted to the habits it knew best – the policing expertise and ideological orientation established in the two previous decades.

Although security screening of industrial workers began at a modest level, involving just twelve plants before 1941, even this degree of security precaution called for increases in clerical help at the RCMP Criminal Investigation Branch (CIB) in Ottawa, which included the Intelligence and Fingerprint sections. On 15 September 1939 Commissioner Wood reported the need for six new CIB stenographers, two of them for Intelligence, because of 'increased duties dealing with precautions respecting Civil Security, the prevention of espionage, sabotage, etc.' By the end of November 1939 three new female clerks had been brought into the Fingerprint Section.[2]

The RCMP's growing reliance on fingerprinting during the early war years seems to have emerged as a response both to this heavy workload of security checks and to the perceived limitations of it. By June 1940 the RCMP was overwhelmed by the demand for civilian and military security checks, and Commissioner Wood decreed that industries should conduct their own initial security checks and submit only the names of those employees and applicants deemed to be suspicious. The force was also worried about the inherent unreliability of passing judgment on the basis of nothing more than names in its subversive index. Deputy Commissioner C.H. King fretted about the force inadvertently giving 'employees a clear bill of health, if we fail to find their names in our records ... for as you know a man might be entirely untrustworthy without his name being in our records.'[3] Fingerprinting, by contrast, held out the tantalizing prospect of certainty: 'We are also checking finger prints of employees, when asked to do so. The result in this case is more definite, because we are positively able to say whether the person, whose finger prints were sent here, has ever been arrested or convicted of an indictable offence.'[4] King was not the only official enthralled by fingerprinting. Ontario Fire Marshal W.J. Scott believed it capable of revealing country of birth, racial origin, and even the war sympathies of employees.[5] When Deputy Commissioner King wrote his memo, the RCMP was checking civilian fingerprints from a dozen companies. The number quickly grew to over 500 plants. The Mounties' conviction that fingerprinting represented the application of scientific certainty to a difficult organizational and human problem contributed to this sweeping expansion of the program.[6]

This unprecedented use of fingerprints quickly overwhelmed the Fingerprint Section. Manual fingerprint processing was inadequate to the task of clearing away the rapidly accumulating backlog. By April 1942 Inspector Butchers complained that the FPS 'is being inundated with finger prints received from various factories,' leaving the section 'daily falling a little farther behind.'[7] By April 1943 the force had received some 450,000 sets of war workers' fingerprints. Over 100,000 of them had not been processed.[8] The impact was felt even beyond headquarters. For instance, in November 1943 RCMP Commissioner S.T. Wood agreed with a report saying the force's Prairie detachments urgently needed competent members with forensic training to perform criminal work, and that they should be obtained from the Fingerprint Section. But he deemed it 'inadvisable to make these transfers until such time as the [Fingerprint] Section has caught up with all Civil Security fingerprint forms. I understand they are several thousand behind.'[9] Thus the Fingerprint Section's inability to keep up with the volume of fingerprint checks was hampering other RCMP duties. Nevertheless, wartime political assignments were deemed more important than criminal tasks.

This huge burden of unclassified fingerprints compelled the RCMP to adopt three innovations. One was the use of IBM tabulating equipment for fingerprint processing. But it was introduced only after two earlier efforts had failed to stem the tide of problems. Initially, the RCMP Fingerprint Section adapted by condensing the time taken to train newcomers in what Butchers called 'the intricate technicalities of fingerprint work.'[10] The second, and more drastic, innovation, was applied after the new training methods alone did not reduce the backlog. This was incorporating women into the fingerprint classification and checking process. Replacing uniformed male RCMP officers performing office duties with female civil servants was in any case a policy pursued by the force during the war, so it must have seemed inevitable that yet another all-male bastion would fall. Beginning in 1942 it did. Women were speedily introduced to the technical side of the Fingerprint Section, and by 1943 there were seventy-eight women in the section, double the 1942 figure. Exactly how many of them were performing technical tasks is unknown, since no distinction was made in the RCMP *Annual Report* between those performing clerical and technical duties.[11] In any case Inspector Butchers declared the experiment a success.[12] Judging from Commissioner Wood's assessment, however, an accumulated backlog still plagued the section in November 1943.

Increasing the number of searchers and classifiers probably contributed to yet another snag in the program – missed identifications. Those occurred when a searcher failed to match a criminal fingerprint form in the RCMP index with a war plant employee who had a criminal record. This was more than an error, it was a blight on the Mounties' good reputation. A paper volcano erupted when Sergeant. R.W. Wonnacott reported in November 1943 that 'one NCO [in the FPS] ... claims to have located one hundred missed identifications in a period of two years.'[13] Assistant Commissioner V.A.M. Kemp, who was also CIB director, admitted to Commissioner Wood that Wonnacott's observation about the missed identifications was 'the most serious reflection of all. If it is true ... this constitutes a definite black eye for our Finger Print Section. Accepting as we do the theory that no two fingerprints are alike, it is the most serious reflection on any fingerprint bureau to acknowledge that they have failed to make an identification, and ... the situation calls for an investigation.'[14]

The inquiry which followed brought to light some 246 missed identifications between 2 January 1942 and 27 November 1943, a period in which 561,696 searches were made.[15] Kemp deemed it 'a very high ratio [which] indicates a need for tightening up.'[16] The probe did, at least, demonstrate the merit of acquiring the female civilian searchers. Female searchers had far fewer missed identifications, although, as Butchers pointed out, differences in the numbers of searchers and time spent searching rendered a strict female-male comparison invalid.[17] One cause of the errors was lack of motivation among the regular RCMP officers doing the searching. Kemp conceded that recruits had gone to the finger print branch to escape even more monotonous routines elsewhere. As a result, 'the bulk of the men in the Finger Print Section are unambitious and lacking in general application to police work.'[18]

Available records on the new fingerprint-processing equipment do not indicate whether this problem helped prompt mechanization. It is true that the equipment was in use before Wonnacott's report was received. Still, it is entirely feasible that the RCMP hoped that at least one benefit of the equipment would be fewer missed identifications and improved motivation. This was certainly a prominent theme in Inspector Butchers's 1943 laudatory pronouncements about the advantages of mechanical processing with IBM equipment. He observed that 'the introduction of mechanical searching ... has been another successful innovation at the Fingerprint Bureau brought on by the war .... the efficiency of searching ... is increased, as a machine does not get tired around four o'clock nor does the tedium of making innumerable cross-searches have any appreciable effect on its morale.'[19] Butchers's statement is doubly fascinating for what it reveals about the RCMP's purpose in mechanizing. He described it as a means 'to cope with criminal ingenuity.' Coping with on-the-job boredom better describes the real internal challenge.

Contemporary accounts would have led the RCMP to expect the IBM machinery to trim search time significantly – hence quickly cutting into the fingerprint logjam – and to register identifications without error. An American article from the time indicated that using IBM equipment reduced the average time required to search the largest sections of a fingerprint file – the all-ulnar-loop group – from about one hour to about seven minutes. In addition, 'automatic searching has been accompanied by an exceptionally high record of identification.'[20] A 1937 article in the IBM publication *Business Machines* claimed a similar improvement in efficiency. With the semi-automated search, it became possible to locate any set of prints in the New York State Department of Correction collection within four minutes, the newspaper boasted.[21]

Remarkably, this speedy, machine-assisted search does not appear to have been brought to bear on one fundamental issue which was supposed to be addressed by fingerprinting – identifying communists. When DMS Dominion Security Officer R.L. Anderson spoke to the Co-ordinating Committee for Security in December 1940, he envisioned fingerprinting as a way to track down the 'communistic chaps' who were moving from factory to factory, organizing unions, and agitating against the war. In order to carry out this mandate, the RCMP Fingerprint Section would have been required to compare factory fingerprint forms with previously received fingerprints in the civilian collection. In fact a method to carry this out was devised. In a January 1941 memo to divisional officers commanding, which detailed how the security screening system would operate, Commissioner Wood specified that employees who were discharged or left under suspicious circumstances would have a 'watch for' notice attached to their fingerprint form in the civilian collection so that such individuals would be identified if they again applied at a war plant.[22] Nevertheless, this was not done, at least not in November 1943, when Sergeant Wonnacott prepared his comprehensive report on the state of fingerprinting in the force. He observed:

When a set of such prints is received they are searched only through the criminal collection and if identified, the record is forwarded ... Should no criminal record be found, the civil collection is not searched to see if he had been previously fingerprinted by any other factory, etc. Thus a person with no criminal record could be fingerprinted ten times, have ten different positions and, because the civil collection is not searched, this information is not known.[23]

Wonnacott did not say why the Fingerprint Section failed to make the search that was vital to achieving fingerprinting's original purpose. Perhaps sheer volume of work made it unfeasible. But its import should not be lost in our discussion of the use of tabulating machinery: almost one year after the equipment was introduced, it was not being applied to deal with one of the system's fundamental goals. Nevertheless, Inspector Butchers, the officer in charge of the section, seemed unperturbed by this fact. He laconically replied that 'recent [federal government] regulations freezing workers to their positions have reduced this situation to a point where it merits no further consideration.'[24] In other words, a legislative act had come to the rescue of an overburdened technical system. An additional factor which Butchers did not cite was the Communist party's changed attitude towards the war after 22 June 1941. The itinerant communist factory organizers feared by Anderson in 1940 were, by mid-1941, devotees of the anti-fascist war effort. Again, politics helped to unravel a technical snag in the fingerprint-based security system.

Mechanization of fingerprint searching gave the appearance of satisfying another of the RCMP's internal wartime priorities. It represented the application of science and technology to modern problems. By automating its fingerprint searching, according to Inspector Butchers, the RCMP demonstrated its capacity 'to grasp the latest scientific inventions' and 'to continually study and revise its operational methods.'[25] The lure of science can also be seen in Sergeant Wonnacott's 1943 recommendation to reorganize the various sections performing identification work into a centralized Scientific Identification Branch, which was done in 1944.[26]

The RCMP's system relied upon three technical developments. One was the Henry system of fingerprint classification, which allows any fingerprint to be expressed in numerical form. The second was punch-card tabulating equipment, whose foremost manufacturer at the time was International Business Machines Limited. The third was the adaptation of IBM business tabulating equipment for use in a fingerprint-processing system, which had been pioneered by the Federal Bureau of Investigation in the United States in 1934. Understanding the RCMP's screening system requires some knowledge of electromechanical tabulating equipment and the FBI's innovative use of it.

Electromechanical tabulating equipment dates from the late nineteenth century, when competing entrepreneurs began to vie for burgeoning commercial and state markets. One of the most successful of them was Herman Hollerith, the founder of International Business Machines Company Limited. IBM had established a presence in Canada by 1917, and henceforth it was served directly by IBM in the United States, unlike Britain and its other colonies.[27]

Describing the steps by which the Canadian business office became mechanized, Graham Lowe identifies punch-card machinery as the third and final stage of the process.[28] This stage had begun by 1920, but its coming of age occurred in the 1930s. Another study of office automation in Canada calls the punch card and its accompanying battery of sorters, collators, reproducing punches, and tabulators 'the most dramatic innovation' in offices during the interwar period.[29] A history of IBM indicates that during the 1930s the card punch, the sorter, and the accounting machine were the company's basic rental unit.[30] In a typical business function, an operator would first punch the cards, entering information on them by making a hole, each standing for a different characteristic. When the time came for retrieval, the cards would be placed in the sorter, where they would pass through at a rate of from 225 to 400 per minute, with the desired cards falling into the proper classification bins. These would be taken out and placed in the accounting machine, which would use the information on them to print invoices or cheques, or to perform other functions. Ease of operation was an attractive feature about the machinery. Learning to operate either the keypunch or the sorter took only a matter of hours. Working an IBM keypunch machine was often the first job that young women did after graduating from high school.[31]

During the Second World War demand for the IBM devices

Engineers of conduct 171

soared. In Canada, where tabulating equipment was IBM's major line of business during the war, sales were so brisk that by 1949 IBM's share of the tabulating-equipment market was estimated to be about 90 per cent.[32] In the United States, the federal government's requirements for accounting machines, tabulators, and related devices expanded so dramatically during the war that IBM was asked to produce these rather than military items.[33] By the time it appeared in the RCMP Fingerprint Section in 1942, IBM electromechanical tabulating equipment was a familiar sight in Canadian business and government offices. The Dominion Bureau of Statistics had Hollerith equipment in 1941, and the RCMP used its own machine to register almost 1.5 million firearms early in the war.[34]

The Hollerith equipment the RCMP installed in the Fingerprint Section was a tabulating card keypunch, a reproducer, and a multiple sorter. The apparatus allowed one trained technician and a semi-skilled helper to duplicate the work of several skilled fingerprint operators.[35] The heart of the system was the multiple sorter, which used an electric current to sort Hollerith tabulating cards. Rather than standard IBM equipment, the RCMP used a specially modified sorter. For this unusual machine, the force owed an immense debt to the Federal Bureau of Investigation, with whom the RCMP had an ongoing liaison during the war. The two agencies routinely exchanged non-criminal fingerprints, and they participated jointly in a working committee dealing with mutual problems.[36] So there was ample opportunity for the FBI to impress the Canadian police with the merit of automated fingerprint searching.

The similarity between the RCMP's sorter and those used by the FBI is apparent from RCMP and FBI descriptions of how the machines worked. Both systems processed only the all-ulnar-loop group, the segment of a fingerprint file containing fingerprint cards with ulnar loop patterns on all ten fingers. For the all-ulnar-loop classifications, IBM cards were punched with the appropriate code. The cards were gang-reproduced to transfer the coded information about the ridge count for each finger from the left hand to the right hand side of the card. (This was necessary for the operation of the cylindrical selection device which was unique to the FBI and RCMP equipment.) The punched cards were mechanically sorted into categories according to classification number. The cards, once sorted into groups made up of only a few, or even just one, classification numbers, were manually compared to the classification numbers in the criminal index by a fingerprint technician.[37] The FBI and RCMP punched cards were virtually identical in form. Although no records show that the FBI passed on to the RCMP information about using IBM business tabulating equipment to process fingerprints, that is probably where the Canadian police acquired the technique. International exchanges of this kind of were not new. Fingerprinting itself was a technology transferred from one police force to another back and forth across the Atlantic Ocean and the 49th parallel.

The IBM machines used by the RCMP appear to have been made specially by IBM, relying on experiments within the FBI and suggestions by that agency.[38] IBM called the machine a Type 076 Searching Sorter.[39] A 1937 article in the IBM corporation's organ, *Business Machines*, explained that the company had made only four of the machines to that point. Three of the 1937 machines were at the FBI and one was at the New York State Department of Correction.[40] There must have been sufficient demand for the machine to merit production of more, because the IBM sales manual for June 1944 includes a Type 076 Searcher Sorter which was 'specially designed' for use under conditions 'such as the counting of ridges in fingerprint work.'[41]

The machinery could be so easily transferable from the FBI to the RCMP because their criminal and subversive indexes were organized along similar lines and were used in comparable ways. The essence of both operations was a matching exercise which compared, on the one hand, all applicants for or incumbents of government and war plant positions and, on the other, criminals and (in a separate index) suspected subversives. The first condition for such a process is an index arranged in some logical way. Having a subversive or criminal card index organized into several categories allowed for a variety of matching options. Machinery merely performed the action faster than humans could.

Computer matching joins hitherto independent pieces of information and is used increasingly to expose a variety of offenders,
from tax evaders to people who neglect to pay their parking tick-
ets.[42] Mass fingerprinting and mechanical processing operated in
a similar way by linking information that was previously discrete
– on the one hand, criminal convictions and subversive records,
and, on the other, lists of factory workers, seamen, civil servants,
and military personnel. In the process a new type of rule breaking
was exposed – not providing complete information on the
employment form. Indeed, this was the primary cause cited when
a person was fired.[43] Matching information that was previously
scattered was a major advance in a process that in the latter half of
the twentieth century helped to erode personal privacy.

THE CRIMINAL-POLITICAL INTERFACE

In deciding to make fingerprinting an integral part of security
screening, the RCMP gave itself a policy dilemma. With its penchant for removing obstacles by resorting to technical measures, it
is no surprise that the force again turned in that direction. The
result was at best pseudo-science, at worst seat-of-the-pants policy making. The problem was this: since the fingerprint check
turned up thousands of people with criminal records, what criteria could the RCMP use to decide which of them should be
excluded from war industry, the military, and the state? Behind
this practical difficulty lay a philosophical contradiction; fingerprints represented a record of people charged or convicted of
criminal offences. How could the force justify using a *criminal*
identification device to ascertain people's *political* attitudes or
their potential for acts of subversion or sabotage? By ingenious, if
self-serving, reasoning the RCMP was able to skirt these problems
and preserve its faith in fingerprinting. The problem and its resolution, however, illustrate the limitations on the technical dimension of security screening. When the technical rationale for
fingerprinting struck a barrier, human decision making had to sal-
vage the program.

Some 5 per cent of industrial job applicants, potentially tens of thousands of people, could be expected to have criminal records.[44] But for all its ability to churn through volumes of fingerprints, the RCMP's machine could not make a distinction between types of criminals; it identified everyone with a criminal record. Since all the workers who fit that category could not possibly be fired, the RCMP had to come up with a formula to distinguish between criminals who posed a security risk and those who didn't. The underlying problem, of course, was that there was no simple, reliable technical test for political loyalty and no scientific instrument that could measure such an imponderable. Yet, in fingerprinting, the RCMP had a tool which was wrapped in the veil of objectivity, which was relatively easily operated, and which the RCMP believed should be more widely applied. The system could not be abandoned.

Commissioner Wood laid out the RCMP's conundrum for divisional commanding officers in January 1941. In deciding which criminal offences would render a worker unsuitable for employment in a war industry, the RCMP would treat some offences differently than others. Crimes of some types were regarded as constituting no security risk to war industry or the state. The fact that a person had a record of them was to be withheld from plant security officers; such a record would not be a bar to employment. Other offences, however, were classified as meriting security attention, and applicants with these records were to be excluded. But which offences were to be placed in the non-risk or benign category, and which in the high-risk category? Wood advised the divisional commanding officers that 'a record showing that the employee had been arrested on a charge of arson, malicious damage to property, rioting and offences under the Defence of Canada Regulations, *etc.*, would ordinarily be considered as rendering the employee unsuitable for employment; whereas a conviction for assault, carnal knowledge, obtaining money by false pretences, *etc.*, would not, generally speaking, render him unfit for such employment.'[45] The high-risk category included crimes such as arson, which might or might not be politically related, and others which were political in nature.

Wood's memorandum did not lay to rest questions about this

ordering of offences. The ambiguity expressed in Wood's *etceteras* must have sorely troubled the divisional commanding officers. Two months later Assistant Commissioner R.R. Tait responded to queries about the procedure from various divisions throughout the country. He added membership in an illegal organization to the high-risk category. But he deemed as less serious such criminal offences as perjury, vagrancy, manslaughter, and narcotic or sexual offences. People with these convictions would not be regarded as security risks. Theft, armed robbery, and drunkenness, declared Tait, fell into grey areas in which the divisional commanding officer ought to take into account the exact type of work performed by the employee. In some jobs they posed a threat, in others not.[46] By 1943 the force had expanded its list of offences that constituted a security risk to include mischief, arson, wilful damage, subversive acts, forgery, crimes of violence, theft, moral offences of a gross nature, and habitual drunkenness.[47]

The decision as to which criminal offences would be placed in the high-risk category appears to have been based upon policing experience in Canada. Some criminal charges had long been treated as ways of dealing with political dissent. For example, using 'insulting, profane and obscene language,' a charge which at a superficial glance seems unrelated to politics, was invoked in the 1930s to harass people speaking at communist-organized events. Under that section in 1934, for example, Gaston Pilon was ordered to serve a year in jail at hard labour in Montreal for declaring that Roman Catholic popes throughout history had been 'thieves, procurers, murderers, pimps and brothel-keepers.'[48] Other criminal acts were often committed in the course of political actions such as demonstrations. The unemployed person who during the Depression joined an 'outlaw shopping tour' – which entailed the invasion of department stores – or who participated in the occupation of the Vancouver post office and art gallery in 1938, for instance, could have been charged with mischief, wilful damage, or any number of the offences the RCMP placed into the high-risk category in the Second World War.

It might be argued that a simpler explanation could account for the RCMP's blurring of the political and the criminal: that is, the

RCMP did not at this time have a sufficient information base on subversion to provide for easy identification of risks. Hence the use of criminal data was the quickest available fix. The more the vetting system expanded, and the longer it persisted, the greater and more detailed would be the database amassed by the police on subversives. Such a database, however, would develop only over time.[49] Yet it should be kept in mind that, by the 1940s, the RCMP Intelligence Section had more than two decades of experience with subversion and identifying subversives. The real problem was not the lack of information on subversion, it was the lack of experience in turning information into prosecution. Security intelligence agencies in general tend to collect information about subversives but not to prosecute them. Greg Kealey has observed that already in 1919 RNWMP Commissioner A.B. Perry had grasped the principle that acquiring data about subversives was more important that putting them behind bars. Certainly the RCMP was very proficient at collecting information. By the 1920s the RCMP had millions of pages on subversives in its central registry.[50] The Second World War security-screening program represented the first time the RCMP Intelligence Section had been given the opportunity – indeed the responsibility – to turn security intelligence into action.[51] In this case action did not mean prosecutions as such, but it did mean issuing judgments about who constituted security risks, which led to dismissals. The Intelligence Section's inexperience at turning information into prosecutions was one reason why the police had such difficulty negotiating the criminal-political interface.

The RCMP's blurring of an already-indistinct line between political and criminal policing casts into doubt Bernard Porter's definition of political policing. In his history of security intelligence in Britain in the modern era, Porter declares that 'a genuine political police' combats 'activities that are defined as criminal because they are political, rather than activities which would be defined as criminal anyway, but are also classed as political because they have political motives or aims.'[52] That is, political crimes are specially designated; they are unlawful because they are political. They are not criminal offences which can be construed to have political associations. The problem with Porter's definition is that it fails to recognize the extent to which police treat politics and crime as overlapping phenomena. According to Porter, very few of the offenses the RCMP regarded as high risk would fit the political category, the most prominent of them being violations of the DOCR. In the operation of Canada's security screening during the Second World War, the RCMP linked the criminal and the political by creating a category of high-risk offences, which included criminal offences that had long been regarded as implicitly political, and by slightly adjusting their vision to regard some other criminal offences as political ones. This allowed it to justify the use of a criminal procedure, finger-printing, in a political matter. This practice was quite consistent with the way that fingerprinting was used from its inception.

Jean-Paul Brodeur persuasively describes the intermingling of criminal and political policing in his discussion of what he calls high policing. One of the basic features of high policing is its use of crime control to generate information which can be used to help the police supervise dissent. As he points out, criminals have long been used as a means to gather social intelligence. This applies particularly to moral crimes such as prostitution, gambling, and drugs. But, more broadly, he contends that counter-intelligence and security work is often performed by police with a background in criminal detection, since the tasks are similar in nature.[53] The RCMP well illustrates this tendency. The force has always been primarily a criminal force with a secondary involvement in security and intelligence. Moreover, the officers in the Fingerprint and Intelligence sections (both part of the Criminal Investigation Branch) were trained criminal investigators. Almost all of them had been thrown into security intelligence duties, usually with no training in the field.[54] It would be of little surprise, then, for them to apply criminal investigation methods to the security-screening system and to see the criminal and political aspects of their work as similar.

Although the fingerprinting system raised difficulties, it also had its benefits, among them the fact that it allowed the RCMP to take the initiative in seeking out security threats. Early in the war the force had been inundated by reports from citizens who had seen suspicious incidents or people. Even though these reports were sometimes the work of semi-official organizations such as the League of Patriotic Action and Civil Protection Committees, the RCMP remained skeptical about the information it obtained: an 'ill-informed public' was letting its 'imagination run riot.'[55] Although tips of this type might still be useful, security screening allowed the police to remain independent of such reports. Screening gave the police more control over the process of generating and accumulating security information.[56] Screening helped the RCMP to accumulate and massage intelligence data, rather than passively receiving it.

Basing its security-screening system upon fingerprinting also gave the RCMP ammunition to refute charges that it was acting like the Gestapo, an accusation that seemed to haunt the force.[57] Fingerprinting had an aura of scientific objectivity which helped refute any argument that the RCMP was acting as a partisan political police.[58] The science and technology of fingerprinting and mechanical searching became what Richard Ericson and Clifford Shearing call 'an ideological tool of justification and excuse.' Scientifically armed police can claim that they are 'technical agents of scientific rationality rather than instruments of particular interests and a morality reflecting those interests.'[59] One characteristic which made fingerprinting publicly controversial was that it bound up everyone in its irrepressible objectivity, attaching to them all the stigma of criminality. This universality was the very factor that made it a valuable shield against charges of RCMP partiality. When people in a war plant were screened, everyone was fingerprinted, 'from the President down to the most junior employee.'[60] And the machinery played no favourites – anyone with a criminal past was exposed. This lent credence to the view that the security police and the process itself were objective. Screening was 'necessary for the protection of *all*,' in the words of the *Globe and Mail* article announcing the program. Fingerprinting became part of 'the constant ideological struggle ... to make sectional interests appear general.'[61] (The sectional interests served by security screening were clear: employers, for whom the RCMP scrutinized their employees on the lookout for troublemakers of several varieties, and the state, which gained labour peace in the private sector and which also had its own employees screened.) According to Ericson and Shearing, this scientific depoliticization of the police is particularly important because 'they are at the forefront of debates about the relationship between the state and the individual and are a primary means by which the citizen can assess the state as acting on his behalf.'[62] In this case the aura of scientific objectivity surrounding fingerprinting helped to convince people that the state was protecting everyone, without regard to class.

Ericson and Shearing also contend that 'The essence of police-work is to penetrate spheres of organized life to set up surveillance mechanisms in human form, technological, or some combination of the two.'[63] By using the plant security officers and their loyal employees as informants, the RCMP greatly increased the state's intelligence network within the private sector. But security screening also allowed the RCMP to penetrate two other spheres of organized life which were previously outside its purview – the civil service (screened since 1931) and the military. The RCMP used both personnel for human penetration (through plant managers and loyal employees) and mechanisms for technical penetration. The data accumulated on workers, civil servants, and military personnel through security screening and fingerprinting represented a rich new source of intelligence on hitherto untapped spheres of Canadian society.

The intensive surveillance and policing of many aspects of life presupposes 'a society that is bureaucratically conditioned and prepared for data processing.'[64] In 1939 Canadian society was not yet accustomed to being numbered and counted on the scale it would be in the Second World War and after. The security-screening system helped condition Canadian society to yield information to the state for monitoring purposes. And it was but one wartime act that fostered an environment conducive to accumulation of data by the state. The RCMP also registered thousands of enemy aliens and 1.5 million firearms, while the government conducted its own unemployment insurance and national resources mobilization tallies of all citizens.[65] Screening, together with these inventories, helped condition Canadians to relinquish voluntarily information that was useful to the state and its political police.

Brodeur identifies several features of high policing, some of which correspond well with security screening. High policing is absorbent; it exerts control by storing intelligence. And it gathers that intelligence from diverse sources, especially from criminal activities and informants among criminals. Like high policing generally, security screening was also a method to gather and store intelligence. It used technical means to divide society into relatively small units, data from which could be processed easily and precisely. As Brodeur puts it, high-policing technique breaks up 'physical and social space into definite coordinates in order to increase the scope and precision of surveillance.'[66] With the results of security screening in its hands, the RCMP was no longer faced with an undifferentiated workforce, civil service, or military. It could discern the peculiarities of the workers in each individual factory. Who had criminal records, who had subversive records, who were aliens? The details were spread out before the Mounties' eyes. The system was not perfect, but it provided the police with better intelligence about the workforce than it had ever previously possessed.

According to Brodeur, high policing also carries the police beyond mere enforcement into a situation in which the police unofficially but nonetheless effectively assume significant legislative, judicial, and executive powers. Security screening in the Second World War confirms Brodeur's observation. The RCMP did use it to take on more than an enforcement role. With no political rein on its screening operation, the RCMP was able to define what constituted a violation as well as to track down and judge who was guilty. Only the execution of its sentence eluded the force – it left the fate of a worker or civil servant deemed suspect up to the person's employer. The RCMP's assumption of the security-screening mandate illustrates a broader trend. From its inception the RCMP carved out its own security intelligence mandate. No government legislation spelled out what powers the force could appropriate. Instead, this authority was pieced together from what Brodeur calls 'a motley array of legal, executive and police internal policy documents.'[67] Security screening merely represents one part of its security jurisdiction which the RCMP initiated and implemented on its own, outside any political control.

Internally, the RCMP appears to have been on a treadmill with the fingerprinting aspect of security screening from the beginning of the war until at least 1944. Each change it introduced seemed to demand another. Fingerprinting first presented itself as a solution to the pressure of security screening and to the force's dependence on subversive indexes organized exclusively by name. Fingerprinting gave security screening an air of scientific certainty. But in adopting fingerprint checks as an important cog in its security-screening machine, the RCMP created a different problem – too many fingerprint classifications to perform. Manual processing proved unequal to the huge volume of fingerprints submitted by hundreds of war plants after January 1941. Three innovations were seized upon to alleviate this problem. The RCMP condensed the training period, brought civilian women technicians into the Fingerprint Section, and acquired IBM tabulating equipment. The first two of these innovations not only failed to break the deadlock, they contributed to a further complication, improperly filed and missed identifications. Another difficulty, low morale and lack of motivation among fingerprint technicians, was no doubt exacerbated by the sheer volume of prints to be processed. The RCMP addressed that problem by automating the search process.

In arranging criminal offences into categories, the RCMP stamped a human solution onto a technical difficulty. The machinery could produce lists of people with criminal records, but it could not predict which of them would be saboteurs. To answer that question the RCMP had to take the machine's list of suspects and apply its own judgment to it. In the end, RCMP officers, with their own understanding of police work and their own biases, were called upon to adjudicate the security risk of workers, civil servants, and military recruits whose criminal records had been brought to light by the screening process. Humans stepped in to sort out a matter which technique could not.

Taken as a whole, the security screening experiment represented a new excursion into the use of technology to monitor the
Canadian people politically. It graphically reveals the Canadian
state's faith that science and technology could help manage its citizens. Never before – and never since – had such a large proportion of the Canadian population been subject to scrutiny by the
political police. An effort of such magnitude was possible only
because the RCMP had an imposing technology and an abiding
faith in it. Experience proved both to be flawed.

8

Security affairs: Liaison with the Allies and provinces

If the friendship among the RCMP, MI5 and MI6, and the FBI was warm before 1939, the war made it intimate. Indeed, on at least one occasion the entanglement became too tight. In October 1942 nurturing it landed the RCMP in trouble. The incident illustrates the RCMP's high regard for its relationship with its fellow agencies.

In January 1942 the three major security intelligence agencies in North America, the RCMP, the FBI, and British Security Co-ordination (BSC), held the first of a series of meetings designed to achieve a 'complete co-ordination of intelligence.'[1] The conferences were top secret. In attendance were the directors of the agencies and other high-level security experts, including specialists from military intelligence. Although the Department of External Affairs had transmitted to the RCMP the initial American invitation to the coordinating meetings, and had sent a representative to the inaugural session, at later councils no one from the department was present. In October 1942, wishing to have an official record of what had transpired at the meetings, the under-secretary of state for external affairs, Norman Robertson, asked the RCMP for a complete set of minutes.

The force, however, was not immediately ready to give them up. Loyal to its colleagues in the other services, the RCMP wrote them to ask if they objected to Robertson's receiving the minutes. When Robertson heard of the request, he delivered a pointed civics lesson. 'I cannot agree that the views of [the outside security

agencies] should be solicited in this matter,' he rebuked the
RCMP. 'The Secretary of State for External Affairs is responsible
for the conduct of the international affairs of this country.' Contri-
tion followed swiftly. The RCMP recalled the letters to its fellow
agencies and yielded up the minutes.[2]

The incident reveals the strength of the security alliance
among Canadian, British, and American security intelligence
agencies, which emerged during the Second World War. The
RCMP esteemed its fellow intelligence agencies so highly that,
until corrected, it was ready to give them higher priority than a
department of its own government. Several authors have commented upon Canada's stepped-up involvement in security
intelligence liaison arising from the war. In Wesley Wark's view,
the war ruptured Canada's prewar pattern of intelligence sharing. Canada would no longer be just a passive recipient of British and American intelligence. During the war Canada became a
partner in a major Anglo-American program to intercept and
decode enemy wireless radio messages. This involvement in signals intelligence would continue and expand after the war.
Wark attributes Canada's active participation in the western
security intelligence network to this cooperation in signals intelligence.[3] Similarly, Peter St John regards this Canadian cryptanalysis effort as a fresh departure in Canadian security intelligence
work.[4] David Stafford has examined the Canadian involvement
in Camp X, a British training school for agents sent into occupied Europe.[5] None of them mention cooperation in the fields of
suppressing internal dissent and security screening, and nothing
has been written about how this work encouraged the three-
way security intelligence liaison. Yet security screening was a
field that stimulated an active collaboration among the allies
during the war.

LIAISON WITH BRITAIN

When Britain made the fateful declaration of war on Germany in
1939 it was fortunate in not having to create a brand new transatlantic intelligence network. Security links that had been tied in the

First World War had not been abandoned in the interwar years. After 1918 subversion replaced counter-espionage as the main international intelligence concern, and the RCMP corresponded directly with MI5, military intelligence, and Scotland Yard on the subject.[6] In the early 1930s, S.T. Wood, a future commissioner, and Superintendent T. Dann made the first official RCMP visit to Scotland Yard. International contacts established in the 1930s were unprecedented in RCMP history, recalled Vernon Kemp, an officer who would himself take part in wartime exchanges.[7]

The threat of war itself encouraged closer communication. In August 1939 RCMP Commissioner Wood assured Justice Minister Lapointe that 'liaison is being maintained in all matters of mutual interest with M.I.5.'[8] But these channels remained relatively unused until the spring of 1940.[9] The German occupation of Europe demanded that the channels be opened. Isolated, Britain looked west and recognized that its security depended upon North American help. Its enemies also knew this. As F.H. Hinsley and C.A.G. Simkins point out, 'the Axis powers would obviously attempt to impede the production and delivery of munitions and essential supplies and to foster a climate of public opinion that was hostile to Great Britain, or at least indifferent to her fate.'[10] Perhaps the most important security intelligence outcome of this delicate situation was the creation of a new agency, British Security Co-ordination.

The BSC grew out of a 1939 British Secret Intelligence Service (SIS) overture to the FBI which was conveyed personally by William Stephenson, a Canadian-born businessman who had lived in England since 1921. The initiative led to the construction of a security intelligence bridge between the two countries – a secret British organization in New York, the BSC. Under Stephenson's guidance, the BSC inhabited a shadow world for the two years that the United States remained neutral. Based in New York, Stephenson gained the collaboration of U.S. President Franklin Roosevelt and FBI Director J. Edgar Hoover only by agreeing to a condition that the organization remain secret, especially to the American government. Under the cover of business affairs, Stephenson was able to forge a close working relationship among the SIS, the FBI, and later the U.S. Office of Strategic Services, the predecessor of the Central Intelligence Agency.[11]

The BSC was also instrumental in inducting the Canadian security intelligence service into the partnership. The RCMP became involved in the work of Stephenson's clandestine unit in 1940, and the two agencies were soon exchanging information. In February 1941 Stephenson made an unusual request of RCMP Commissioner Wood, asking him to release the officer in charge of intelligence, Superintendent E.W. Bavin, to work at the BSC's New York office. Wood and Bavin's relationship had been fractious, which probably encouraged the commissioner to expedite the transfer. Within a month Bavin was working at BSC headquarters. Once there, he proved as useful to the RCMP as to the BSC, since he discovered information of Canadian interest in BSC files and sent it north.[12]

The BSC had a security division which was engaged in vetting people and companies. Operating out of the BSC New York office, this division had a daunting responsibility: 'protecting British property and British and Allied shipping, vetting the companies working on Britain's account and individuals proceeding to British territory or joining the British and Allied Services, supervising the execution of anti-sabotage measures for factories, railways and docks and investigating suspected sabotage and subversion among labour unions and merchant seaman.'[13] To carry out these functions it assigned agents to all the major ports in the United States.[14] The BSC continued to vet on behalf of MI5 throughout the war.[15] Before the United States entered the war, the BSC also screened seamen and kept watch against sabotage in New York. After December 1941 American authorities took over that duty. But the BSC remained in charge of protecting British shipping in American ports and trained its industrial security officers in Canada.[16]

The British security-screening machine was similar to the model that operated in Canada. Far more than a million Britons were screened by the domestic security intelligence agency, MI5.[17] And the vetting was highly political; communists were seen to be the primary threat to the state. Communist party membership grew considerably after 1941, and its influence in British political life rose correspondingly. The British state also had reason to fear that communists were passing on information to the party, information which would ultimately reach Moscow.[18] The similarity between Britain and Canada also extends to another sphere – the healthy suspicion between the security intelligence agency and other political authorities. Politicians saw MI5 as overzealous in its pursuit of communists; MI5 tended to dismiss its critics as naïve, even dangerously so, about the menace of communism.[19] A similar distrust marked the relationship between the RCMP and bureaucrats in the prime minister's office and the Department of External Affairs.

In one important respect, however, British experience differed from Canadian practice. In Britain, the debate about vetting went right to the highest levels of the government and helped to set policy. That political involvement, in turn, tended to restrain MI5's hand. Frequently, the government rejected MI5's appeals to purge the civil service of communists.[20] In other words, politicians, the people elected to make political decisions, actually had the courage to make them. During the war the Canadian cabinet, on the contrary, did not address the security-screening issue, much less establish a policy on it.

British-Canadian security liaison was intimately bound up with restraining, regulating, and scrutinizing merchant seamen. Behind that need lay one of the thorniest of Canada's Second World War security puzzles: how to ensure security in Halifax and satisfy the British and Americans that the port was safeguarded. The British in particular were scathingly critical of security provisions at Halifax, and no Canadian palliative appeared to mollify them.[21] In September 1941, at the request of the Security Executive, Winston Churchill asked Mackenzie King to give the problem his personal attention and offered to send experts to help.[22] This lack of confidence in Canadian capacity to prevent the port from being a treasure house of vital intelligence to German U-boats in the Atlantic plagued the Canadian cabinet war committee, the military, and the RCMP.

Yet this troublesome seed bore positive fruit. It brought the

RCMP and other Canadian agencies into closer alliance with British security intelligence. The British sent at least four port security specialists, one of them Sir Connop Guthrie, head of the BSC Security Division. Two others were dispatched after Commissioner Wood appealed directly to Sir David Petrie, head of MI5.[23] Two British experts on industrial security also toured Canada and the United States in 1942.[24] The RCMP, in turn, sent officers across the Atlantic to observe British security procedures. Assistant Commissioner Vernon Kemp and Sub-Inspector F.A. Regan visited England in 1943 to study port security, a subject Norman Robertson admitted was 'knotty.'[25] Their visit also strengthened the RCMP's ties with the British security services. While there they consulted with MI5 about techniques to combat subversion, sabotage, and espionage.[26] Kemp came away believing that British War Office intelligence agents were 'definitely in the front line with respect to security matters.'[27]

Through the wrangling over port security the formalities of security intelligence liaison between the two countries were fleshed out. When the problem first arose, William Stephenson suggested the establishment of a BSC office in Ottawa. However, the British Security Executive decided that the subject was one that should be handled through political levels – the high commissioners or even prime minister to prime minister. Lord Philip Swinton, the head of the British Security Executive, also broached the subject of posting a permanent MI5 liaison officer in Ottawa. This proposal took firmer shape in May 1942, when an MI5 representative visited St John's and Halifax and pressed the RCMP to accept an MI5 training mission. In November of the same year, the RCMP attempted to operate the first German spy captured in Canada as a double agent and urged MI5 to send an officer to act as adviser. Cyril Mills, the representative who came to assist, remained for the rest of the war in Canada, where he also became an important liaison link between MI5 and the FBI.[28] It is indicative of the relatively unequal relationship between the RCMP and MI5 that the RCMP did not reciprocate by arranging to locate its own liaison officer in London. No officer was stationed in London until October 1946.[29]

Port security was not just the subject most likely to cause friction among the three allied countries; invariably that animosity also crept into dealings between the RCMP and other Canadian government departments and agencies. In March 1943 Tommy Stone of the Department of External Affairs, who specialized in intelligence issues, lamented the Canadian record on the subject of port security:

We are in a very vulnerable position vis-a-vis both the United Kingdom and the United States. For two years and a half now the United Kingdom has been trying in a co-operative and friendly manner to suggest the unsolved security problems to Canadian authorities and to help in their solution. To this end they have sent one after another of their best security men to Canada. The record of these visits on our files is a most discouraging one.[30]

Stone placed the blame for the port security disasters directly on the shoulders of the RCMP: 'It seems to me intolerable that an agency of the Canadian Government primarily responsible for a really vital war measure for the successful operation of which co-operation with other agencies of the Government is absolutely essential should thus refuse to co-operate.'[31] The RCMP, he sniped, 'do not really consider security in its larger aspects as their responsibility.' Moreover, the force had a seventy-five-year history 'of working completely by itself and of keeping its general activities secret even from its own Officers.'[32] Stone's suggestion to alleviate these problems was radical: form a government security executive, like the British had, to coordinate all aspects of security in the country, leaving the RCMP to execute the decisions of an interdepartmental authority. The plan would certainly have infuriated the RCMP. As the under-secretary of state for external affairs, Robertson, admitted, 'formal responsibility for coordination in this field rests with the R.C.M.P.' If the police would admit it couldn't handle port security, 'then perhaps we could take an initiative in the matter of a "security executive." Otherwise I'm stumped.'[33] The RCMP was no happier about the situation. The federal police were so sharply scolded about port security at one interdepartmental security coordinating meeting in 1943 that Commissioner Wood ordered Assistant Commissioner Mead not to attend a later meeting of intelligence directors. Wood was reported to have said that 'he was sick and tired of criticism of the R.C.M.P. and generally sick and tired of security organization.'[34]

In one important way British wartime security practice influenced Canada, especially with regard to vetting. While the Canadian government did not see fit to create a body to establish policy on security screening during the Second World War, the Department of External Affairs was highly impressed by the British Security Executive's sure hand on the controls of security policy, and it recommended the same type of body here. No action was taken on that suggestion then, but when the crisis of the Gouzenko defection struck, a Security Panel was quickly set up, using the British model.[35] Thus British experience helped to guide the Canadian government after the war.

In addition to the dealings over port security, a steady stream of intelligence, advice, and tips flowed between London and Ottawa. Warnings of impending sabotage waves, news about the movements of suspected enemy agents, and suggestions about methods to deal with sabotage and espionage were all part of the flow of intelligence back and forth across the Atlantic.[36] The RCMP received the British Overseas Security Bulletin regularly.[37] Hence a vibrant, if relatively lopsided, transatlantic security intelligence exchange developed, some of it related to security screening.

Security-screening dealings between Canada and Newfoundland were a special case of international liaison. Newfoundland was a British colony, run by a commissioner appointed from London. Moreover, its location made it an important link between North America and embattled Britain. This led to the construction of substantial defence facilities, including two large naval stations and five air bases, the biggest of which, Gander, was used by British, Canadian, and American forces. Building these defences required considerable labour, much of it provided by Canadian workers employed by companies from the mainland. Screening them compelled the RCMP and the Newfoundland Rangers to pool their information 'concerning the comings and goings of suspected enemy agents.'[38] This collaboration was already underway by 1941, but, when construction picked up in that year, coping with the influx of workers led to a spate of problems. When taken together, they demonstrated the limitations of security screening.

In July 1941 Inspector R.D. Fraser, the chief of the Newfoundland Rangers, asked the RCMP to vet a list of Canadian workers, some of whom he believed had been in a riot in Montreal shortly before and had also been implicated in strikes in Gander. Deputy RCMP Commissioner R.L. Cadiz explained to Fraser the procedure the RCMP used to screen workers, which relied on the standard Department of Munitions and Supply employment history form and fingerprinting.[39] But neither force appeared to take steps to implement the system. In December 1941 the Newfoundland Department of Justice complained to the Canadian high commissioner that 'men have got into this country who never should have been permitted here.' Although some of them had been deported, the Newfoundland government wanted the Canadian government and construction companies to ensure that no undesirables would be allowed to leave Canada. But the contractors vigorously objected, arguing that it was already extremely difficult to find skilled workmen willing to go to Newfoundland. If they 'were required to undergo a police examination they simply would not come.' Still, the Canadian contractors agreed to have their workers vetted by the RCMP and accepted rules about who would be barred: 'It is understood that no Naturalized Germans will ever be sent down or Communists.' Italians and Japanese were also to be excluded and former citizens of other enemies carefully scrutinized.[40] Some enemy aliens were allowed into Newfoundland because they were 'required as a specialist, a foreman, or to perform work of a class for which a qualified Newfoundlander is not available.'[41]

To enforce this agreement the Canadian high commissioner in St John's suggested that the RCMP send two officers to Newfoundland 'to assist in the weeding out of any undesirable employees of the Canadian contractors in this country.' This would be equivalent to the scrutiny the FBI already had in place on Americans. The American government had agreed in 1941 to investigate all employees of its contractors before they left the United States. When this was not carried out, the FBI sent agents to investigate the workers, some of whom were later deported. For their part, the FBI agents remained in Newfoundland.[42] Yet in April 1942, when the two RCMP officers arrived in Newfoundland, they encountered problems. Although their specific goal was to vet Canadian workers, the Newfoundland commissioner of justice and defence had other ambitions. He appeared to believe that their greatest value would be to make a public presence at airports. As Commissioner Wood complained, the men were not selected for their skills in 'the investigation of sabotage, espionage or security of airports. Had I known at the beginning that the duties were for the purposes just mentioned, I would have selected different personnel who had experience in this line of work.' Screening was clearly becoming a specialized skill within the RCMP.

To make matters worse, the Newfoundland government accepted a British offer to organize an airport and seaport security service, and the staff for it were on their way from England. 'Port security' and 'Britain' were words guaranteed to sting Wood. Within weeks, the Mounties were recalled to Nova Scotia until their exact role could be agreed upon.[43] Three months later, the Newfoundland government was still complaining about the entry of enemy aliens from Canada.[44] When the RCMP was questioned about it, Assistant Commissioner Mead brought out his letter to Inspector Fraser of the Newfoundland Rangers, which explained that employers had to submit the names and fingerprints of workers in order to have them screened. The matter rested there.[45] Later complaints about Canadian-based enemy aliens being in Newfoundland, however, suggest that a thorough security-screening system was not implemented for the balance of the war.[46] The conflict points out some of the salient features of the system. When it came to screening which required international cooperation, harmony was not always certain. Competing jurisdictions, insistence that bureaucratic regulations be observed, and the demand for labour, especially skilled labour, all helped to limit the impact and scope of the system.

Regular liaison between the FBI and the RCMP began in 1937 under the initiative of Commissioner James MacBrien, who was the first RCMP commissioner to visit the FBI.[47] Representatives of the two security intelligence forces met occasionally later in the decade and after September 1939. One of them was very high level. In November 1940 FBI Director J. Edgar Hoover and Assistant Director Edward Tamm travelled to Ottawa to meet with the RCMP commissioner and discuss matters of common concern with Canadian police and political authorities. The topics dealt with were almost exclusively devoted to security: subversive organizations, sabotage prevention, informants, and nazi fifth columnists.[48] Preventing criminals and subversives from moving across the border also figured in the discussion.[49]

The RCMP and FBI actively exchanged intelligence methods. For instance, in August 1940 the FBI produced a primer on industrial security, *Protection of Industrial Facilities*, an update of an earlier and more elaborate *Plant Protection Manual*.[50] The similarities between the FBI's *Protection of Industrial Facilities* and the RCMP's November 1940 *Protection of Industry in Time of War* are so remarkable that the FBI work must be considered to be the model for the RCMP's pamphlet. The topics covered and their organization were virtually identical. Much of the text in *Protection of Industry in Time of War* duplicated word for word the text in *Protection of Industrial Facilities*.[51] The RCMP did introduce several new sections, including 'Labour Sabotage,' 'Security Officer,' and 'Internal Security Service.' But perhaps the most important addition to the RCMP booklet was a section on fingerprinting, in which contractors for the Canadian or British governments were 'strongly advised to have all present and prospective employees fingerprinted.'[52] By contrast, the August 1940 FBI manual did not mention fingerprinting. This was merely a legal nicety; fingerprinting was in full force at the time. The omission was corrected in the

December 1941 edition of the same pamphlet, in which the FBI announced that the attorney general had authorized it to suggest that all munitions suppliers fingerprint their employees.[53]

Cooperative intelligence work was advanced considerably once the United States was thrown into the war. In late December 1941, just two weeks after the Pearl Harbor attack, American authorities invited Allied agencies to attend a meeting to coordinate intelligence in the Western Hemisphere. The purpose of the conference was 'to formalize and regularize contacts previously existing between' the FBI, the RCMP, and 'security organizations of one or two other ... countries.'[54] From that invitation, three Western Hemisphere Intelligence Conferences were held, in January, March, and August 1942, the first two in Washington, the last in Ottawa. These were high-level meetings; Commissioner Wood and Assistant Commissioners R.R. Tait and F.J. Mead attended the Ottawa session. Minutes of one meeting refer to three services, so it is probable that BSC agents were at the table beside senior FBI and RCMP officers.[55] The security topics taken up were wide ranging: measures to counteract sabotage and espionage, communism, a radio communications set up (probably between the RCMP and the FBI), port security, Alaska highway and Norman Wells pipeline construction and security problems attached to it, prisoners of war, and internment camps for enemy aliens.[56]

One of the important outcomes of the conferences was the exchange of permanent liaison officers between the RCMP and the FBI. In April 1942 Assistant Commissioner W.V.M.B. Bruce became the first RCMP liaison officer with the FBI in Washington.[57] Bruce was given access to all FBI files and senior branch personnel, and travelled frequently between Washington, New York, and Ottawa.[58] The FBI also sent an officer to Ottawa in 1942.[59] The duties of the liaison officers were set out in a March 1942 Western Hemisphere Intelligence Conference. The liaison officers were assigned to interpret the policies of one force to the other and to give advice on what investigations could usefully be taken on.[60] Soon the officers were in place, and safe and rapid communication was established between the offices through the telekrypton system, a cipher machine that automatically scrambled teletype messages. So there was probably less need to hold regular conferences, and the Western Hemisphere sessions ended after the August 1942 meeting.[61]

Exchanging liaison officers was the idea of the RCMP intelligence officer, Superintendent E.W. Bavin, who proposed it to the FBI at an October 1940 meeting in Washington. But when Bavin broached the idea with the Department of External Affairs, the hostility must have been tangible. Norman Robertson wrote the then under-secretary of state, O.D. Skelton:

> My own feeling is that if the R.C.M.P. had any one man who could do a useful job as general liaison officer with the F.B.I., he would be an invaluable aid and reinforcement to their present Intelligence Division. In a field where speed and secrecy are all important, I would really be doubtful whether intermediaries between the organized Police forces of the two countries would help more than they would hinder the direct and informal communications which are now taking place all the time.[62]

Robertson is one of those who have contributed to the myth of RCMP incompetence in security intelligence matters. Others did not share his derisive view of RCMP intelligence officers. Four months after this letter William Stephenson asked the RCMP commissioner to release Bavin to work at the BSC headquarters in New York. The request was quickly approved, and Bavin went to the BSC, where he served as an informal liaison officer.[63]

The enormous logistical and personnel challenges posed by building a military defence system in Alaska called for considerable intelligence liaison between Canadian and American police and military officials. There were no significant industrial plants in Alaska, but immense construction projects were undertaken. Foremost among these were the Alaska Highway, most of it in Canada, much of it driven through the subarctic wilderness by Canadian labour, and the Canol pipeline project. Those projects, plus the construction of docks, bridges, railroads, tank farms (at Norman Wells), and an oil refinery at Whitehorse, required thousands of workers. Although many of them were Canadian, the Intelligence and Protective Security Office of the U.S. Northwest

Service Command was responsible for screening the civilian employees of contractors. But this could only be carried out through close cooperation with the RCMP, the British Columbia Provincial Police, and police departments of the larger Canadian cities.[64] The Industrial Security Branch of the Canadian Department of Munitions and Supply also worked with the American military to vet American workers who came to Canada to work on the Alaska Highway.[65]

The high degree of collaboration between the RCMP and the FBI must have contributed to the remarkable similarity between the American and Canadian wartime security-screening systems. The American system evolved through the 1930s and matured early in the 1940s. Informally, it was well in place by 1940, when Congress authorized the secretaries of war, navy, and state to remove summarily any person who, in the opinion of the secretary, constituted a risk to national security.[66] From July 1940 to June 1941, the FBI received 2.6 million fingerprints of civil servants, munitions employees, and armed service personnel. In 1941–2 the bureau 'conducted thousands of investigations of applicants for vital positions in ... government war agencies.'[67] In industry, fingerprinting uncovered 'many cases' of individuals 'who have been convicted in the past of such crimes as disloyalty and arson,' the FBI reported.[68] In the year 1941–2 the number of non-criminal fingerprints in the FBI's possession grew from 12.2 million to almost 42 million. Another 5 million fingerprints of civil servants were on record.[69] By June 1945, 64 million non-criminal fingerprints and another 7.6 million prints of civil servants were on file.[70]

Acting upon directions from Congress in the 1942 appropriation bill, the FBI also began legally to investigate federal employees who were 'members of subversive organizations.' During the 1941–2 year the bureau made almost 4500 inquiries of this type.[71] In 1942–3, the FBI conducted over 5000 such investigations, although it added that they were 'predicated upon specific complaints.' As a result of those 5000 investigations, fifty-three people were discharged and forty-four others were disciplined in other ways.[72] These investigations of civil servants continued right to the end of the war. In 1944 there were 1145 cases, resulting in thirteen firings. In 1945 there were 549 investigations, and sixteen people were dismissed and seventeen others resigned or were disciplined.[73]

American and Canadian vetting differed from the British routine in one important way: the British system was not nearly so dependent upon fingerprinting. British police were authorized under the defence regulations to take fingerprints during the Second World War.[74] But they did not have the Americans' fingerprinting zeal. This is evident from the numbers of fingerprints in the central collections of British and American police. Although it began using fingerprints in 1901, by 1954 Scotland Yard had just over one million fingerprint sets on record, whereas the FBI held one hundred times that number in 1946.[75] The Canadian and American security-screening routines shared more than just reliance upon fingerprinting. As discussed in chapter 7, the RCMP adopted the FBI's innovation of using Hollerith tabulating machinery to process fingerprints. Significantly, the equipment arrived at RCMP headquarters in December 1942, shortly after the two police agencies exchanged liaison officers.

The Hollerith equipment represents one example of the RCMP borrowing security methods from south of the 49th parallel. Intelligence also flowed from north to south. At the second Western Hemisphere Intelligence Conference in March 1942 the FBI, RCMP, and BSC talked about methods to investigate and prevent sabotage.[76] In this field, the Americans looked to the RCMP for advice on civil security and the protection of factories and essential public facilities.[77] At the meeting, Inspector Alexander Drysdale, representing the RCMP, gave a complete report on methods to protect factories. The RCMP's two years of wartime experience in dealing with subversion and sabotage threats clearly made it an authority for the FBI. Other Canadian agencies also shared their knowledge about security. In October 1942, for instance, a U.S. legation military attaché asked for the industrial security questionnaire that DMS circulated to all industrial plants. In December 1942 Colonel H.G. Reynolds, of the U.S. Security Staff in Washington, visited the DMS Industrial Security Branch to discuss security measures in Canadian munitions plants with an eye to using the same. In May 1943 a delegation of military officials from the United States visited and inspected security and safety installations at DMS explosive and shell filling plants 'and reported favourably on our methods.'[78]

Once both countries were at war, pressure mounted to harmonize screening practices north and south of the border. The RCMP, however, proved itself capable of resisting efforts to conform entirely to American methods. For example, FBI policy was to inform the police of the city in which an industrial plant was located of an employee's or an applicant's criminal record, even if the offences involved were relatively minor. The local police would then pass this information on to the plant authorities. The consequences for the applicant or employee could well be imagined. After several disastrous experiences with a similar policy, the RCMP resolved to let far less intelligence out of its hands. Inevitably, industrial security officers of Canadian plants made trips to the United States where they learned of FBI policy. Seeking the same information, they informed the Department of Munitions and Supply, as a way to have the RCMP reverse its policy.[79] The DMS, in turn, took the matter up with the RCMP. After he visited American munitions plants, E.J. Johnson, the Canadian DMS Industrial Security Branch director general, tried to bring the RCMP commissioner into line, saying American authorities' 'ideas on this subject are practically the same as ours.'[80] The RCMP, however, did not change its policy.

The RCMP was informed about but rejected another element of the FBI's security system – placing undercover agents in factories. In 1940, before the Americans were at war, the FBI had 263 agents in manufacturing plants in Detroit alone to report suspicious people and incidents.[81] In addition to FBI members going undercover in plants to keep workers under surveillance, the bureau had between three and thirty employees serving as confidential informants in every defence plant. In this way the FBI mustered a veritable army of informers, since it monitored 7700 defence suppliers.[82] Ontario Fire Marshal W.J. Scott enthusiastically reported this information to RCMP Assistant Commissioner R.R.

Tait.[83] But the Canadian force opted for a more low-key approach. It urged employers to form an internal corps of security watchers.[84] In at least two ways, therefore, the RCMP resisted pressure to follow the FBI's lead. The force was not so overawed by American methods that it adopted them willy-nilly.

Moreover, although the RCMP shared political intelligence on communists with the FBI, it did so with some selectivity. In 1941, for example, the force received a letter from the commissioner of internment operations, which had been intercepted on its way from a communist internee to a relative in the American army in Alaska. The internment commissioner believed that the information might be of value to the FBI. But RCMP files showed that the soldier to whom the letter was addressed had no record of subversive activities in Canada. Replying to the internment commissioner, the assistant intelligence officer, Inspector C. Batch, explained that 'if we communicate with the Federal Bureau of Investigation simply because the writer is a detained Communist, it might result in directing suspicion against a member of the American Forces, who may possibly have no sympathies whatever with the Communist viewpoint.' The FBI never received the letter.[85]

Three other significant differences stand out between Canadian and American security-screening systems. The first was the high degree of political involvement in the American screening system. As outlined in chapters 4 and 5, Canadian politicians had little to do with the Canadian system. In the United States screening was politically sanctioned even before the war began. In 1939 the Hatch Act was amended to make it illegal for a person to be employed by the federal government if he or she was a member of any political party or organization which advocated the overthrow of America's 'constitutional form of government.' In June 1941, the Justice Department set aside $100,000 for the FBI to investigate federal employees who might be members of subversive organizations.[86] Although the FBI had been engaged in security screening long before that time, with this official approval it enlarged its network.

In addition, the American cabinet vigorously debated fingerprinting, while its Canadian counterpart avoided the subject. Harold Ickes, secretary of the interior in the Roosevelt administration, recalled cabinet meetings in December 1939 and January 1940 in which the topic produced spirited disagreement. Attorney General Frank Murphy favoured fingerprinting war workers while Ickes, Solicitor General Robert Jackson, and Labor Secretary Frances Perkins expressed principled opposition. Their objection was based upon the iniquitous application of the fingerprinting law – it would be applied to and stigmatize only workers – and 'the disgraceful connotation connected with fingerprinting.'[87] The resulting cabinet stand-off was resolved in February 1942 when the U.S. War Department ordered that munitions plant employees and applicants be both fingerprinted and photographed.[88] Despite the political debate, the outcome in the United States was the same as in Canada – vastly increased fingerprinting. It appears that whether or not politicians could agree on mass fingerprinting, or even whether or not they were aware of it, police and military authorities could agree among themselves about implementing it and did so.

Political involvement also meant that the police did not independently set policy for security screening. Interdepartmental committees were appointed to advise departments and coordinate their efforts in handling disloyalty accusations. These committees helped to establish policy on how FBI reports were to be handled. Together with the Civil Service Commission's policy statements, these guidelines helped bring some degree of fairness to the security-screening process.[89]

A second difference between Canada and the United States was the extent of publicity about vetting. Once it got the political authority to conduct security screening, the FBI published detailed reports on its efforts. In each year of the war it calculated the number of investigations and, in an impersonal way, enumerated the consequences by listing the number of people dismissed. The figures were then printed in the FBI *Annual Report*. Candour like this was unknown in the northern dominion. The RCMP *Annual Report* tabulated the thousands of people fingerprinted during the war, but it mentioned nothing about more elaborate security investigations and shunned entirely any hint about the repercussions of these investigations.

The third distinction between the United States and Canada was the depth of objection to security screening. People in the top echelons of the American political élite, principled liberals like Harold Ickes, Robert Jackson, and Frances Perkins, despised the program and stated their opinions about it. Articles examining the system were also printed in prominent magazines and journals.[90] By contrast, opposition to the state security-screening program from Canadian politicians was minimal, and no journalist went on record as opposing the system.

One other comparative point stands out, and that is the relative equality between Canadian and American security intelligence agencies. Canada's superiority in certain matters – some of it gleaned from the British – must have given it some reflected authority in the United States. The fact that the RCMP and the FBI were both police forces that had grown into security intelligence work also gave them grounds upon which to found an egalitarian relationship. Agencies in Britain had decades of experience as exclusively security intelligence bodies, and in 1939 they were clearly superior to either the Canadian or American counterparts. The RCMP and the FBI's background as police forces and as subordinates to the British intelligence organizations gave them similar backgrounds, common approaches, and approximate equality. This common experience, plus their long-standing and frequent liaison, undoubtedly helped them build wartime security-screening systems that were remarkably similar, with fingerprinting being a central element.

LIAISON WITH THE PROVINCES

In 1939 the RCMP was the police force in all provinces except British Columbia, Quebec, and Ontario, where provincial police forces operated. Newfoundland, of course, was a British colony and was policed by the Newfoundland Rangers. The RCMP was responsible for the security of the country, although provincial forces also assisted to some extent. The most energetically engaged was the Ontario Provincial Police (OPP), which had long experience in security matters. The Communist party had been the object of its attention for years before the war. Left-wing influence in the growing industrial union movement was the OPP's special interest. During the formative 1937 auto workers' strike in Oshawa, for instance, the OPP had received inside information from an informer, Jim Wolansky. He was also a favourite of the Toronto Red Squad, 'who look upon him as one of the best men in Canada for such work,' according to the OPP's chief inspector.[91] By 1940 the force had established a Special Branch in charge of measures to prevent sabotage. One of its duties was to supervise the special constables guarding hydroelectric dams and stations.[92] But the squad also helped companies screen their personnel. One which took advantage of this assistance was Defence Industries Limited of Pickering. The company sent lists of its workers to both the RCMP and the OPP, but in spite of this, or perhaps because of it, vetting was slow. In 1943 it complained about delays by police which had resulted in it hiring people 'the plant would have been better without.' The OPP responded by speeding up the processing of key personnel for the company.[93]

Submitting lists of employees to both the RCMP and the OPP might be seen as excessive caution. It could also be a tacit recognition that the federal and provincial police had not integrated their vetting operations. This lack of integration should not, however, be taken to mean that the federal and provincial police forces were engaged in a battle over security intelligence jurisdiction. No such turf war seems to have broken out. The same cannot be said for their counterparts in government. Almost from the moment the war was declared, Ontario Premier Mitchell Hepburn was up in arms about federal security measures. For close to a year, the two sides bickered over some new dispute: the reliability of the guards at the vital hydroelectric facilities in the province; who would pay for the guards; whether more suspected subversives ought to be interned; why the federal government would not create and arm civilian defence committees.[94] The police forces, at least, avoided such conflict, even though they maintained separate security organizations when one would have been more efficient.

Having used its list of some 500 suspected subversives for security screening early in the war, the OPP turned it to more ominous purposes after 1943. On the instructions of Attorney General Cross, the OPP Anti-Sabotage Branch was closed in June 1943. But three months after the Conservative government of George Drew came to power, a Special Branch was revived, with a new object of scrutiny. Under the pretext of investigating 'Communist activities, C.I.O., CCF,' the officer in charge of the branch, William Osborne-Dempster, set up a unit to keep tabs on the Ontario CCF, led by E.B. Jolliffe. Osborne-Dempster submitted reports on CCF members of the Ontario legislature directly to Premier Drew and the provincial attorney general, John Blackwell. The intelligence was also given to Conservative stalwarts in the business community, who used it to publish advertisements condemning the CCF and to attack CCF speakers at public meetings. The judgment of long-time CCF and New Democratic Party notable David Lewis is entirely proper: 'it was political espionage at public expense, against a party which happened to be the Official Opposition in Ontario.'[95] This improper appropriation of OPP intelligence facilities went on until May 1945, when the issue was made public and a royal commission appointed to investigate.[96] The OPP's security operation, and its wartime involvement in security screening, had helped to build up a database which was turned to partisan political advantage. By contrast, there is no evidence to suggest that the RCMP misused its political intelligence. Still, RCMP Superintendent George McClellan was aware that the OPP was waging a campaign of dirty tricks.[97] And it must be acknowledged that wartime security screening helped to foster an environment in which intelligence was abused.

In Quebec the provincial police also engaged in security screening independently of the RCMP. Its efforts appear to have been initiated through requests by war plants for checks of their personnel. In 1941, the Sûreté du Québec (SQ) conducted 6377 inquiries into the backgrounds of munitions plant workers, most of them in the Montreal district. This exceeded the number of criminal investigations it carried out that year. In 1942 employers made 6700 requests for the Sûreté to investigate employees, although it was able to carry out just 3629 inquiries. It was soon apparent that the SQ could not continue the burden of this work, and in 1942 it abandoned the task. Thereafter security officers in the plants themselves carried on the screening.[98]

The British Columbia Provincial Police (BCPP) also conducted its own inquiries into subversives, but it placed a much heavier emphasis on cooperating with the RCMP. The BCPP had files of its own on communists, which went back to the early 1930s. In 1932, for example, the provincial force reported that the 'names and descriptions of all the [communist] leaders are on record and their movements as far as possible have been watched and their presence in any part of the Province made known to the Officer Commanding.'[99] The BCPP also investigated the backgrounds of citizenship applicants for the RCMP in the early 1930s.[100] In addition, in April 1939 provincial police intelligence reports had urged that names of Germans active in the German Culture Club be checked against the 'Payrolls at [the Cominco smelter in] Trail, Boeing Aircraft [in Vancouver] and any work being undertaken by the Federal Department of National Defense.'[101] Hence when it came time to conduct vetting inquiries on a larger scale during the Second World War, the BCPP was experienced. The war emergency did, however, put new security demands upon the police, and the BCPP responded by inaugurating a Special Branch distinct from the Criminal Investigation Branch.[102] Perhaps because there were fewer munitions producers in British Columbia than in Ontario and Quebec, the BCPP was less involved in security screening than the OPP and the SQ. With the outbreak of war, the BCPP began to check the antecedents of industrial security guards.[103] The force's vetting of security guards included searches of criminal fingerprint records. These turned up 'a number of men with bad records,' and they appear to have been fired.[104] In all, 657 industrial guards, 197 civil security guards on vulnerable points, and 1509 special BCPP reservists were fingerprinted and registered in 1940.[105] The screening involved more than criminal checks. At the height of the fifth column scare in May 1940, the commissioner authorized all divisions to form special auxiliary squads, and advised that corporations might also wish to form their own police. But the specials were to be strictly screened. 'Headquarters will check the names of all specials against our secret lists,' the commissioner advised, but 'the companies themselves should have a pretty good idea of whom they propose to sponsor.'[106]

The bulk of the BCPP work appears to have been liaison with the RCMP, the intelligence branches of the Canadian Armed Forces and American security intelligence agencies. Indeed, collaboration became so important that a new liaison designation was added to the organizational chart in 1940.[107] In 1942 the BCPP commissioner reported that

since the war commenced in September, 1939, hardly a day has passed but what one or other of the three Forces has not asked the Criminal Investigation Branch to perform some task for them or investigate individuals who have been reported to their Intelligence as possible subversive agents or engaged in anti-British activities of some kind or other. As an instance, during the year we searched our indexes for 2,504 names sent in by Pacific Command Security Intelligence, and in many cases we were able to supply enlightening information.[108]

Beginning in 1942 cooperative security work with American intelligence agencies also required attention. In that year United States Army intelligence submitted 165 sets of fingerprints for search in the BCPP records, 17 of them identified as having criminal records.[109] The next year U.S. Army intelligence submitted 500 sets of fingerprint records, 36 of which were identified.[110]

OUTCOMES

The outcomes of security intelligence efforts are frequently nebulous or cannot be revealed, especially in wartime. The 1942 RCMP Intelligence Section Annual Report nonetheless dared to disclose that a case had been resolved which 'showed the importance of international co-operation between the services of the various countries concerned with the responsibility of checking subversive activities.'[111] The details were omitted, but the report went on to caution that 'should the case be considered for inclusion in the official annual report, consideration [should] be given to using fictitious names of the principals concerned in order to avoid any possible criticism from our Overseas contacts.'

The case proved that international security intelligence collaboration could produce results. Yet collaboration had its drawbacks. Each partner was forced to respect its colleagues' sensitivities. By 1942 the RCMP had absorbed that lesson – too well, if we can judge from Norman Robertson's outrage upon being told that the RCMP had asked the FBI and BSC if they objected to the Canadian under-secretary of state for external affairs receiving minutes of the Western Hemisphere Intelligence Conferences.

The war significantly advanced the RCMP's experience in interacting with other security intelligence agencies and gave it a relatively high level of competence. This can be judged by an issue in which it was not involved – signals intelligence. It was a field which the Department of External Affairs, whose members were known to disparage the RCMP's skill in the world of intrigue, was anxious to enter. But External Affairs' first venture therein was a fiasco, marked by what Wesley Wark has labelled 'cryptographic innocence.' In 1941 the department formed a signals intelligence monitoring team in Ottawa called the Examination Unit. It did so without approval from the military Chiefs of Staff and without fully discussing the issues with cryptographic experts in Britain and the United States. Worse still, it hired a maverick cryptanalyst whom the U.S. Army Signal Corps regarded with extreme suspicion, and then attempted to conceal his identity behind a transparent alias. Herbert O. Yardley had tweaked the Americans' nose by publishing a sensational exposé of the corps' black chamber, which operated during the First World War. Determined to mark its own path in a new intelligence enterprise, External Affairs kept the U.S. State Department in the dark about hiring Yardley. It did not even ask the RCMP to screen him. When the British deduced Yardley's identity, External Affairs still naively hoped that cooperation would continue. After months of *opéra bouffe* the department realized it had no choice but to fire Yardley and coordinate the Examination Unit's work with that of its British and American counterparts. The department's failing, Wark observed, was its innocence about security measures and its naïveté about the need to consult with its allies.[112] Although the RCMP had its own security failings, it was as astute as the Department of External Affairs in some fields.

Carl Betke and Stan Horrall point out another aspect of the RCMP's relationship with its fellow agencies. They argue that 'implicit in this liaison between the R.C.M.P. and these intelligence services was the vital recognition by them that Canada was capable of protecting its own internal security.'[113] One of the fields in which the RCMP demonstrated this competence was security screening. It had much to learn about some aspects of the work – counter-espionage and port security in particular. But in screening factory workers, civil servants, and armed forces personnel it was at least the equal of its fellow agencies. The fact that the RCMP reported on its screening and anti-sabotage methods at one of the Western Hemisphere Intelligence Conferences in 1942 shows that it was regarded as having expertise that was valuable to the other agencies.

Collaborative though it was, the relationship that emerged by the war's end was not a relationship of equals. Before the Second World War Britain was the senior partner; after it the United States came to the fore. Christopher Andrew and David Dilks point to the postwar UK-USA agreement to divide worldwide signals intelligence collection and analysis as the confirmation that a palace coup had brought the Americans to the throne. Britain could no longer afford to keep the lead.[114]

Britain also slipped from being Canada's senior security intelligence partner during the war. Canada became dependent upon the United States, a condition that persists today.[115] There does not appear to be anything in the nature of wartime liaison between the RCMP and the FBI which suggests why the United States assumed this security intelligence leadership *vis à vis* Canada. Disparities of wealth and power account for most of it, since the United States emerged as the dominant Western power after 1945. The transition in security intelligence leadership also corresponded with a broader shift in Canadian relations towards the United States during the war years. But one particular factor can partly account for why Canada took the United States as its primary security intelligence partner. This was the growing similarity of interests between the RCMP and the FBI. The two had been established as police forces and had only later taken up security intelligence. They had a similar interest in applying techniques like fingerprinting, which had originated as forensic methods, to security intelligence problems. With such characteristics in common, they established a formal liaison with each other by exchanging officers. MI5, by contrast, tried to handle liaison with the FBI through an officer stationed in Ottawa, but who divided his time in Washington. This arrangement must have made effective interaction difficult to achieve.

Betke and Horrall contend that 'the intelligence contacts consolidated with British and American security agencies [during the war] prepared the groundwork for postwar international liaison.'[116] One example they raise to illustrate this postwar cooperation was the problem of screening the large number of war refugees seeking to enter Canada. In this task, the RCMP found information from its partners to be exceedingly valuable.[117]

Liaison among the RCMP, the FBI, and MI5 was established before the Second World War began. The crisis of the war, however, added strong momentum to the inter-service cooperation. The three agencies, plus the BSC in New York, introduced several innovations designed to improve communication. They organized joint conferences, established encrypted teletype communication, and exchanged liaison officers. By 1945 a new cooperative environment had been created among security intelligence agencies in Canada, Britain, and the United States. Geography alone meant that most of these efforts brought together the RCMP and the FBI. The result was a change in the nature of the international relationships. Before 1939 the RCMP saw MI5 as its security intelligence mentor. The RCMP's interaction with British intelligence services, of course, remained close. But by 1945 its strongest relationship was with the FBI.

This high-level cooperation was characterized by effective sharing. In some respects the RCMP was subordinate – to the experienced British security establishment at the beginning of the war, and to the Americans by the end. Yet the RCMP had its strengths, and these were acknowledged by its partners. Its knowledge of security screening of factory workers and prevention of sabotage was one area of RCMP expertise that the Americans in particular appeared to respect.

The frequent and respectful American contact with the RCMP with regard to security screening casts doubt upon an idea which was popular in Canadian government circles at the time and which has since become accepted wisdom. This is the belief that the RCMP was incompetent in security intelligence. Officials in the Department of External Affairs and the Prime Minister's Office were active proponents of this view, and it is often repeated today.[118] While the RCMP was certainly inexperienced and probably incompetent in some aspects of the security intelligence field – especially counter-espionage – quite the opposite verdict must be rendered in the area of security screening. Hence, when it comes to assessing the effectiveness of the RCMP in security intelligence endeavours, it is important to look more closely at how the force performed in discrete components of the enterprise. In security screening it appears to have been relatively capable.

9

'The first to come under suspicion': Popular response to security screening

Security screening gave the Canadian state a powerful new instrument to control its own people. It was a device the RCMP and other government departments did not always wield with care, as John Kisko of Welland, Ontario, learned to his dismay. In 1941 Kisko lost his job – maintenance work on the Welland Canal – because of an RCMP investigation. He had one strike against him. He had come to Canada from Hungary in 1925, and in 1941 Canada was at war with that country. But the RCMP reports did not list Kisko's country of birth as a reason why they considered him a security risk. He did not even have a criminal record. What the RCMP reported to the Civil Service Commission was that Kisko had a wife and two children but lived in a common-law relationship with another woman. RCMP Commissioner S.T. Wood acknowledged that 'on account of an unsatisfactory report from this Force, this man is unable to secure any employment either with the Government or with anyone else.' To the RCMP's consternation, Kisko engaged a lawyer and with his lawyer's assistance appears to have been rehired at the Welland Canal. But the incident did not cause the RCMP commissioner to doubt the program. His sole complaint was that someone in the Civil Service Commission had released confidential information to Kisko and that 'charges of "Gestapo" methods' had been flung at the force.[1]

The depth of the security investigation, which probed Kisko's personal life, and the deplorable consequences of the screening, do not appear to have been uncommon. Unfortunately, we know of only those few cases that emerged from the shadows, usually when security reports saw the light of day through error and the state's still-primitive understanding of how to handle sensitive intelligence. In December 1941 Commissioner Wood reproached the CSC for lapses which had allowed John Kisko and other job applicants to learn not only that adverse RCMP reports had cost them jobs but, in some cases, even the names of persons who had given information to the police.[2] In October 1942 he again chastised the commission for allowing the subjects of security screenings to learn information from RCMP reports on them. Wood cited two cases, one in which a Vancouver man appointed to the Wartime Prices and Trade Board was fired because of a critical security report, and another in Saskatoon.[3] The fired men 'complained bitterly to this Force of reports made upon them,' and Wood demanded that the CSC act 'to prevent the Royal Canadian Mounted Police being placed in an invidious position.'[4]

In Halifax another case blew up in the RCMP's hands. In 1943 a Haligonian working for the Department of Munitions and Supply (DMS) was able to obtain a security report on himself prepared by the RCMP, which he said contained incorrect information. He complained to the RCMP that the adverse report had prevented him from obtaining work with the Controller of Aircraft for Canada.[5] Also in 1943 George Ross, member of parliament for Calgary East, brought to the attention of Justice Minister Louis St Laurent two cases of people losing jobs or job opportunities because of adverse security reports.[6]

W.C. Bryan, a constable in the RCMP in Halifax during the early years of the war, described another case which had injurious personal consequences. In the course of conducting background security checks for the navy, Bryan had occasion to investigate a 'fairly senior' Canadian officer. 'Homosexuality was considered a risk in those days,' Bryan noted. 'And we had to come up and report ... that he was a practicing homosexual.' Did the RCMP report hurt the officer's military career? 'Oh there was no doubt about it, because our report ... went back to naval headquarters. He was considered not reliable from a security point of view.' His homosexuality made the officer potentially subject to blackmail, the RCMP believed.[7]

The fingerprinting and security screening of all 5000 civil servants in the DMS also forced people out of their jobs.[8] The inquiries revealed that some employees of the department had criminal records, a few with a large number of convictions. Except in cases where the employee was a 'repeater' and the crime serious, these people were allowed to stay. However, employees were advised that their directors had been told of their criminal record, placing a threat over their heads.[9]

There were many other casualties of the program. The Scarborough, Ontario, plant of the General Engineering Company, for instance, hired some 9500 people during its four years of munitions production. All were fingerprinted and photographed. Among them, 100 (1 per cent) had criminal records of a type that the RCMP believed made them unsuitable for employment at the factory, and they were not hired.[10] If that same proportion of wartime workers were turned away throughout Canada, given that the RCMP checked the fingerprints of some 1 million war plant workers during the war, 10,000 applicants would have been rejected. That estimate is probably high, however, because General Engineering, as a manufacturer of explosives, was especially careful about its employees. Still, it reveals the number of people who might have been negatively affected by the vetting program.

For many workers and civil servants, the consequences of security screening were less immediately punitive than firing. For them security screening introduced the indignity of being under the scrutiny of a supervisor who knew about their past. The RCMP realized that intimidation might result. In February 1941 the officer in charge of the Civil Security Branch, Inspector R.S.S. Wilson, assessed some of the early problems of the security-screening program. One of them was that prior to January 1941 the RCMP had released all the details of employees' criminal records to twelve private sector employers. With the expansion of the program at the beginning of 1941, this policy was changed; the RCMP would now release criminal intelligence only selectively, at least for private employers. Government departments still received full criminal records.[11] In his justification of the new policy, Wilson noted with distaste the practices of one of the twelve participants in the pre-1941 program, the Ottawa Car and Aircraft Company. He reported that the firm 'makes a practice of calling every employee whose record they receive from this Force, before [name deleted], who tells him that he has received his criminal record from the police and, while he will be permitted to continue working, he will be watched and, if any trouble occurs in the plant, will be the first to come under suspicion.'[12] Wilson cited an example of an applicant who had a criminal record for carnal knowledge. If the person knew the RCMP would reveal it to Ottawa Car and Aircraft, 'he would likely refuse [to be fingerprinted] and [would] probably be discharged as a result.'[13]

Despite the new policy not to release full criminal records to employers, the RCMP continued to provide confidential intelligence to a company which the force recognized had used it to intimidate workers. Ottawa Car was quietly exempted from the RCMP's general policy until December 1942.[14]

Ottawa Car president Redmond Quain's incentive to obtain extensive background information on his employees and applicants was not that he had found his workforce to be riddled with miscreants. By fingerprinting its 200 employees soon after the war's outbreak, Ottawa Car ferreted out just one with a criminal record. By March 1940 the company had hired 300 new workers; 16 with a criminal record were identified. Quain told Ontario Fire Marshal W.J. Scott that among the revealed convictions 'there were very few of a serious nature[,] some of them being very young men with charges of theft.' Despite the absence of criminality among his employees, Quain concluded that the exercise was worthwhile. His reasoning showed that the value of fingerprinting lay in the power it gave the company to isolate and discipline potential troublemakers: 'It has indeed been gratifying to us that we instigated the finger print system as we have found in a number of instances employees with records which *have given us an opportunity of scrutinizing them very carefully,* or if necessary dismiss them after advising of the reasons for so doing.'[15] At peak war production, some 2400 people laboured in the construction of aircraft wing tips and bomber doors at Ottawa Car and Aircraft; many of those with criminal records worked under the scrutiny of a president who was armed with detailed personal information about them provided by the RCMP. The information served Quain in exactly the way Wilson had described it, 'as a club to be held over his [employee's] head, or as an excuse to discharge him.'[16]

Elsewhere in industry, tens of thousands of people worked under the same threat, judging by RCMP records. Inspector H.R. Butchers, officer in charge of the RCMP Fingerprint Section, reported in November 1943 that since the beginning of 1942, 562,000 civilian fingerprint searches had been made, 60,000 of them resulting in criminal records being disclosed.[17] It is true that employers were told about their employees' records only if the crimes were judged by the RCMP to be serious ones. But that simply removed the threat one step, because the DMS Industrial Security Branch maintained a list of war plant employees whose criminal records had been revealed by their fingerprinting.[18]

The attitude of some industrialists towards their employees is vividly illustrated by R. Flynn, superintendent of investigation at the Canadian National Railroad. At a meeting to discuss the program, Flynn bluntly asserted that 'any man of ours that has a conviction registered against him is fired, even for drunk driving, that fellow is fired. It does not matter whether the offence was on his own time or anything else.'[19] Flynn was speaking at a meeting of senior police, government, and industrial representatives organized by the Ontario Provincial Police. At this Co-ordinating Committee for Security session, the DMS dominion security officer, R.L. Anderson, acknowledged that the caveat of fingerprinting being voluntary was little or no protection to plant employees or applicants. He admitted that employees would be under considerable pressure to submit to fingerprinting: 'There are a lot of employees that do not want to have their fingerprints and photogrphs [sic] taken but they feel that if they do not they will be out of a job. [As for prospective employees], they either have their fingerprints taken or they do not get the jobs.' To Anderson, refusing to submit to identification measures was itself grounds for suspicion. When A.W. Manby of the Hydro-Electric Power Commission of Ontario reported that 'we have had cases where a man objected to having his picture taken,' Anderson shot back 'I would be inclined to suspect that person, gentlemen.'[20]

People with criminal records were but one target of the Canadian state's wartime security-screening program. Communists and others on the political left were the preferred quarry. Again, we have no figures on how many people suspected of being dissidents became casualties of the Canadian state's wartime security-screening system. But some cases show the circumstances under which loyalty inquiries would lead to firings. For instance, a Montreal woman who applied to perform temporary editorial work for the Nationalities Branch of the Department of National War Services was rejected because an RCMP security report concluded that she was a subscriber to the Communist party newspaper, *Canadian Tribune*, and secretary of the local branch of the Writers, Artists and Broadcasters War Council, an organization 'the Communists are taking some interest in.'[21] Fred Kostyck ran afoul of security screening because he had been a volunteer in the Spanish Civil War. He was taken on at a munitions plant in Winnipeg; three weeks later he was fired because of his Spanish Civil War service. When he complained, he was told to keep quiet or he would be blacklisted and would never get a job.[22] In fact, the blacklist already existed, operated out of RCMP headquarters in Ottawa.

UNION OBJECTIONS

Despite the low-key way in which it was announced, the RCMP's scheme to use mass fingerprinting for security screening sparked immediate opposition. At least some of the workers targeted by the program were not convinced that it had been implemented 'for the protection of all,' as *Globe and Mail* announcement article in March 1941 contended. The same month the measure was revealed publicly, the United Auto Workers District 26 Council, speaking for all the auto worker locals in Canada, expressed its 'unqualified opposition to the fingerprinting of workers in industry' and called on the government 'to immediately rescind any orders or instructions it may have issued in this respect.' The autoworkers feared that fingerprinting would give employers a 'drastic weapon' to maintain a national blacklist, and foresaw its being used 'to browbeat employees into the acceptance of whatever wages and conditions the employer cares to establish.'[23] Toronto shop stewards of the United Electrical, Radio and Machine Workers' Union also damned the fingerprinting program, calling it another example of the state's 'democracy-destroying regimentation.' The stewards, representing fifteen plants in the Toronto area, contended that fingerprinting was 'a drastic weapon' which could be used by 'anti-union and unscrupulous employers ... to set up and maintain a national blacklist' of unionists. The shop steward's council forwarded copies of the resolution to all members of the House of Commons.[24]

The next month, April 1941, unionists at the Fairchild Aircraft plant at Longueuil, Quebec, launched a protest that went directly to the prime minister. Lodge 712 of the International Association of Machinists fired off an angry telegram to Mackenzie King on 7 April 1941: 'Employees at Fairchild Aircraft plant in Montreal greatly resent having to fill out Nazi like questionnaire and be finger printed Stop Union members have been instructed to actively resist the carrying through of this scheme.' The telegram immediately brought the assistant deputy minister of labour, followed by the minister of labour, onto the scene to try to suppress an impending explosion. The reason for their haste was obvious: both the RCMP and the union executive were aware that dissatisfaction among the Fairchild workers was infecting employees in other plants.[25]

The machinists saw a deeper purpose behind the 'Nazi like questionnaire' and fingerprinting. According to the RCMP, 'the Union is afraid that it will enable employers of labour to establish Blacklists of men active in Union affairs.' Not aware that the screening effort had been initiated by the DMS, the union members believed that fingerprinting 'was but another manifestation of the company's arbitrary methods in dealing with their employees.' They had good cause for concern. Fifteen men had refused to submit to fingerprinting, and the plant manager was convinced that this alone was evidence of their 'subversive tendencies.' And he was only constrained from firing two others whom the RCMP had informed him were subversives by an agreement with the union which forbade dismissal without cause.[26]

The machinists' resistance was probably short-lived. Gerald Brown, the assistant deputy minister of labour, told the RCMP that 'if the fingerprinting system was properly explained to them we would probably have no further trouble.' Two executive members of the union were mollified when Brown and RCMP Detective/Sergeant W.M. Brady appeared to explain the measure and assure them that it was intended to prevent sabotage.[27] Nevertheless, one month later a conference of the machinists' union executive and shop committees decided to inaugurate a country-wide campaign against the practice of fingerprinting workers in war plants. The results of the campaign are unknown. If it had little impact, there are tangible reasons why, since other issues preoccupied the union. The government had recently passed an order in council freezing wages at the 1926–9 level, and the union itself was opening negotiations with five aircraft firms in the Montreal area for a blanket agreement covering wages and working conditions.[28] Although the program proceeded, it did not do so entirely smoothly. As late at August 1942 the DMS recorded some cases of labour leaders who objected to fingerprinting and even '"hold out" industries' who refused to go along with it.[29]

By mid-war, unionists had yielded to the 'Nazi-like,' 'democracy-destroying' screening operation. Part of the reason why their initial vehemence cooled to lukewarm is apparent: the war was a period of great challenge for unions. They were simultaneously striving to organize new locals among the hundreds of thousands of new industrial workers, defeat the resistance of employers and the state and win contracts that would protect and make gains for their members. In addition, just before the fingerprinting issue became public the labour movement was directly threatened by the arrest under the Defence of Canada Regulations (DOCR) of picketers at the Chrysler auto plant in Windsor, an act observers even outside the labour movement saw as calculated to 'hamstring Labor's rights.'[30] The internment of prominent left-wing labour leaders like C.S. Jackson and Pat Sullivan also occupied the labour movement's attention in 1941 and beyond. Clearly unions had more than enough to absorb their full efforts on the civil liberties front.

The waning opposition of unions to fingerprinting and security screening could also be related to communists' attitude towards the war. Unions objected to the measure most actively in the period before the German attack forced the Soviet Union into the war. Moreover, of the three unions that showed the strongest aversion to fingerprinting, two of them, the United Auto Workers and the United Electrical Workers, were very influenced or controlled by communists at the time.[31] Three months after these unions first objected to fingerprinting the Soviet Union joined the war, and communists within the union movement reversed their position. Whereas before June 1941 they encouraged any strikes or other union dislocation of the war effort, after June 1941 the communists were indefatigable advocates of all-out war, and this went as far as urging a no-strike policy for labour.[32] This might help explain the lack of a persistent union challenge to fingerprinting.

One of the puzzling aspects of wartime security screening and fingerprinting was that it was never actively challenged by most Canadians. Although there is ample evidence from before the war that many Canadians objected to the expansion of fingerprinting, the wartime program generated no serious opposition from the population as a whole. One factor stands out as an explanation for why most Canadians did not contest it – wartime conditions. The devastating successes of the German *blitzkrieg* terrified people in Britain and North America. At huge demonstrations in the spring of 1940, Canadians insisted on active measures to win the war and asserted that sacrifice was necessary from all levels of Canadian society.[33] In the face of the emergency, public opinion strongly favoured the surrender of 'certain ... liberties temporarily in order that all ... liberties might be preserved.'[34] Government acts hitherto seen as too intrusive now became politically acceptable. With the public in this mood, universal adult registration under the

National Resources Mobilization Act proceeded in August 1940, and it was accepted even in Quebec, where resistance had been anticipated.[35] Under such circumstances, when it came to fingerprinting and security screening, many Canadians must have agreed with Kingsley Ferguson, who, as an applicant for the Royal Canadian Naval Reserve, was fingerprinted, screened, and cleared by the RCMP. Ferguson would later relate that 'I did not at the time, nor do I now, see anything sinister or "abusive" in these procedures, and I feel that if a volunteer is eventually to be given a weapon, it is not unreasonable to ascertain that he is unlikely to misuse it.'[36]

While the state of public opinion and the popular perception that wartime emergencies required people to temporarily surrender some democratic rights could explain the lack of widespread opposition to fingerprinting, a more critical approach might have been expected from civil libertarians. Yet those who were prepared to question and stand up to the government on matters such as the DOCR – and it was only a handful of politicians, periodicals, and civil liberties' organizations – were virtually silent on the issue of fingerprinting and security screening. Why didn't this particular civil liberties violation generate more opposition? Answering this question requires an examination of the civil liberties movement in Canada during the Second World War.

CIVIL LIBERTIES ORGANIZATIONS' RESPONSE

Before 1963, Canada did not have a national civil liberties organization of a modern type. Such a body has several essential characteristics: political non-partisanship and non-involvement and a willingness to defend people without distinction as to their class, creed, or race.[37] Contemporary civil liberties organizations focus on political rights considered universal within liberal democratic societies: freedom of speech, association, and worship, the right to a fair and impartial trial, and equality before the law, among others.

Civil libertarian concern about the operations of the RCMP security service emerged during the 1920s. What helped stimulate this, according to Betke and Horrall, was the shift in the security police's focus from the external enemy of the nineteenth century to the internal enemy, 'made up of Canadians themselves who sought for ideological or other reasons to bring about a change in the institutions of the state.' Canadians were united against foreign intrigue, represented, for example, by the Fenians in the 1860s and 1870s. Hence they perceived 'no need to be concerned about the operations of a security service, or fear that civil liberties were threatened.' Inadvertently, in turning towards the internal enemy, the RCMP helped to create 'a small but at times influential body of opinion that has constantly criticized the security service.'[38] Hence the RCMP's conclusion that it could not trust Canadian citizens provoked a corresponding suspicion of the security service within the population. The most prominent individual critic was parliamentarian J.S. Woodsworth, who in the early 1920s issued his first broadside against the RCMP for spying on labour organizers, unions, and left-wing activists. This criticism from individuals probably reached its peak after the arrest of eight leaders of the Communist party in 1931, arrests which ultimately caused the infamous Section 98 of the Criminal Code to be revoked.[39] Still, this criticism was a minority opinion. Having studied four civil liberties cases in Toronto in the early 1930s, Suzanne Skebo concluded that 'the majority opinion lay on the side of "authority" rather than of "liberty."'[40]

Before 1939, what civil liberties organizations existed for more than a brief time were created by members and supporters of the Communist party. The best known of these bodies was the Canadian Labor Defense League. The CLDL was born in 1925, and, as its name suggests, became an advocate for workers, immigrants, and, not incidentally, communists facing arrest, jail, and deportation by the Canadian authorities. The league had some success as a civil liberties bulwark; at the very least it slowed the sorrowful parade of deportations in the 1930s.[41] Even a CCF supporter like Frank Underhill acknowledged that the league led the civil liberties struggle in Canada in the 1930s.[42]

Whatever its accomplishments, the CLDL was not a liberal civil liberties alliance in the contemporary sense. For one thing it defended only workers and those on the political left; it did not pretend to follow the dictum of making no distinctions about whose liberties it defended. Mutual animosity between communists and social democrats also hampered the CLDL. Underhill observed that cooperation between them was unlikely: 'there isn't much use for the despised bourgeoisie trying to work along with the Communists.'[43]

Something more closely approximating a modern civil liberties organization arose in the late 1930s, although again with considerable input from the Communist party. At the instigation of the party, the Montreal branch of the Canadian Civil Liberties Union was formed in 1937. A Vancouver branch was founded in May 1938, although communists had considerably less influence in it. The Montreal branch had both English- and French-language committees.[44] It functioned as a tenuous alliance between communist, social democratic, and liberal members. It also attracted conservatives. For instance, Jean-Charles Harvey, editor of Le Jour, who used the newspaper as a platform to decry communism, was an executive member of the union in the early years of the war. Despite this relatively broad representation of political opinion within the CCLU executive, the RCMP consistently regarded it as a communist front.[45] It also considered the CCLU the Communist party's most effective weapon before the union's demise in 1941.[46]

The Montreal CCLU sponsored the most prominent public civil liberties action of the war, a national conference in Montreal in May 1940. The conference brought together 500 people, virtually all of them left wing, to discuss issues such as censorship, civil liberties, and the law, as well as the rights of labour, aliens, and minorities.[47] The CCLU also continued to produce leaflets and campaigned against internment. Yet there is no indication that it had anything to say about security screening or fingerprinting.

In June 1940, at the height of the fifth column scare, the government banned the Canadian Labor Defense League as part of its effort to suppress the Communist party and its popular front organizations. With the CLDL outlawed, its guiding spirit, the Reverend A.E. Smith, put his energies into a new organization, called the National Committee for Democratic Rights (NCDR).

Founded in 1941, it soon had units in practically all Canadian cities from Montreal to Victoria. The NCDR concentrated its efforts on winning the release of anti-fascist internees and raising the ban on the Communist party.[48] As was the case with the CCLU, there is no record of the NCDR opposing the Canadian state's security-screening program.

Social democrats had dreamed and plotted throughout the 1930s to create a civil liberties league that would be, in the words of CCFer Graham Spry, 'the most polite, democratic, white-tie, liberal sort of an affair, to champion "British freedom etc."'[49] The war gave them their chance. Unlike the communist-inspired civil liberties organizations established before the war, the fledgling societies created after 1939 were led by social democrats, liberals, and some conservatives. These were the Democratic Rights Movement in Victoria, which appears to have been short-lived, the Toronto Civil Liberties Association, founded in 1940, and the Winnipeg Civil Liberties Association, founded the same year. Council members of the Toronto group included prominent CCF members like Andrew Brewin, G.M.A. Grube, and J.W. Noseworthy. The Winnipeg organization was founded by liberal-minded academics like A.R.M. Lower. But both also welcomed conservative members and indeed sought them out in order to gain respectability. Lower, for instance, reported that he would make changes to a 1940 appeal for civil liberties he intended to submit to the government 'in order to secure important signatures' on it. Anglicans were 'always good names ... as they are so damned respectable.'[50]

Indirectly, the Canadian state stimulated the growth of these organizations. Early in the war the Canadian government presented them with generous, if inadvertent, assistance. First, the DOCR enacted under the War Measures Act at the outset of the war contained many restrictions on accepted democratic freedoms. People who feared both the comprehensive power of the regulations and the repressive trend they represented soon banded together in defence of 'British freedom etc.' The government assisted these organizations again in June 1940 when it banned the Communist party and many institutions connected to it, including the CLDL. The impact of the ban was two-fold. Most immediately, it opened a vacuum in the field of civil liberties, which could be filled by social democrats. In addition, it made communism more than just a heretical political movement; now it was also an illegal one. Barring communists from civil liberties organizations would henceforth be much easier.

The newly formed civil liberties organizations in Toronto and Winnipeg made great efforts to keep communists out, or at least to exclude them from executive positions.[51] According to Ramsay Cook, left-wingers attempted to control them using the tactic of 'boring from within.'[52] In February 1941, shortly after it was founded, the Civil Liberties Association of Toronto was engulfed in an internecine clash. A group associated with the communist newspaper *Canadian Tribune* made a determined but unsuccessful effort to win executive seats.[53] A year later another attempt so rattled the non-communists that the organization's president made a direct appeal to the prime minister in an effort to shore up his support.

In early February 1942 B.K. Sandwell, managing editor of *Saturday Night*, wrote a remarkable personal letter to King, frankly mapping the political terrain of the group. Writing as president of the association but on *Saturday Night* stationery, Sandwell reminded the prime minister that the association had earlier requested a meeting with him. The political schism within the association now required an immediate meeting. Sandwell warned King that a group of about one third of the association's membership, who desired nothing more than 'to have it make loud noises at frequent intervals about any case,' no matter what its merit, had almost pulled off a coup: 'This faction came within two votes, on Monday last, of the necessary two-thirds majority to effect a radical change in the constitution which would make it almost impossible for the "conservative" element to retain any control over the Association's activities.' If further trouble was to be avoided, it was imperative that the promised meeting between the association and King occur soon. The consequences of failure were serious, Sandwell stressed, and especially for the government: 'It is my personal desire, and it is, I think, in the interests of the Government, that the Civil Liberties Association of Toronto should be maintained as a serious, careful and responsible body; but unless we can show our members that we are doing something useful we may be unable to keep it so.'[54] Duly warned, King acted quickly. The delayed meeting took place less than two weeks afterwards. At it, King declared himself 'wholly sympathetic with their aims.'[55]

Despite their influence with the government, the social democratic civil liberties movements did not campaign against the state's security-screening system and its concomitant fingerprinting. On the contrary, in the pages of *Saturday Night* Sandwell advocated a system even more comprehensive than what the RCMP implemented: a national registration system based upon universal fingerprinting, a centrally held dossier on each citizen and RCMP investigations of suspicious people.[56] So it should come as little surprise that when the Toronto assembly met with representatives of the federal cabinet in February 1942 it had other complaints. The association judged arbitrary application of and appeals to internment to be the outstanding problem.[57] The delegation did not see fit to mention the state's experiment in mass fingerprinting and vetting.[58]

Among Canadian publications, *Canadian Forum* was one of the most consistent in campaigning for civil liberties. It recorded the abuses of democratic freedoms virtually monthly from the beginning of the war to May 1942. Prepared by the Civil Liberties Association of Toronto, the articles described a host of Defence of Canada Regulations prosecutions, ranging from the absurd to the outrageous. Yet, in marking civil liberties abuses, it never strayed beyond those prosecutions. The regulations were an easy target, since they were often applied in an arbitrary and heavy-handed way. A farmer in Saint-Polycarpe was fined $50 under the regulations for failing to remove the weeds from his field. A British pamphlet titled 'Is War Christian?' was banned, even though it circulated freely in that country.[59] It is little surprise, then, that defenders of civil liberties would give the regulations their primary attention. Moreover, prosecutions under the DOCR were conducted in open court, which gave them considerable publicity.

Dismissals and job denials under the security-screening program, to the contrary, were always private matters, imposed far from public view. Being buried made them uncontroversial. This may explain why *Canadian Forum* devoted just one editorial to the issue of security screening of Canadian workers, without mentioning fingerprinting.[60]

One newspaper which could have been expected to sound the alarm about the security inquiries was *Canadian Tribune*. It was established in January 1940 by the Communist party to replace its banned newspaper, *Clarion*. A lively weekly paper, *Canadian Tribune* followed the Communist party line of opposition to the war, which changed in June 1941 when Germany attacked the Soviet Union. Thereafter, it raised the communists' cry for the release of interned communists, aid to the Soviet Union, and the opening of a second front. During the eighteen months of its oppositional phase, the *Tribune* took a constant interest in civil liberties' violations and often damned the government for its draconian use of the DOCR. Yet the sum total of the *Tribune's* coverage of the security-screening issue was two articles reporting on union objections to fingerprinting; even those were not followed up with editorials.[61]

The *Tribune's* lack of criticism can be explained partly by state repression. The federal government closed the *Tribune* only once in the war, for three weeks beginning 27 February 1941. Ostensibly, the suspension was for failing to support the Canadian war effort and for publishing references to speeches of a communist member of the British House of Commons.[62] Yet, by remarkable coincidence, during that three-week closure the fingerprinting of industrial workers was publicly announced.

The Canadian state's fingerprinting and security-screening system was the subject of just one extended debate in the House of Commons during the course of the war.[63] The exchange was initiated by CCF member of parliament Angus MacInnis, one of the small group of MPs whom the *Canadian Forum* praised as civil libertarian 'stalwarts' in parliament.[64] In March 1941 MacInnis surprised the minister of labour by questioning him about the program. Putting a false face on it, Norman McLarty replied that this fingerprinting was benign. 'It is not for any policing purpose; it is a purely voluntary undertaking, providing a convenient method of identification in the event of injury or death as the result of sabotage.'[65] This was a rationale the RCMP itself never used, and MacInnis expressed scepticism about it. Yet however much he distrusted the fingerprinting program, MacInnis's complaint was not that it assaulted both the law and inviolable rights. He saw the issue not as a civil liberties question but as a labour-management problem. MacInnis simply objected to the lack of consultation: 'If the government thinks it necessary to finger-print the employees of any Canadian industry, why not consult with the officials of the trade union movement? ... I am satisfied that they will be found to be reasonable and ready to give their consent to *anything* that may be necessary in this emergency.'[66] According to MacInnis, the government need only put the case for fingerprinting to the union – the war's exigencies would convince them. Whether or not the workers would have been so mollified, it is a striking comment about attitudes towards civil liberties during the wartime emergency. To MacInnis – and possibly to the CCF – fingerprinting and security screening was not a profound civil liberties violation. By convincing union leaders of its importance as a war measure, the state could calm workers' fears of the procedure.

There was remarkable agreement with MacInnis's approach to the issue in the social democratic labour press and the *Canadian Forum*. Both the *Canadian Unionist* and the *Canadian Congress Journal* quoted at great length MacInnis's statement to the House of Commons, and the *Canadian Forum* devoted an editorial to it. Although the labour journals did not comment editorially on the statement, their extracts emphasized the conclusion drawn by the *Canadian Forum*: 'there is no doubt that the government is completely failing to learn ... that an efficient war effort requires the active cooperation of labor.'[67] This message was consistent with the cry which organized labour had raised from the beginning of the war: prosecution of the war demanded that representatives of labour be brought into the government's councils and planning boards.

Hence, neither of the two publications most likely to speak out against the mass security-screening program paid the issue any sustained attention. The communist *Tribune* mentioned it only twice while the CCF and labour journals used the problem as a reminder that the government must bring union leaders into its confidence. Clearly they had different priorities than opposing security screening. This attitude probably helped to confine the issue to those who were immediately and negatively affected, in that way limiting its popular perception as a civil liberties' violation.

WHY DID CIVIL LIBERTIES ORGANIZATIONS NOT ADDRESS SECURITY SCREENING?

What explains the silence of civil liberties organizations on security screening? Any satisfactory answer demands an inquiry into several factors. One of them is the weakness of the civil liberties associations. Ramsay Cook's thesis on civil liberties during the Second World War demonstrated that these groups had little impact, although he saw one trace of success in the fact that the handful of people who launched the organizations were able to attract others to their cause.[68] Even this claim is doubtful. Cook limited his vision only to two civil liberties organizations, in Toronto and Winnipeg. Those two did gain strength, at least in the early war years. But the Winnipeg group was inactive after 1942, and neither association was able to extend its reach beyond the two cities. The most influential organization which existed before 1939, the Montreal branch of the Canadian Civil Liberties Union, did not survive past 1941. By the end of the war none of the civil liberties bodies was more than a shell, and no national body had risen in response to the wartime challenge.[69]

These facts beg the question of why the civil liberties movement in Canada was so feeble. One answer proposed by Cook was that 'the roots of liberalism have not grown deep in the arid soil of Canada's heterogeneous community.'[70] He attributed this to the nature of the Canadian population, including the absence of a liberal democratic tradition within the large French Canadian national group, the fact that English Canadians have not had to fight for their freedoms and the influx of non-British newcomers who came from societies with little regard for human rights.[71] Curiously, Cook's observations about the lack of a concern for civil liberties among French Canadians disagree with the observations of one industrial worker who was subject to wartime fingerprinting. Fred Hicks, who was employed at the Canadian Ingersoll Rand Company in Sherbrooke, Quebec, from 1934 to 1974, recalls that francophone workers were highly suspicious of the purpose of fingerprinting. 'A lot of the French boys thought they were tagging them as criminals,' Hicks remembers. 'I don't recall any of the English boys objecting.'[72] Part of this wariness was doubtless French Canadians' long-standing resistance to conscription. At least some francophones must have seen registration through fingerprinting as part of, or equivalent to, registration for conscription. But this mistrust of fingerprinting at Ingersoll Rand did not appear to reflect a widespread sentiment among the majority of Quebecers, since there is no evidence of francophones vigorously opposing security screening.

Another possible explanation for the minimal civil libertarian resistance to wartime security screening comes from Edgar Friedenberg's *Deference to Authority: The Case of Canada*. His book approaches the issue from an American perspective and was written before the Charter of Rights was written into the constitution, an event which arguably has created a 'rights culture' in Canada. Nonetheless, his ideas may have some explanatory value with regard to Canada prior to 1945. In *Deference to Authority*, Friedenberg contended that the Canadian political consciousness lacks the conviction that the state is the natural enemy of freedom. There is no Canadian tradition of distrust for the state and asserting individual rights against it. This respect for authority extends in particular to the RCMP, one of the country's most venerated government institutions. Canadians think the RCMP is the law, and they clearly have more respect for the law than Friedenberg considers healthy.[73]

Canadians' respect for the state and the RCMP undoubtedly helped to muffle the outcry against the security process. The positive image of the Canadian state shone especially brightly during the Second World War. The state earned new respect through its initiation of social security ventures such as unemployment insurance and its intervention in the economy. Even the popular resentment of rationing, price and wage controls, and higher taxes was mitigated by a confidence that the cause was good and that such authoritarian measures were a temporary expedient to ensure victory.[74] In any case, the war demanded discipline. Sacrifices were necessary and everyone expected to have restrictions imposed upon them. The distinguished civil libertarian F.R. Scott has observed that in Canada 'it is commonly ... assumed that there is no place for the assertion of fundamental freedoms in wartime.'[75] This view must have coloured Canadians' attitude towards fingerprinting and security screening. While the procedure was contrary to law and a violation of personal privacy, within the context of the war it could be tolerated.

Friedenberg's theory has some merit, but it grasps only one side of the relationship between Canadians and their state. It neglects to take into account the attitude of the state towards citizens. As the main state agency overseeing security screening, the RCMP dealt with opposition in two ways. Coercion was one route. But the RCMP also took the opposite tack, and managed the system with some circumspection.

Coercion took two forms, political and economic. Within the state the RCMP used its weekly *Intelligence Bulletins* to campaign against civil liberties associations, especially those it deemed to be communist controlled.[76] It also made the same effort in the open media and at public meetings. The 1940 RCMP *Annual Report*, for example, labelled the Canadian Civil Liberties Union an affiliate of the Communist party, which did 'a great deal of work in circulating the Communist literature.'[77] In addition, Superintendent H.A.R. Gagnon, the commander of C Division in Montreal, where the CCLU was most active, spoke to a branch of the Imperial Order of the Daughters of the Empire and, according to a *Montreal Gazette* article, blasted the CCLU as 'Communist-motivated.'[78] The CCLU also contended that RCMP officers had visited the employers of several members and told them to fire their employees because they belonged to a subversive movement. Members at the 1941 annual meeting of the Montreal Branch were advised that 'we have lost many of our [executive] members through intimidation.'[79]

Another form of coercion which the security-screening program made available to the state and employers was economic compulsion. This took various forms. Fred Hicks succinctly summed up one obvious form of economic pressure: 'If you were hired you were sent over to the police station to be fingerprinted. If you didn't want to do that, you weren't hired.'[80] This simple equation – no fingerprints, no job – must have convinced thousands of people to set aside their concerns about the practice.

The RCMP also helped to defuse objections to security screening by administering the system with considerable sensitivity and by obscuring its role in security assessments. This was not primarily motivated by concern for the civil liberties of the individuals caught up in the system. The federal police were acutely aware that fingerprinting civilians was contrary to law.[81] Because there was no statutory authority to fingerprint workers, the RCMP became preoccupied with the possibility that the issue 'was liable to "back-fire" at any moment with unpleasant results to the Force.'[82] Such a controversy might also sting the government, which could be embarrassed by unions or opposition politicians. Moreover, strong union protests 'might well prove more injurious to the war effort than the sabotage we are trying to prevent,' observed one astute officer.[83] The RCMP did express some consideration for the predicament of people who had 'paid the penalty for their misdemeanours [and were] endeavouring to rehabilitate themselves.' But it was not motivated exclusively by concern for the individual. The state could also suffer because of overzealous enforcement: 'A man who has been thrown out of work due to his past record and knows his chances of obtaining another job are negligible, constitutes fertile ground for an enemy agent to work on. Moreover, his productive services, at a time when every man in industry counts, are lost to the country.'[84]

As a result the RCMP resolved to restrict employers' access to intelligence about their workers. Ever vigilant to maintain their reputation and the highest pace for the war effort, the Mounties reined in overzealous employers who wanted every available detail on their employees.[85] The RCMP also refused to advise an employer to fire a labourer when he was discovered to have a criminal record which made him unsuitable. It dodged responsibility for the dismissal by proclaiming that it had declared him a risk; that label 'should speak for itself.'[86] For the same reason, the RCMP also put strict limits on government departments' use of security intelligence. It found that confidential reports it forwarded to government departments, especially the Civil Service Commission, were being disclosed to the subjects of the reports. The person was then discharged. Consequently, the RCMP commissioner complained, 'we are gradually building up a Gestapo reputation and dislike across the country.'[87]

The problem came about because an untried screening process was being conducted on a formidable scale. This made it necessary for the RCMP to accord considerable access to sensitive security records on individuals to government departments. Not surprisingly, the departments were unaccustomed to handling such intelligence. The resulting leaks of information and – even more appalling to the RCMP – the names of sources, prompted the force to begin to exercise strict control over the type of information that passed out of its hands. The RCMP was also apprehensive that its intelligence was being used by some employers to make up for their own managerial shortcomings. It was being asked to relay data about personal and work habits that the employer ought to have known about.[88]

Bureaucratic infighting was another reason why the RCMP zealously guarded its intelligence. As Reginald Whitaker has pointed out, after 1945 the force took pains to monopolize the field of security intelligence by establishing exclusive control over the files and the knowledge it had accumulated. By so doing it enhanced its power over other government departments.[89] There is no reason to believe that the RCMP would have been any less concerned during the war about keeping intact its hold over security intelligence.

The RCMP's reluctance to release data accumulated through

security screening was more than just a jurisdictional squabble over confidential information. The issue was that the state's security transcended both the rights of individuals and the interests of corporations or government departments. The RCMP did not articulate the problem in such terms. But in an inchoate way its officers realized that the state's security police had to maintain authority over its privileged information. It simply could not allow the intelligence it had painstakingly gathered and nurtured to be put to petty and inopportune use. This *caveat* applied to both demanding and influential employers and incompetent government bureaucrats.

The RCMP was also careful to avoid being implicated in any decision to fire an employee. W.C. Bryan recalled that the RCMP made no recommendation about firing: 'we only reported the facts.' It phrased its security reports to say that

this person should not have access to any matter of a classified nature and that any action that they [government departments and employers] took on the strength of this information was not to be associated with a police investigation. In other words, they hired him, he was their man, and they had to think of an excuse to either move him somewhere else or dismiss him.[90]

By masking its involvement in a dismissal, the force disguised the existence of the screening system and made it more difficult for victims to mount an effective protest.

Hence the major constraint on the security-screening system was its author, the RCMP. Its reluctance to take the system to its limits undoubtedly moderated the effect of security screening, even though abuses occurred. Still, it was not primarily concern for individual civil liberties which tempered the RCMP's use of its elaborate security-screening system. The RCMP's restraint resulted from the potential harm to its own reputation, the difficulty of ensuring that security reports would be kept confidential, and the possible consequences for the war effort if a negative security report exploded in the face of the force.

In the light of this we must reassess Friedenberg's concept of

Canadian deference to authority. Certainly it offers a clue to the lack of protest against wartime security screening. But, for a more complete explanation, one must also stand his proposition on its head: Canadians' deference to authority, yes; but, equally, the deference of authority to Canadians. The authorities were anxious to ensure that security screening never become a *cause célèbre*. Their deference, it should be noted, was purely pragmatic. They feared for the effect on the state and its war effort if security screening became controversial.

The security-screening system was also tempered by some employers and by the work of unions. Clearly, an adverse security report from the RCMP did not always lead to an employee losing his or her job. Early in the war the RCMP encountered resistance from some employers to acting on information from the RCMP. In December 1940 Commissioner Wood criticized industrial firms who continued to retain the services of employees in spite of criminal records or connection with what the police considered to be subversive organizations. Wood claimed to know of 'numerous cases' of this kind, adding that 'this renders the investigation futile.'[91] And, as noted above, even as late as 1942 some employers refused to implement security screening, while unions prevented many workers from being fired.

Explaining why civil liberties organizations reacted with such docility to security screening also demands an examination of their internal politics. For the entire decade before the war, they had been crippled by antagonism between social democrats and communists, and this partisanship carried on after 1939. In February 1940, for example, the Canadian Labor Defense League invited A.R.M. Lower to attend a meeting on civil liberties under the War Measures Act. With characteristic venom Lower jotted at the bottom of the invitation: 'These people horning in, as usual. A fat chance they would have to convince anyone of their sincerity in such a cause.'[92] So great was the bitterness that Lower insisted that communists – 'just one degree removed from traitors' – be barred from the Winnipeg organization.[93] In order 'to keep this movement in safe hands,' Lower declared, 'all our members are carefully chosen ... There have been half a dozen attempts made by people of Communist sympathies to get in but so far we have managed to keep them out, and intend to do so.' In the same vein, the Toronto society discussed conducting a 'serious investigation of prospective members' after communists attempted to gain executive seats.[94] This was a momentous development: the civil liberties organizations were screening members! How could they be expected to object to screening communists from industrial plants and the civil service when they did the same themselves?[95]

The communists were also partisan in their civil liberties efforts. Despite their record of struggle for democratic rights spanning more than a decade, after 1941 they squandered their leadership by paying attention almost exclusively to issues that benefited the Communist party and war assistance to the USSR. For example, in their strategy for labour set down after their about-face of June 1941, the communists included a section demanding 'full democratic rights.' But what the party identified as full democratic rights was more oriented to its own needs than to the needs of workers. Specifically, the party insisted that 'release of all anti-fascist internees and prisoners, legality of the Party, freedom of the press, etc., are necessary if the war against fascism is to be won.'[96] Yet no opposition was raised to security inquiries and mass fingerprinting, issues that directly attacked the civil rights of many workers.

The peculiar bent of the Communist party position on civil liberties was revealed at a national convention on democratic rights held in Ottawa in February 1942. At it, A.E. Smith and a delegation from the National Committee for Democratic Rights met Justice Minister Louis St Laurent. They called for an all-out war program, declared their support for a 'Yes' vote in the impending referendum on conscription,' and demanded that interned anti-fascists be released.[97] In one respect this is an *anti*–civil liberties platform – calling for conscription is contrary to the usual stand of a civil libertarian.

In this mixture of causes, appeals, and grievances – all-out war, release of interned anti-fascists, and democratic and trade union rights – civil rights matters took second place. After 1942, with the communist internees freed and a pragmatic compromise reached with the government over the ban on the Communist party, the communists set aside their struggle on the civil liberties front.[98] Having championed the cause of civil liberties in the prewar period, the communists abandoned the field and submerged the movement within their wartime campaign for assistance to the Soviet Union. In the end this was inimical to the civil liberties of Canadian workers, since issues such as mass fingerprinting were lost in the scramble for all-out war. This may help explain why civil liberties were in such a feeble state during the war.

Indeed, it was about this time that the oldest, most active and most influential of the civil liberties organizations was liquidated. The demise of the Montreal branch of the Civil Liberties Union was swift. It had some 3000 members in September 1939 and still claimed to have 1500 in June 1941.[99] Why it abruptly collapsed is instructive.

One of the central figures in the Montreal CCLU was R.A.C. (Campbell) Ballantyne, who served as executive secretary of the union from 1938 until 1941. He was also closely aligned with the Communist party, working as a contributing editor of the *Canadian Tribune* from its founding in January 1940 to April 1941. Ballantyne has offered contradictory explanations for the collapse of the CCLU in 1941. In a recent book on civil liberties organizations in Quebec, Ballantyne is quoted as saying that repression, fear of arrest, and lack of dues throttled the organization.[100] But in a candid private letter to Frank Park, Ballantyne painted an entirely different portrait. The letter was hastily written about 1947 as another round of partisan rivalry heated up over the creation of a new civil liberties group in Montreal, and it was clearly a communication between communist insiders. In it Ballantyne argued that far from fading once the war broke out, the CCLU led a spirited attack on the DOCR and the internments conducted under the regulations. What brought the end of the CCLU was not harrassment but the dramatic shift in the Communist party's position on the war in June 1941:

In mid-1941, with the change in governmental policy toward the war, the issue of civil liberty assumed a different character. The newly-created national unity made the Defence Regulations less of a menace to civil liberty ... the energies of the country began to be concentrated on winning the war. A natural consequence was the diversion of energy from the civil liberties movement into movements aimed at the consolidation of national unity against the common enemy. It was *agreed* that the Union should therefore *suspend operations* until a need for it should again become apparent.[101]

So there is considerable truth to Lester Phillips's blunt declaration that the CCLU was 'choked from within by Communists.'[102] In short, Canada's liveliest civil liberties body was gutted in the name of rousing the country to a total war effort. The RCMP had been attempting to discredit the union for years, and regarded it as the Communist party's 'most effective weapon.' They needed to worry no longer. The communists voluntarily killed it. Some of Canada's gravest wartime civil liberties violations – the ongoing persecution of Jehovah's Witnesses and the mass security-screening program – were occurring even then, and others – the internment of the Japanese Canadians, for instance – were mere months away. Yet the Montreal branch of the Civil Liberties Union was deemed unnecessary.

It is doubtful whether the Communist party's goal of assisting the Soviet Union's struggle against the Nazi invader required such a concession. But the communists' readiness to overlook Canadian problems provides another reason why protest against security screening was insignificant. Once the Soviet Union was threatened, the communist-led Civil Liberties Union, and indeed the whole Communist Party of Canada apparatus, ignored the fingerprinting and security screening of millions of Canadian workers and armed forces members.

The exact nature of the security-screening system offers another possible explanation for why civil libertarians did not make mass fingerprinting a contentious public issue. It is well to recall that there was considerable protest against internment, suppression of publications, and other repressive acts under the DOCR. What conditions specific to fingerprinting and vetting might have mollified the civil libertarians? The salient characteristic of security screening was that it was not applied even-handedly. The targets of the operation were specifically selected – industrial workers, civil servants, and armed forces personnel. The program was clearly biased against low-status members of society. Fingerprinting was a class-based violation of civil liberties, and as such was a rarity. Usually civil liberties are seen as rights held by everyone. In this case, lawyers, university professors, teachers, business leaders, and the other solid citizens who made up the civil liberties organizations were the least likely to have the abhorent procedure imposed on them. Is it any wonder that they found cause to complain about violations of the right of free speech but not about violations of the fingerprinting law? Discriminatory application of the law corresponded to an imbalance in objection to it. Those who did protest the procedure were unions and people who suffered abuse at its hands. The civil liberties organizations, made up of a privileged élite, found other problems more objectionable.

In addition, civil rights are rarely invoked in the context of the workplace. As citizens, people enjoy the protection of a variety of rights, either enshrined in law or established through long-standing practice. As workers, by contrast, they are stripped of most of those freedoms. In the words of *Harvard Business Review* editor David Ewing, people on the job have rights 'so compacted, so imploded by the gravitational forces of legal tradition' that their status is like a black hole in space.[103] Workers did not expect to have rights at their workplace, so being fingerprinted there was not surprising to them. Moreover, the one organization that might be expected to protest an injustice applied prejudicially to working people, the Communist party, threw off its oppositional habit early in the war.

The outcome of the wartime security-screening system based on fingerprinting was in some ways predictable, and predicted. The auto workers' immediate response was suspicion that the system of fingerprinting would be used by employers to create a blacklist of dissidents and to coerce their employees and make them accept intolerable working conditions. Judging from the comments expressed by senior executives at the Ontario Co-ordinating Committee for Security, workers' fears were not far off. In some cases, such as at the Ottawa Car and Aircraft Company, the information which the security-screening system put into the hands of management was used to intimidate workers. Evidence of firings and employment rejections shows that the security-screening system was responsible for wartime injustices. The fingerprinting of millions of Canadians and inquiries into their personal and political behaviour constitute a larger civil liberties transgression.

If the program's existence and grasp are unsettling, more worrysome still is that it proceeded virtually unopposed by the country's guardians of basic freedoms. It is true that civil liberties associations were hard-pressed to keep up with the pace of authoritarian regulation implemented under the Defence of Canada Regulations. Nevertheless, time and energy could be found to point out the idiocy of punishing, under regulations intended to safeguard national security, a farmer who failed to weed his field. Yet civil libertarians did not muster a whimper against the state's violation of the fingerprinting law and personal prying on a grand scale. This anomaly occurred for several reasons, foremost among them that civil liberties defence groups were weak and politically divided. But the Canadian state, particularly the RCMP, realizing the potential for trouble inherent in a program this invasive, also operated it with considerable care. Their concern was not for the individual but for the preservation of the state and its security intelligence capacity.

Chapter 10
Outcomes, developments, and significance

The quest for an infallible machine to determine loyalty goes back centuries. Kings, feudal lords, and modern bureaucratic states alike have devoted considerable effort to devising a means, in the words of Canada's Mackenzie Commission, to obtain 'an objective judgment of the subject's future loyalty, reliability and character.'[1] Until the twentieth century oaths of allegiance were the primary means by which authorities sought to guarantee their subjects' fidelity. Oaths were always fallible, but new conditions in the early years of this century made them appear more dubious than ever. The event that most dramatically reinforced the demand for a new apparatus to ascertain loyalty was the Bolshevik Revolution. It led to an ideological split within Western society, undermining the belief that most members of society held common convictions, which was the implicit foundation of loyalty oaths. The Bolshevik Revolution and the creation of the Communist International, along with parties affiliated with it, also introduced the threat of a potent internal enemy whose allegiance was to a foreign country, the socialist motherland, the Soviet Union.

Until now, the prevailing view has been that, in its search for a test of true loyalty, the Canadian state introduced security screening only in 1946, and under duress. The event thought to have launched the system was Igor Gouzenko's 1945 defection from the Soviet embassy in Ottawa, carrying proof that Canadian civil servants were spying for the Soviet Union. The tale of the origin of state security screening is now so familiar that it has become part of a Canadian mythology. It goes like this: before Gouzenko we were simple folk, naïve in the ways of the intelligence world. Soviet spying ripped away our naïveté and left us naked in our shame before the entire world. We thus had no choice but to clothe ourselves in a security-screening system.

A radical rethinking of that fanciful image is in order. Rather than 1946, we must look to 1931 as the date at which the Canadian state began systematically to screen civil servants. Security investigation of naturalization applicants began even earlier, in the 1920s. This knowledge is important for more than the fact that it pushes back the creation of the system more than fifteen years. It forces a re-evaluation of what motivated security screening. The evidence shows that the RCMP did not begin to screen civil servants to search for Soviet spies. What gave birth to the machine was the fear of domestic communism. Hatred for communism preoccupied the RCMP and the Canadian state virtually from the moment the Communist Party of Canada was formed in 1921. Under vehemently anti-communist commissioners like James MacBrien and S.T. Wood, the force began to adopt new methods to address the party's influence. Security screening was one such measure. The same motive prompted the RCMP and the Department of Munitions to expand the system at the beginning of the Second World War by incorporating war plant employees and armed forces personnel.

In addition to the fear of communism, we can point to another factor in the genesis of the infernal machine – technology. While technical developments of the early twentieth century did not specifically provoke security screening, they made it feasible. Foremost among these innovations was fingerprinting, which provided the police with a scientifically grounded method to establish identity. In the 1920s fingerprinting became a central element in the Canadian state's screening mechanism. So valuable did it appear to be to the police that, during the Second World War, they dramatically expanded the number of people fingerprinted. Some 2 million Canadians yielded their fingerprints to the state during the war. For at least half of them – workers in munitions plants – the procedure contravened the Identification of Criminals Act. Although many workers agreed to be finger-printed by signing an employment application form, the pressure on them to comply was very real, and the RCMP itself acknowl-edged its coercive power.

Police and other state authorities in Canada justified wartime security screening with arguments that can be placed into two cat-egories. Political arguments – one category – were expressed first. The primary rationale offered to the public was vetting's power to detect saboteurs. The RCMP claimed that fingerprinting, the heart of security screening, frustrated sabotage in the following way. The enemy worked through criminals, who could be blackmailed into carrying out sabotage. Once unmasked by a fingerprint check, criminals could be kept out of positions where they might do damage. But as the war continued and enemy-organized sabo-tage proved to be chimerical, sabotage was not abandoned as a reason to scrutinize workers. Instead, sabotage came to be rede-fined in economic terms – as 'exceedingly slow work.'

The other major political rationale was that screening would detect communists in industry and government. In private dis-cussions the police and industrialists particularly emphasized this as a benefit. Yet, in practice, the communist threat to sabotage or subvert industry evaporated after the Soviet Union entered the war on 22 June 1941. After that the communists became zealously pro-war. This did not cause the RCMP to abandon vetting. The police carried on with screening, partly because of long-standing anti-communist bias and partly because they believed the truce with communism would be short-lived. Some fear also persisted that communists in government could spy for the Soviet Union, and this doubtless remained a political motive for continued vigi-lance.

The other category of explanations for vetting reveals a desire to impose social and economic control on workers. This purpose lay behind several justifications for screening. The Department of Munitions and Supply believed vetting helped to monitor labour turnover and absenteeism. The RCMP contended that in a mass society anonymity made identification difficult. This problem was compounded by the war's demand for labour, which caused hundreds of thousands of workers to move from their homes to distant employment. This dislocation of labour worried the state and employers. Security screening met their needs to monitor the movements of workers, and it satisfied employers' desire to curb union efforts to improve working conditions. And communists, it should also be noted, were well represented among union organizers.

Social and economic explanations for security screening were frequently indistinguishable from political ones. The director general of the Industrial Security Branch of the DMS, for instance, believed that agitators and saboteurs were responsible for labour turnover and lost time. To bridle labour it was necessary to rein in militants, particularly the communists, who, at least until June 1941, also happened to be enemies of the war effort. Principles and pragmatism were thus intertwined. In short, although the arguments for security screening can be grouped into two categories, neither category was hermetically sealed. The political category contained explanations which spilled into the realm of economics, and vice versa.

Little of this rationale was laid out by Canadian state authorities in their justifications for security screening. An explanation for this deficiency is not hard to identify. Before the RCMP dramatically expanded screening at the beginning of the Second World War, it did not draw up a theoretical plan for the program. No one within the force charted in any detail the purposes and possible repercussions of screening. Like many wartime measures, the system simply evolved and grew, amorphously. Even at the close of the war the RCMP did not evaluate its security-screening system and weigh its consequences. Neither did anyone else in the Canadian state. Up to 1946 the system does not appear to have ever received political approval or scrutiny.

In assessing the impact of wartime security screening we must ask blunt questions: Did it amount to anything more than a huge stack of IBM tabulating machine cards? Was it effective? Did it influence Canadian society? Returning to the motives behind the creation of the machine will help us respond to those queries.

Preventing wartime sabotage was one of the claims made for the system. Here there is little evidence to bring to bear. As security and intelligence agencies frequently point out, only their failures become public; no one ever learns what sabotage, assassination, or espionage they thwart. Sometimes the agencies themselves do not know. That general rule also applies to security screening. During the entire war period the RCMP cited just two cases of screening being linked to the apprehension of saboteurs. Significantly, the RCMP reported those two successes in a meeting of its peers, a Western Hemisphere Intelligence Conference, where it could confidently reveal security details. In each case the offender was employed in a succession of war plants, where his special skill allowed him to attain a vital position quickly. After making a crucial 'mistake' which held up production, the delinquent quit and moved to another plant. But the astonishing aspect is that each suspect worked at a number of factories (four in one instance, ten in the second) before being apprehended. Moreover, it is not certain that the vetting system deserved credit for isolating the culprit; sharp-eyed employers might have been equally responsible.[2] In any case, catching two saboteurs was a small achievement for a system that absorbed an immense amount of the state's effort.

Measuring the impact of a security program often involves weighing intangibles. The test is not what did happen, but what did not, not who was caught in the act, but who was discouraged from acting. In this regard, one fact is certain: Canada saw no organized sabotage during the war. Should security screening be given credit for the achievement? Seen in a rational light, the claim is dubious. The patient was healthy not because of the medicine's potency but because there was no disease. No significant potential perpetrator of sabotage existed in the first place. Canadians were remarkably loyal to the strategic war aims of the state. Those few who were not were isolated and neutralized in the first months of the war by traditional methods of political intelligence and restraint – infiltration of opposition groups and selective internment of opponents. Concentrating on security screening and fingerprinting probably had no more effect than to divert the

RCMP from the proven methods which had produced results early in the war.

As for its aim of identifying communists, the security-screening system was probably of little value. We have seen earlier that the RCMP did not carry out the laborious cross-checking of new fingerprints with those already in the existing civil collection, a process which would have been necessary in order to identify itinerant communist organizers. The existence of the screening system, however, would have been obvious to communists, as it was to others. This obvious level of surveillance – if communists needed to be reminded of it – might have convinced sympathizers of the danger of heeding the Communist party's bold talk about turning the imperialist war into revolutionary war. The net effect, then, was probably some reduction in expressions of anti-war dissent.

It is somewhat easier to evaluate the impact of the third major aspect of security screening, social control. Screening performed a variety of tasks. Authorities believed that vetting was effective in disciplining labour and stifling economic dissent because it made 'people think that we ... have some check on them.'[3] Security screening identified who worked where. It safeguarded private property by preventing theft and acts of individual sabotage bred of personal frustration. It maintained industrial authority by keeping potential troublemakers in check. In certain circumstances, vetting was also used to uphold conventional moral standards. Thus security screening became at least as important as a measure of social and economic control on ordinary workers as it was a restraint on politically motivated saboteurs. Disciplining labour might not have been vetting's theoretical aim, but it ultimately served that purpose.

Security screening also had a political impact on Canadian society. Establishing a direct correlation between security programs and political characteristics is difficult. This is so in part because modern surveillance coerces people by inducing fear of the unknown rather than by overt punishment. Michel Foucault observed this trend in the evolving methods of punishment. Where once they relied upon inflicting pain on a transgressor's body, authorities during the nineteenth and twentieth centuries resorted to observation, surveillance, and inspection as a means of control.[4] Pressure to conform came from the fear of a pervasive and omnipresent panoptic eye, the very type of surveillance system implemented in security screening. Whether or not they read Foucault, security intelligence forces appear to understand this knowledge. Their usual practice is to maintain a high level of surveillance but only rarely to act upon the intelligence gained by it. Implicitly they grasp that placing people under scrutiny tends to constrain their actions. It may also alter the ideological climate in a society by legitimizing one set of political ideas and rendering other views unacceptable. As James Littleton points out, the knowledge that one must pass a security test to gain certain employment has a remarkable ability to induce political conformity and intellectual self-censorship. This exerts ideological control by narrowing the scope of public discourse.[5] In the years before 1945, it is clear that security screening put Canadian society under some ideological and political pressure.

Vetting represented a new intrusion by the state into the lives of its citizens. Never before had the state mounted so sweeping a campaign of inquiry into people's activities, an inquiry in which people were made aware that their past actions and associations were being scrutinized. There is ample evidence that people in private corporations and government departments across Canada were fired and refused jobs because of the security-screening system. Moreover fingerprinting of one million Canadian workers was contrary to the law, and the inquiries into the personal and political behaviour of some two million Canadians went on without political approval. This was a significant violation of citizens' rights. Certainly other states during the Second World War were more aggressively abusive of their citizens; political police rounded up innocents en masse, imprisoning, interning, and killing millions. Those regimes subjected people to the ultimate in extermination technology – gas, drugs, and germs included. But those were dictatorships and police states. Canada prided itself on upholding 'British freedom,' and it is within that context that the Canadian screening system must be evaluated. Judged by the norms of the Canadian democracy of the day, vetting, especially in its use of mass fingerprinting, was an offence.

Security screening represented the covert side of the Canadian state's wartime measures to restrain its citizens. The overt means were the Defence of Canada Regulations, which gave the prime minister and cabinet highly autocratic powers. Canadian civil libertarians concentrated their efforts on attempting to put constraints on the use of the DOCR. This strategy was understandable, given that some of the state's actions under the DOCR were significant violations of civil liberties. But in opposing the open suspension of traditional liberties, defenders of civil rights paid little attention to the covert infraction.

Security screening was an iniquity precisely because it was *sub rosa*. In contrast to actions taken under the DOCR – which, for all their arbitrariness, at least had the virtue of being somewhat public – security-screening punishment was meted out in secret. There was no publicity about the people fired or not hired because of security reports. Security screening led to uncontrolled and informal punishment. It lacked any acknowledged rules or regulations. It was administered outside the courts, beyond the protection of due process. It was not amenable to the elementary principle that an accused has the right to know the charges against him or her and face his or her accuser. It allowed for no appeal. Observers today might take comfort from the fact that there were few victims and their punishment was mild. How tragic, after all, was it to lose or be denied a job in a period of full employment? But the issue is not the number of victims or the severity of their punishment. The point is that the *very process* was contrary to the accepted principles of openness and fairness which are fundamental to Canadian democracy. The machine was wrongful, damnable, infernal.

Canadians regarded fingerprinting with deep suspicion, and political authorities understood this well. Throughout the 1920s and 1930s Canadians were hostile to fingerprinting and resisted it, even in cases where the RCMP was on firm legal grounds to proceed with it. The military brass rejected fingerprinting for more than two decades before 1939, and even at the opening of the war they expressed reluctance to begin fingerprinting because they believed it would harm recruitment. Norman Robertson, the country's most senior civil servant, looked askance at a proposal to fingerprint Allied aliens entering the Canadian forces. But perhaps the most telling argument that non-criminal fingerprinting was not acceptable to the Canadian people came from the RCMP. The police were highly sensitive to a possible backlash against fingerprinting and security screening during the Second World War. Following objections from people who had been fired because of adverse security reports the RCMP commissioner expressed fears that the force was acquiring 'a Gestapo reputation.' Although it was stung by such criticism, the RCMP did not stop screening. Instead it changed the screening methods slightly, endeavouring to allow as little security information as possible out of its hands. It should be noted that this caution arose only in small part from concern for the individual. The RCMP's primary motives were avoiding conflict to preserve the pace of the war effort and keeping its security intelligence capacity intact. But the fact that the Horsemen trod so gingerly around the issue means that the RCMP perceived that Canadians did not like being fingerprinted and nor did they relish the police prying into their private lives.

After the war the RCMP remained aware that its civilian fingerprint collection was itself a potentially explosive device. In 1947 a flame came near its fuse when CCF MP Alistair Stewart asked a series of pointed questions of the minister of justice. The first was simple: 'How many fingerprints of individuals are in the files of the Royal Canadian Mounted Police?' Justice Minister J.L. Ilsley's reply was startling: '(a) Criminal collection – 766,723; (b) civil collection – 1,147,585.' Fingerprinting had been developed as a criminal procedure; the Identification of Criminals Act allowed fingerprinting only for serious criminal charges. Yet the RCMP admitted to having one and a half times as many non-criminal fingerprints as it had criminal fingerprints. Stewart pressed home the point: why were the fingerprints of non-criminals held by the RCMP? Ilsley's disingenuous answer must have convinced no one: 'To identify unknown dead persons or amnesia victims when so requested by an authorized source.' On how many occasions had that need arisen? Since 1936, just 284 times.[6] The minister said nothing about the civil collection being the core of a vast screening system. The exchange seemed to be enough to cause anxiety within the government and the RCMP; soon afterwards the civil collection was destroyed.[7] The RCMP continued to fingerprint civilians as part of security screening, but once it had checked its criminal files it returned the fingerprints to the government department or private corporation from which the prints had originated.[8]

Canada's early experience with fingerprinting calls into question Edgar Friedenberg's claim that Canadians, unlike Americans, exhibit deference to authority. The record shows that, when it comes to fingerprinting, Canadians have displayed no deference to authority. Aside from the extraordinary conditions of the war, they have not supported or yielded to a series of police efforts to fingerprint more widely.[9] Indeed, they have consistently exhibited more resistance to fingerprinting than their American counterparts. This resistance has not been showy. There was no public campaign against universal fingerprinting in Canada like that waged by the American Civil Liberties Union in the 1930s. And while it is true that 2.3 million Canadians were fingerprinted during the Second World War, far more Americans, absolutely and relatively, were fingerprinted during the war. In 1939 the RCMP held about 18,000 fingerprints in its civil collection, and that grew to 1,148,000 in 1947.[10] By contrast, from 30 June 1941 to 30 June 1945, the number of non-criminal fingerprint sets held by the FBI rose from 11 million to 83 million.[11]

These figures, particular that from the United States, are extraordinary. Considering the populations of each country, about 20 per cent of Canadians had been subject to non-criminal fingerprinting by the end of the Second World War, while almost 60 per cent of Americans had their fingerprints in the FBI's civil collection. In both cases the police must have held a number of duplicate fingerprints, which might have been an especially significant factor in the United States, where the FBI had conducted an active civilian fingerprinting campaign before the war. Whether the percentages are perfectly accurate is probably less important than the great disparity between the Canadian and American figures. It casts doubt upon Friedenberg's formula that Canadians show deference to authority, while Americans do not.

An important long-term impact of the security-screening program was that it became the model for the postwar system. The cessation of hostilities in Europe did not bring on the dismantling of the state's screening system. Security inquiries into government employees carried on apace. In July 1945, after victory in Europe had been secured, and only a month before Japan would fall, Intelligence Officer C.E. Rivett-Carnac reported that the RCMP was continuing to check National Research Council employees.[12] They were not the only ones; the RCMP retained a great variety of security-screening duties. Refugees, applicants for the armed forces, persons in the employ of British and American governments, as well as employees of the United Nations Relief and Rehabilitation Agency were all vetted by the RCMP.[13] In short, it was business as usual.

What ended business as usual was a political earthquake, which shifted the sedimentary relationship between the Canadian government and the RCMP security service and forced a fundamental change in security intelligence policy and practice in Canada. That shock was the defection of Igor Gouzenko from the Soviet embassy in Ottawa in September 1945. His revelations had a double impact upon security screening. First, they presented the Canadian state with a signal opportunity to inaugurate a properly constituted security-screening program. Beginning in February 1946, the government observed careful protocol with regard to security screening. It established a royal commission under Supreme Court justices R.L. Kellock and Robert Taschereau, who held formal hearings investigating Gouzenko's charges. In view of the evidence of spying, the commission's report recommended coordinated and uniform security measures within the government. 'Out of these recommendations,' Reg Whitaker has written, 'grew the formidable machinery of the government's internal-security system.'[14] On 22 May 1946 the cabinet created a new security coordination organization, the Security Panel, to oversee the vetting program.[15] At the beginning of 1947 the cabinet approved the panel's proposals for vetting. 'Henceforth,' according to Robert Bothwell and Jack Granatstein, 'the political views held by individuals could be deemed sufficient reason for firings, shiftings to less sensitive posts, or decisions to deny employment in the civil service.'[16]

This tidy picture of proper procedure, however, is sullied by the knowledge that the Canadian state already had a functioning security-screening system. The Security Panel had a model upon which to base its policy for vetting civil servants. It could follow the practice worked out by the RCMP during the previous fifteen years of loyalty inquiries. Moreover, the government could afford to leisurely plan and weigh the consequences of a screening system because vetting of civil servants was ongoing, as it had been since 1931.

To illustrate how smooth the security-screening transition was, on 22 May 1946, the very day the cabinet constituted the Security Panel, the officer in charge of the RCMP Special Section reported: 'We are and have for some time past, as you are aware, been engaged in vetting persons for the Civil Service Commission, concerning not only persons to be employed directly by the Civil Service Commission but also those persons who are temporarily or permanently assigned to other Government departments.'[17] As they had been since 1931, the political views of civil servants were an important standard against which they were judged. Clearly there was no hiatus period between the end of the war and the formal commencement of screening in 1947. Moreover, the security-screening method used then and for the next twenty years was virtually identical to what had already been practised in the years before and during the Second World War.[18]

One element of the wartime loyalty inquiries was much reduced after 1945. That was the vetting of private sector employees. Although the RCMP continued to screen employees of a small number of crown corporations and companies supplying strategic materials, as well as Great Lakes seamen, after 1945 the focus shifted to civil servants.[19] Why did the police scale back private sector fingerprinting and screening after 1945? One reason was that with the end of the war the number of plants producing war materials fell drastically. Probably more important was that the screening system, especially the fingerprint aspect of it, was of dubious legality. Under such conditions, it is little surprise that the RCMP reduced its scope.

Gouzenko's second significant impact upon security screening has not been widely recognized. Gouzenko has been credited with many things, foremost among them starting the Cold War.[20] Yet no one has acknowledged him to be the unlikely instigator of a civil liberties' breakthrough in Canada. Certainly his defection gave the Canadian state the opportunity officially to set up a screening system for civil servants. But, in doing so, the Canadian state was forced to make a profound admission. When the cabinet issued Directive 4 on security screening in 1948 it formally recognized *for the first time* the existence of a functioning vetting system. Government recognition of screening was accompanied by some rudimentary operating rules for it. It would be years yet before principles of natural justice were introduced into security screening.[21] But at least politicians were forced to accept responsibility for the screening system, a responsibility they had shirked for many years.

Without the chance occurrence of Gouzenko defecting, little would have changed in Canadian state security screening. All evidence points to the conclusion that in September 1945 the Canadian state had no intention of abolishing the existing procedure. Neither did it have any plan to legitimize the practice. On the contrary, barring interruption, the same secretive, iniquitous, and unaccountable technocratic process would have prevailed for years to come. The infernal machine, which was sparked to life by the Canadian state's fervent determination to identify and suppress the supporters of domestic communism, was built without brakes, and roll on it did.

Appendix 1
Application for employment

APPLICATION FOR EMPLOYMENT

(NAME OF FIRM)
DEPARTMENT or WORKS...
(LOCATION)
EMPLOYMENT No........

NAME.:...
(Surname)   (Given Names)   (Maiden Name if Married WOMAN)

ADDRESS..
(Present Address)   (Permanent Address)

BIRTHPLACE......................DATE OF BIRTH...........NATIONALITY...................

NUMBER OF YEARS IN CANADA.........MARITAL STATUS................RELIGION..............

HEIGHT......WEIGHT......EYES.......HAIR......COMPLEXION...........MARKS or DEFORMITIES..

IF FOREIGN BORN

NAME USED WHEN ENTERING CANADA..........................NAME OF SHIP................

PORT OF ENTRY...DATE OF ENTRY................

IF NATURALIZED

WHEN NATURALIZED..........WHERE NATURALIZED.............CERTIFICATE PRODUCED.........
NO. OF CERTIFICATE.........
(Yes or No.)

BIRTHPLACE AND ADDRESS OF NEAR RELATIVES

	Name in Full	Birthplace	Present Address if Living
FATHER....................	....	....	....
MOTHER....................	....	....	....
WIFE or HUSBAND.......... (Give Wife's Maiden Name)	....	....	....
FATHER OF WIFE or HUSBAND..	....	....	....
MOTHER OF WIFE or HUSBAND .	....	....	....
BROTHERS...	....	....	....
SISTERS.	....	....	....
CHILDREN.................	....	....	....

OTHER NEAR RELATIVES
NOW LIVING IN
FOREIGN COUNTRIES...
(Name in Full)   (Address)   (Relationship)
RELATIVES EMPLOYED BY
GOVERNMENT OF CANADA..
(Name in Full)   (Address)   (Relationship)
RELATIVES EMPLOYED BY
ANY FOREIGN GOVERNMENT..
(Name in Full)   (Address)   (Relationship)
PRESENT EMPLOYMENT OF WIFE or HUSBAND...

NAMES OF EMPLOYEES KNOWN TO APPLICANT..
PERSON TO BE NOTIFIED
IN CASE OF EMERGENCY..
(Name)   (Address)   (Phone)   (Relationship)

MILITARY, NAVAL or AIR SERVICE (In Canada or any other Country)

UNIT...............REG.NO........RANKS.................PRESENT STATUS..................

WHERE ENGAGED.....................WHEN ENGAGED.........WHERE DISCHARGED...............

WHEN DISCHARGED...................WHY DISCHARGED.......................................

Source: Justice Access A89-00061

EDUCATION

	Name of School	Location	Period of Attendance	Course	Degree or Diploma
Elementary or Public Schools......					
High Schools........					
Colleges or Universities........					
Trade, Business or Night Schools					

FORMER EMPLOYMENT

Employer	Address	Kind of Work	Period of Employment	Reason for Leaving
Present or Last..				
Previous........				
Previous........				
Previous........				

RESIDENCES DURING PAST FIVE YEARS

Period	Address	Period	Address

REFERENCES

(References MUST be British Subjects who have known applicant for at least one year. They MUST NOT be relatives or former employers).

Name	Address	Phone No.	Occupation
1.			
2.			
3.			

NATIONAL REGISTRATION

NAME ON CERTIFICATE...........................ADDRESS ON CERTIFICATE.......

DATE OF REGISTRATION...............ELECTORAL DISTRICT NAME and NUMBER..................

POLLING DIVISION NAME and NUMBER.........CERTIFICATE PRODUCED (Yes or No)...............

WHERE WERE YOU DURING THE PERIOD 1914 - 1918 ?...

HAVE YOU EVER BEEN CHARGED WITH A CRIMINAL OFFENCE?.............................IF SO:..

NAME OFFENCE (OR OFFENCES).....................................DATE..................

PLACE.................DISPOSITION..

TO WHAT ORGANIZATIONS (OTHER THAN LABOUR UNIONS) HAVE YOU BELONGED AT ANY TIME DURING THE PAST TEN YEARS?..

ARE YOU WILLING TO HAVE YOUR FINGERPRINTS & PHOTOGRAPHS TAKEN FOR RECORD PURPOSES?..

It is understood and agreed that any misrepresentation by me in this application will be sufficient cause for cancellation of the application and/or for separation from the Company's service if I have been employed.

(Witness)..(Signed)...........................
        (Official conducting interview)   Date............................

Appendix 2
Non-criminal fingerprint form

( ) MALE   NON - CRIMINAL

Name:

Place

Application for

Class

Ref.

RIGHT HAND				
1 RIGHT THUMB	2 R. FORE FINGER	3 R. MIDDLE FINGER	4 R. RING FINGER	5 R. LITTLE FINGER

LEFT HAND				
6 LEFT THUMB	7 L. FORE FINGER	8 L. MIDDLE FINGER	9 L. RING FINGER	10 L. LITTLE FINGER

Left Hand
Plain impressions of the four fingers taken simultaneously

Right Hand
Plain impressions of the four fingers taken simultaneously

Thumb   Thumb

Impressions taken by .... Date .... Place

Classified at F.P.S. by .... Date

Checker .... Searcher .... Date

Signature ....

Address ....

Year of birth ....
Place of birth ....
Height .... ft. .... in.
Weight ....
Eyes ....
Complexion ....
Hair ....
Amputations. (State date) ....

RIGHT FOREFINGER PRINT
TO BE IMPRESSED
IMMEDIATELY AFTER
SIGNATURE IS WRITTEN

Marks, scars or deformities ....

Remarks ....

Employed by ....

Source: Justice Access A89-00061

Notes

Introduction

1 Canada, *Report of the Royal Commission on Security* (Mackenzie Commission) (Ottawa: Queen's Printer 1969), p. 10
2 *Ibid.*, p. 11
3 By political control I mean the maintenance of the existing state's hegemony and the stability of its attendant institutions and supporting economic and social structure.
4 Mackenzie Commission, p. 30
5 A succinct definition of security was provided by the British Security Executive in 1942: 'the defence of national interests against hostile elements other than the armed forces of the enemy; in practice against espionage, sabotage and attempts to procure defeat by subversive political activity.' F.H. Hinsley and C.A.G. Simkins, *British Intelligence in the Second World War*, 4 vols. (London: Her Majesty's Stationery Office 1990), vol. 4: *Security and Counter-Intelligence*, p. 3. Roy Godson defines intelligence as 'the effort of a government, or of a private individual, group or body, devoted to:
   1. collection, analysis, dissemination, and exploitation of knowledge and information affecting its own interests which relates to any other government, political group, military force, movement, or individual;
   2. protection against similar initiatives on the part of other governments, political groups, parties, military forces, movements, or individuals...' Roy Godson, 'Intelligence: an American View,' in

British and American Approaches to Intelligence, ed. K.G. Robertson (London: Macmillan 1987), p. 4

6 Godson, 'Intelligence,' pp. 4, 20–1 and John Bruce Lockhart, 'Intelligence: a British View,' in *British and American Approaches*, ed. Robertson, p. 43

7 Nigel West, *A Matter of Trust: MI5, 1945–1972* (London: Weidenfeld and Nicolson 1982), p. 51

8 Since it focuses upon security screening – the search for hidden subversives within the Canadian population – this study does not deal with separate security issues, such as internment, registration and supervision of aliens, and censorship.

9 By political police, I mean a specialized police force or sub-force whose primary objective is not to accumulate evidence leading to criminal prosecution. Instead, the attention of political police is focused on those in conflict with official ideology; their cases usually involve no victim (individual or corporate, real or potential) other than the state itself.

10 Jeff Sallot, *Nobody Said No: The Real Story about How the Mounties Always Get Their Man* (Toronto: James Lorimer 1979), and Robert Dion, *Crimes of the Secret Police* (French ed., 1979; Montreal: Black Rose 1982) deal exclusively with the 1970s events. John Sawatsky's *Men in the Shadows: The Shocking Truth about the RCMP Security Service* (Toronto, Doubleday 1980) is a journalistic chronicle of the history and contemporary activity of the RCMP Security Service which relies largely on interviews and eschews the McDonald and Keable Commission testimony.

11 Reg Whitaker's *Double Standard: The Secret History of Canadian Immigration* (Toronto: Lester and Orpen Dennys 1987) effectively dissects the screening of immigrants in the postwar era.

12 Reginald Whitaker, 'Origins of the Canadian Government's Internal Security System, 1946–1952,' *Canadian Historical Review* 65, no. 2 (June 1984): 154–83; Lawrence Aronsen, 'Some Aspects of Surveillance: "Peace, Order and Good Government" during the Cold War: The Origins and Organization of Canada's Internal Security Program,' *Intelligence and National Security* 1, no. 3 (September 1986): 357–80

13 Wesley Wark, 'Security Intelligence in Canada, 1864–1945: The History of a 'National Insecurity State,'" in *Go Spy the Land: Military*

Intelligence in History, eds. Keith Neilson and B.J.C. McKercher (Westport, Conn., and London: Praeger 1992), p. 172

14 Canada, Commission of Inquiry Concerning Certain Activities of the Royal Canadian Mounted Police (McDonald Commission), Second Report, *Freedom and Security under the Law,* vol. 1 (Ottawa: Ministry of Supply and Services 1981) (hereafter McDonald, Commission of Inquiry, vol. 1), p. 61

15 Wesley Wark, 'The Evolution of Military Intelligence in Canada,' *Armed Forces and Society* 16, no. 1 (1989): 65–6

16 Peter St John, 'Canada's Accession to the Allied Intelligence Community, 1940–45,' *Conflict Quarterly* IV, no. 4 (fall 1984): 6, *passim*

17 Stuart Farson, 'Schools of Thought: National Perceptions of Intelligence,' *Conflict Quarterly* IX, no. 2 (spring 1989): 78

18 One of the curious features of security intelligence practice on both sides of the Atlantic is that although security-screening procedure is very similar the labels are not. When it comes to ascertaining the political trustworthiness of civil servants and others, Canada, Britain, and the United States have clung to idiosyncratic titles. What is called security screening in Canada is vetting in Britain and loyalty testing in the United States. Since each name describes a standard procedure, I shall use the labels synonymously.

19 Roy Godson, 'Introduction: The New Study of Intelligence,' in *Comparing Foreign Intelligence: The U.S., the USSR, the U.K. & the Third World,* ed. Roy Godson (Washington: Pergamon-Brassey's 1988), p. 2

20 A pioneering study of the FBI, Max Lowenthal's *The Federal Bureau of Investigation* (London: Turnstile Press 1950), probably contains more any other work about the bureau's security-screening efforts up to 1945. More recent studies include Frank Donner, *The Age of Surveillance: The Aims and Methods of America's Political Intelligence System* (New York: Alfred A. Knopf 1980), and Athan Theoharis, *Spying on Americans: Political Surveillance from Hoover to the Huston Plan* (Philadelphia: Temple University Press 1978), both of which contain penetrating insights into how the FBI used deception to gain a political intelligence mandate. In Britain, the 1980s saw the publication of several probes into that country's extensive security network. In addition to *A Matter of Trust,* Nigel West has produced *MI5: British Security Service Operations, 1909–1945* (New York: Mili-

tary Heritage Press 1981). By far the most authoritative study, however, is Christopher Andrew's *Secret Service: The Making of the British Intelligence Community* (London: Sceptre 1986). Bernard Porter has produced two valuable studies of the development of British security intelligence capacity, *The Origins of the Vigilant State: The London Metropolitan Police Special Branch before the First World War* (London: Weidenfeld and Nicolson 1987) and *Plots and Paranoia: A History of Political Espionage in Britain, 1790–1988* (London: Unwin Hyman 1989).

21 David Caute, *The Great Fear: The Anti-Communist Purge under Truman and Eisenhower* (New York: Simon and Schuster 1978); Harold Hyman, *To Try Men's Souls: Loyalty Tests in American History* (Berkeley: University of California Press 1959)

22 Edward A. Shils, *The Torment of Secrecy: The Background and Consequences of American Security Policies* (Glencoe, Ill.: Free Press 1956); Mark Hollingsworth and Richard Norton-Taylor, *Blacklist: The Inside Story of Political Vetting* (London: Hogarth Press 1988)

23 Books written with the assistance of the act include: William Kaplan, *Everything That Floats: Pat Sullivan, Hal Banks, and the Seamen's Unions of Canada* (Toronto: University of Toronto Press 1987); Gregory S. Kealey and Reg Whitaker, eds., *R.C.M.P. Security Bulletins: The War Series, 1939–1941* (St John's, Nfld: Canadian Committee on Labour History 1989); Gregory S. Kealey and Reg Whitaker, eds., *R.C.M.P. Security Bulletins: The War Series, Part II, 1942–1945* (St John's, Nfld: Canadian Committee on Labour History 1993); John Bryden, *Deadly Allies: Canada's Secret War, 1937–47* (Toronto: McClelland and Stewart 1989); John Bryden, *Best-Kept Secret: Canadian Secret Intelligence in the Second World War* (Toronto: Lester Publishing 1993).

24 Canada, Access to Information Act, 29-30-31 Elizabeth II, c. 111, sections 13(1), 15(1), and 19(1)

CHAPTER 1 The last recourse of liars

1 Archives of Ontario (AO), MU 6286, Engineering Records Foundation, Industrial Relations Division, box 2, British Counterpart, 1915

2 S.D. Trivedi, *Secret Services in Ancient India: Techniques and Operation* (New Delhi: Allied Publishers 1984), p. 151 and *passim*

3 Goran Therborn, *What Does the Ruling Class Do When It Rules?: State Apparatuses and State Power under Feudalism, Capitalism and Socialism* (London: NLB 1978), p. 49

4 Marc Bloch, *Feudal Society,* trans. L.A. Manyon (Chicago: University of Chicago Press 1961), vol. 1: *The Growth of Ties of Dependence*, pp. 146, 157–8

5 Harold M. Hyman, *To Try Men's Souls: Loyalty Tests in American History* (Berkeley and Los Angeles: University of California Press 1959), p. 3

6 Michael Hill, *The State, Administration and the Individual* (Totawa, N.J.: Rowman and Littlefield 1976), p. 23

7 Peter Richards, *Patronage in British Government* (London: George Allen and Unwin 1963), pp. 60–1

8 Geoffrey K. Fry, *The Growth of Government: The Development of Ideas about the Role of the State and the Machinery and Functions of Government in Britain since 1780* (London: Frank Cass 1979), p. 115

9 Harold Hyman, *Era of the Oath: Northern Loyalty Tests during the Civil War and Reconstruction* (Philadelphia: University of Pennsylvania Press 1954), p. 207 n27. A glance at early use of the phrase 'ironclad oath' confirms how divorced Britain had become from the practice by 1885. The *Pall Mall Gazette* of 6 June 1885, for example, recorded that 'The British parties ... may try ... to follow the American precedent, and make "an ironclad oath" to preserve the union of the two countries [Britain and Ireland] a condition of election.' Cited in *Oxford English Dictionary,* 2nd ed., vol. VIII, s.v. 'ironclad oath.'

10 Sidney and Beatrice Webb, *The History of Trade Unionism* (1894; Clifton, N.J.: Augustus M. Kelley Publishers 1973), pp. 28–9

11 Philip Bagwell, *The History of the National Union of Railwaymen* (London: Allen and Unwin 1963), cited in Mark Hollingsworth and Richard Norton-Taylor, *Blacklist: The Inside Story of Political Vetting* (London: Hogarth Press 1988), p. 9

12 Bernard Porter, *The Origins of the Vigilant State: The London Metropolitan Police Special Branch Before the First World War* (London: Weidenfeld and Nicholson 1987), pp. 3–4

13 Bernard Porter, *Plots and Paranoia: A History of Political Espionage in Britain, 1790–1988* (London: Unwin Hyman 1989), p. 120

14 *Ibid.*, p. 125
15 *Ibid.*
16 *Ibid.*, p. 133. Christopher Andrew, by contrast, argues that a political police emerged in Britain in the early 1880s as a response to Irish republican bombings in London. This threat declined in 1885, and anti-Fenian surveillance fell off. Nonetheless, the Special Branch of the London Metropolitan Police was created in 1887, and it turned its attention to the British wing of the European anarchist movement in the early 1890s. But Andrew agrees that by the turn of the century the Special Branch 'had little of importance left to do,' and that it would take the spy scare of the prewar years to bring the branch back to the prominence the Special Irish Branch enjoyed in the early 1880s. Andrew, *Secret Service*, pp. 43–7.
17 Porter, *Plots and Paranoia*, pp. 137, 400, 409–11; Nicholas Hiley, 'Internal Security in Wartime: The Rise and Fall of P.M.S.2, 1915–1917,' *Intelligence and National Security* 1, no. 3 (September 1986): 399
18 Porter, *Plots and Paranoia*, p. 127
19 David Saunders, 'Aliens in Britain and the Empire During the First World War,' in *Loyalties in Conflict: Ukrainians in Canada during the Great War*, ed. Frances Swyripa and John Herd Thompson (Edmonton: Canadian Institute of Ukrainian Studies 1983), pp. 102, 105
20 *Ibid.*, p. 105
21 Hinsley and Simkins, *British Intelligence*, vol. 4, p. 5
22 *Ibid.*
23 E.H. Carr, *The Soviet Impact on the Western World* (London: Macmillan 1946), pp. 73–4
24 Hinsley and Simkins, *British Intelligence:*, vol. 4, p. 18
25 Nicholas Hiley, '"Not Necessarily a Crime": The Development of British Counter-Espionage during the First World War,' cited in Porter, *Origins of the Vigilant State*, p. 180
26 Hyman, *To Try Men's Souls*, p. 4, and Arthur Doughty, *The Acadian Exiles: A Chronicle of the Land of Evangeline* (Toronto, Glasgow Brook and Co. 1920), pp. 28–9
27 Cited in Hyman, *To Try Men's Souls*, p. 115.
28 *Ibid.*, p. 112
29 Hyman, *Era of the Oath*, p. 1
30 *Ibid.*, pp. 1–2

31 *Ibid.*, pp. 22–3
32 *Ibid.*, pp. 20, 47, 150
33 *Ibid.*, p. 155
34 David Caute, *The Great Fear: The Anti-Communist Purge under Truman and Eisenhower* (New York: Simon and Schuster 1978), p. 267
35 Hyman, *To Try Men's Souls*, pp. 268–70
36 Caute, *The Great Fear*, pp. 403–4
37 Ontario Legislative Library (OLL), W.J. Scott, *Sabotage Prevention*, War Emergency Bulletin No. 8 (Toronto: Ontario Fire Marshal's Office 1940), p. 5
38 Jules Witcover, *Sabotage at Black Tom: Imperial Germany's Secret War in America 1914–1917* (Chapel Hill, N.C.: Algonquin Books 1989), pp. 21, 193, *passim*. Ironically, the legal case for compensation in those two incidents was resolved only after the beginning of the Second World War, in October 1939. At the time, a Washington newspaper concluded: 'The whole sordid Black-Tom-Kingsland episode has served one good purpose, however. It has shown the need in this country of an efficient counter-espionage system in time of peace as well as war.' Witcover, *Sabotage*, p. 308
39 Scott, *Sabotage Prevention*, p. 5
40 Hyman, *To Try Men's Souls*, p. 286
41 *Ibid.*, p. 295
42 *Ibid.*, pp. 308–10
43 David B. Davis, 'Internal Security in Historical Perspective: From the Revolution to World War II,' in *Surveillance and Espionage in a Free Society*, ed. Richard Blum (New York: Praeger 1972), p. 15
44 *Ibid.*, p. 13
45 Naomi Griffiths, *The Acadians: Creation of a People* (Toronto: McGraw-Hill Ryerson 1973), pp. 27, 53
46 A.L. Burt, *The Old Province of Quebec*, 2 vols. (Toronto: McClelland and Stewart 1968), vol. 1, pp. 15–16, 23; Leonard Woods Labaree, ed., *Royal Instructions to British Colonial Governors, 1670–1776* (New York: D. Appleton-Century Co. 1935), vol. I, pp. 38, 501
47 Burt, *Old Province of Quebec*, vol. 2, p. 80
48 C.E. Cartwright, ed., *Life and Letters of the Late Honorable Richard Cartwright* (Toronto: Belford Brothers 1876), pp. 96–7, cited in David

Mills, *The Idea of Loyalty in Upper Canada, 1784–1850* (Kingston and Montreal: McGill-Queen's University Press 1988), p. 21
49 Mills, *Idea of Loyalty*, pp. 132, 137
50 Jeff Keshen, 'Cloak and Dagger: Canada West's Secret Police, 1864–1867,' *Ontario History* 79, no. 4 (December 1987): 353; McDonald, *Commission of Inquiry*, vol. 1, pp. 54–5
51 McDonald, *Commission of Inquiry*, p. 55. The government's security efforts included surveillance of Indian nationalists in the years before and during the First World War. But while this spying resulted in court prosecutions, it did not lead to the creation of a security-screening initiative. On the surveillance of East Indians, see Hugh Johnston, 'The Surveillance of Indian Nationalists in North America, 1908–1918,' in *BC Studies* 78 (summer 1988).
52 Porter, *Origins of the Vigilant State*, p. 69
53 Desmond Morton, *The Canadian General: Sir William Otter* (Toronto: Hakkert 1974), p. 325
54 Martin Kitchen, 'The German Invasion of Canada in the First World War,' *The International History Review* 7, 2 (May 1985): 251–5; Witcover, *Sabotage at Black Tom*, p. 68; OLL, Arthur Slaght, *War-time Sabotage*, War Emergency Bulletin No. 6 (Toronto: Ontario Fire Marshal's Office 1940), pp. 10–11
55 Morton, *Canadian General*, pp. 326–8; Donald Avery, *'Dangerous Foreigners': European Immigrant Workers and Labour Radicalism in Canada, 1896–1932* (Toronto: McClelland and Stewart 1979), p. 66
56 At least in the first years of the war, the internment operation may have been as much a way to cope with high unemployment among recent immigrants as a security measure. See Morton, *Canadian General*, pp. 328, 333–4.
57 *Ibid.*, pp. 327, 334, 341
58 Myer Siemiatycki, 'Munitions and Labour Militancy: The 1916 Hamilton Machinists' Strike,' *Labour/Le Travailleur* 3 (1978): 133
59 Craig Heron, 'Hamilton Steelworkers and the Rise of Mass Production,' *Canadian Historical Papers*, 1982, p. 121
60 Siemiatycki, 'Munitions and Labour Militancy,' p. 139
61 McDonald, *Commission of Inquiry*, vol. 1, pp. 56–8
62 Siemiatycki, 'Munitions and Labour Militancy,' p. 144
63 McDonald, *Commission of Inquiry*, vol. 1, p. 57

64 S.W. Horrall, 'Canada's Security Service: A Brief History,' *RCMP Quarterly*, 50, no. 3 (summer 1985): 43

65 Porter, *Plots and Paranoia*, p. 142

66 RCMP, *Annual Report*, 1922, p. 47

67 Hyman, *To Try Men's Souls*, p. 337

68 Jeffrey Simpson, *Spoils of Power: The Politics of Patronage* (Toronto: Collins 1988), pp. 126–7

69 Edward Shils, *The Torment of Secrecy: The Background and Consequences of American Security Policies* (Glencoe, Ill.: The Free Press 1956), p. 124

70 Canada, Royal Commission to Investigate the Facts Relating to and the Circumstances Surrounding the Communication, by Public Officials and Other Persons in Positions of Trust, of Secret and Confidential Information to Agents of a Foreign Power, *Report* (Ottawa: King's Printer 1946) (hereafter Kellock-Taschereau Commission, *Report*), pp. 72–3

71 Cited in Anthony A. Thompson, *Big Brother in Britain Today* (London: Michael Joseph 1970), p. 62.

72 Cited in John Schaar, *Loyalty in America* (Berkeley and Los Angeles: University of California Press 1957), p. 132.

73 Cited in Gabriel Kolko, *Main Currents in Modern American History* (New York: Harper and Row 1976), p. 30

74 Horrall, 'Canada's Security Service,' p. 45

75 Kolko, *Main Currents*, pp. 92–3, and Barbara Roberts, *Whence They Came: Deportation from Canada, 1900–1935* (Ottawa: University of Ottawa Press 1988), p. 38

76 Even the crudest of security assessors perceived the change – consciously or unconsciously. Senator Joseph McCarthy was distinguished from all previous right-wing demagogues by the fact that he denounced no specific racial, ethnic, or religious group. Disloyalty, for McCarthy, was synonymous with communism, and it was a vice of choice, not of birth. See Caute, *Great Fear*, p. 21.

77 In 1957 John Schaar concluded from his examination of the American security screening experience that 'the program was hampered by ambiguity, vacillation, and indecision' because 'no authority ... has yet ... taken the time and trouble to define the meaning of loyalty, prescribe reliable criteria for determining its presence or

absence in a particular human container, and elaborate the relations between loyalty and security.' Schaar, *Loyalty in America*, p. 134. In the breach, communist affiliation made do.

78 Hinsley and Simkins, *British Intelligence:*, vol. 4, p. 3

79 CSIS Access 117-90-107, Betke and Horrall, 'Canada's Security Service' (Ottawa: RCMP Historical Section 1978), p. 354. Once a researcher has obtained documents under the act, they are effectively open. Other researchers may therefore obtain the same material by citing the appropriate access number. Hereafter these sources will be listed by government department or agency and access request number.

80 Lowenthal, *Federal Bureau of Investigation*, pp. 36, 71, 113; Homer Cummings and Carl McFarland, *Federal Justice: Chapters in the History of Justice and the Federal Executive* (New York: Macmillan 1937), p. 429

81 Cited in Roger Price, 'Techniques of Repression: The Control of Popular Protest in Mid-nineteeth-century France,' *The Historical Journal* 25, no. 4 (1982): 864.

82 *Ibid.*, pp. 859–61

83 Betke and Horrall, 'Canada's Security Service,' p. 352

84 McDonald, *Commission of Inquiry,* vol. 1, p. 57

85 Horrall, 'Canada's Security Service,' p. 43

86 Avery, '*Dangerous Foreigners,*' p. 118

87 Hyman, *Era of the Oath*, p. 151

88 Michel Foucault, *Discipline and Punish: The Birth of the Prison*, trans. Allan Sheridan (New York: Vintage Books 1979), p. 281; Betke and Horrall, 'Canada's Security Service,' p. 318; Lowenthal, *Federal Bureau of Investigation*, p. 90; Cummings and McFarland, *Federal Justice*, p. 429

CHAPTER 2 The politics of identification

1 National Archives of Canada (NA), RG 18, Acc. 83-84/321, box 25, file 234-2, Circular Memorandum No. 173, 22 October 1931

2 S.W. Horrall, *The Pictorial History of the Royal Canadian Mounted Police* (Toronto: McGraw-Hill Ryerson 1973), pp. 195–7

3 Betke and Horrall, 'Canada's Security Service,' p. 435

4 CSIS Access 87-A-39, Foran to MacBrien, 28 September 1931, and MacBrien to Foran, 9 November 1931

5 NA, RG 18, Acc. 83-84/321 box 25, file 234-2, Brown to the Officer Commanding Saskatchewan District, 14 November 1931. Emphasis added.

6 *Ibid.*, Wood to Officer Commanding Saskatchewan District, 17 January 1932. It is not clear why all the recorded cases of officers refusing to submit to fingerprinting were in the Saskatoon subdistrict of Saskatchewan.

7 RCMP, *Annual Report*, 1941, p. 56; 1946, p. 39; CSIS Access 89-A-63, RCMP Intelligence and Liaison Section Annual Report, 1941

8 NA, RG 18, vol. 3462, file 0-252 (vol. 1), Personal file of Drysdale, Alexander, Drysdale to Officer Commanding Saskatoon Sub District, 31 October 1931. Emphasis added.

9 NA, RG 18, Acc. 83-84/321 box 25, file 234-2, Kemp to the Director, CIB, 11 March 1932

10 'New credit card security system scans shoppers' veins,' *Globe and Mail*, 29 December 1988, p. B11

11 NA, RG18, vol. 3754, file 1920-(139) International Association for Identification Minutes – 1920, A.J. Renoe, 'The Commercial Value of Finger prints,' pp. 24–6. Emphasis added.

12 Herschel first used palm prints to enforce a commercial contract, demanding that a road construction contractor affix his palm print along with his signature to ensure that an obligation to the state would be fulfilled. He later gravitated toward fingerprinting as a more adaptable system. See Sir Percival Griffiths, *To Guard My People: The History of the Indian Police* (London: Ernest Benn 1971), p. 334.

13 *The Times*, 21 February 1931, p. 7

14 John Berry, 'The History and Development of Fingerprinting,' in *Advances in Fingerprint Technology*, ed. Henry C. Lee and R.E. Gaensslen (New York and Amsterdam: Elsevier 1991), p. 25

15 U.S., Department of Justice, Federal Bureau of Investigation, *Fingerprint Identification: The Identification Division of the FBI* (Washington, D.C.: U.S. Government Printing Office 1986), p. 3. E.H. Henry wrote that it was rejected at the time because it 'had not then been sufficiently popularized.' Griffiths, *To Guard My People*, p. 334,

citing E.R. Henry, *The Classification and Uses of Fingerprints* (London 1900), p. 4.

16 Berry, 'History and Development of Fingerprint,' p. 25

17 *The Times*, 21 February 1931, p. 7

18 'Criminal' must be understood in a broad way. For example, in 1871 the Madras state administration passed the Criminal Tribes Act (amended in 1911), which designated certain tribes as criminal. David Arnold indicates that 'in one way or another these "criminal tribes" were at odds with an expanding and assertive economic and administrative order.' The act provided for special settlements to be set up for such tribes, confinement that a 1946 provincial inquiry compared to Nazi concentration camps. Members of the tribe were required to register and be fingerprinted. Refusal to submit to fingerprinting itself constituted a criminal offence, punishable by six months' imprisonment or a fine of Rs 200 or both. David Arnold, *Police Power and Colonial Rule: Madras, 1859–1947* (Delhi: Oxford University Press 1986), pp. 142–4

19 FBI, *Fingerprint Identification*, p. 4

20 Richard Popplewell, 'The Surveillance of Indian Revolutionaries in Great Britain and on the Continent, 1905–14,' *Intelligence and National Security* 3, no. 1 (January 1988): 57. Henry is an outstanding example of what E.P. Thompson calls the 'feed-back of imperialism ... to the streets of the imperial capital itself.' Describing an earlier chief commissioner of the London Metropolitan Police, Sir Charles Warren, Thompson writes that 'he reminds us of the inter-recruitment, cross-posting, and exchange of both ideology and experience between those who learned to handle crowds, invigilate subversives, and engage in measures of "pacification" in the external empire, and those who struggled with the Labour Problem, the Unemployed Question, the Women Problem, and sometimes just the People Problem, at home.' State Research Working Group, *Review of Security and the State 1978* (London: Julian Friedmann 1978), p. v. The words equally apply to Henry.

Bernard Porter points out that the connection between the British empire and the early British secret service is strong. Many senior officers of the security services were recruited from colonial, usually colonial military, backgrounds. Henry was merely part of a long

line. The one exception to this was self-governing dominions, such as Canada and Australia, from whom Britain acquired no secret police or espionage chiefs. Porter, *Plots and Paranoia*, p. 124.
21 *Dictionary of National Biography, 1931–1940* (London: Oxford University Press 1940), pp. 421–2
22 *The Times*, 21 February 1931, p. 7; FBI, *Fingerprint Identification*, p. 6
23 Renoe, 'The Commercial Value of Finger prints,' p. 23
24 FBI, *Fingerprint Identification*, p. 7
25 NA, RG 18, vol. 3754, file 1920-(139) International Association for Identification Minutes – 1920, pp. 23–4
26 U.S., Department of Justice, Federal Bureau of Investigation, *The Science of Fingerprints: Classification and Uses* (Washington, D.C.: U.S. Government Printing Office 1984), pp. 80–2, 83
27 *Ibid.*, p. 103
28 'Fingerprint Identification Devices,' *Scientific American* 147, no. 3 (September 1932): 177
29 Survey of *RCMP Quarterly*, 1933–8
30 *Globe and Mail*, 14 October 1991, p. A7
31 Canadian Association of Chiefs of Police (CACP), Minutes of Chief Constables' Association of Canada (CCAC), 8th Annual Convention, 1912, p. 9
32 Richard Ericson and Clifford Shearing, 'The Scientification of Police Work,' in *The Knowledge Society: The Growing Impact of Scientific Knowledge on Social Relations*, ed. Gernot Bohme and Nico Stehr (Dordrecht, Holland, and Boston: D Reidel 1986), pp. 132–3
33 *Ibid.*, p. 133
34 Michel Foucault's study of the changes in the nature of discipline and punishment during the past three centuries suggests another fruitful way of looking at the scientific aspect of fingerprinting. In *Discipline and Punish* he speaks about the subjugation of the human body, which helps mould people into willing or unwilling participants in the capitalist economy. This pressure is applied not only through 'instruments of violence and ideology' but also through science. Discipline, he contends, 'may be calculated, organized, technically thought out; it may be subtle, make use neither of weapons nor of terror and yet remain of a physical order. That is to say, there may be a "knowledge" of the body that is not exactly the science of

its functioning, and a mastery of its forces that is more than the ability to conquer them: this knowledge and this mastery constitute what might be called the political technology of the body.' There is no better example of a political technology of the body than fingerprinting. It is a technology that constructs a meaningful social map from the apparently random tangle of lines on people's fingertips. It identified a person and tied him or her to a past and to other places. Today fingerprinting is one of many such technologies. But beginning at the turn of the twentieth century, when it demonstrated its mastery over the Bertillon system, fingerprinting was *the* political technology of the body. It kept that exalted status for half a century, enjoying a singular authority in the minds of public and police alike. Viewing fingerprinting in a Foucauldian way as a political technology of the body merits greater elaboration, although this is not appropriate or possible here. See Foucault, *Discipline and Punish*, p. 26.

35 *Ibid.*, p. 6
36 Frederick R. Cherrill, *The Finger Print System at Scotland Yard: A Practical Treatise on Finger Print Identification for the Use of Students and Experts and a Guide for Investigators When Dealing with Imprints Left at the Scenes of Crime* (London: Her Majesty's Stationery Office 1954), p. 8
37 Berry, 'History and Development of Fingerprinting,' p. 35
38 Greg Marquis, *Policing Canada's Century: A History of the Canadian Association of Chiefs of Police* (Toronto, Buffalo, London: University of Toronto Press 1993), p. 6
39 Royal Canadian Mounted Police, *Fifty Years of Fingerprinting: The RCMP Identification Branch* (n.p. n.d.) (first published in the *RCMP Quarterly* 26, no. 3 [January 1961]), pp. 1–2; Marquis, *Policing Canada's Century*, pp. 68–9.
40 *Ibid.*, p. 4
41 NA, RG 18, vol. 3754, file 1920-(139) International Association for Identification Minutes – 1920, Inspector James Anderson, 'Finger Print Identification in Canada,' pp. 31–2
42 Eugene B. Block, *Fingerprinting: A Magic Weapon against Crime* (New York: David McKay 1969), pp. 119–20
43 NA, RG 76, vol. 568, file 812274, Blair to Smith, 24 Nov. 1922; RG 18, vol. 3754, file G-516-26-1, CCAC Minutes, 1928

44 RCMP, *Fifty Years of Fingerprinting*, pp. 1, 6, 11
45 NA, RG 18, Acc. 84-85/084, file G-516-26-1 (vol. 1 Supplement), Report on the 1927 annual convention of the CCAC and synopsis of the 1929 CCAC annual convention
46 NA, RG 18, Acc. 85-86/048, box 54, file S-955-4 (1961), Jennings to MacBrien, 15 July 1932
47 *RCMP Quarterly* 5, no. 3 (January 1938): 175
48 NA, RG 18, Acc. 85-86/574, box 9, file G-537-1, Wood to Commissioner, 8 August 1939
49 RSC, 1927, c. 38, p. 1097; NA, RG 18, Acc. 84-85/84, box 30, file G-516-26-1 vol. 1, Aylesworth to the Governor General in Council, 15 March 1911
50 Department of Justice Access A87-00067, letter to solicitor general of Canada, 1 Sept. 1982, and 8 Nov. 1982 reply; NA, RG 18, Acc. 84-85/084, file G-516-26-1 (vol. 2), Wonnacott to Commissioner of the Metropolitan Police, London, 9 Sept. 1946
51 Marquis, *Policing Canada's Century*, p. 73
52 *Globe and Mail*, 29 Dec. 1988, p. B11
53 Canadian Association of Chiefs of Police, *Canadian Police Bulletin*, 1928, pp. 70, 73
54 Richard Enright, 'Everybody Should Be Fingerprinted: A System of Universal Registration Would Benefit Especially Those Who Were Recorded,' *Scientific American* 133, no. 4 (October 1925): 225
55 *Canadian Police Bulletin*, 1928, p. 66
56 G.B., House of Commons, *Debates*, 17 November 1937, p. 403
57 'Fingerprints,' *Civil Liberty* No. 7 (July 1939): 7
58 Lowenthal, *Federal Bureau of Investigation*, p. 375
59 Herbert Fearon, 'Uncle Sam, Ace Detective,' *Scientific American*, 151 no. 4 (October 1934): 174; NA, RG 18, vol. 3565, file G-537-20, Wonnacott to Kemp, 18 November 1943
60 Ryley Cooper, 'Fingerprinting for Protection,' *Reader's Digest* 35 (August 1939): 75
61 Lowenthal, *Federal Bureau of Investigation*, p. 375
62 FBI, *Fingerprint Identification*, pp. 4–5, 9
63 Lowenthal, *Federal Bureau of Investigation*, pp. 380–2
64 U.S., Department of Justice, Federal Bureau of Investigation, *Report of the Director for the Fiscal Year 1942* (hereafter FBI, *Annual Report*),

p. 14. The report records that by the end of 1941, when the United States entered the war, the FBI had almost 22 million fingerprints in its files, half of them non-criminal.

65 *Thumbs Down!: The Fingerprint Menace to Civil Liberties* (New York: American Civil Liberties Union 1938), p. 4

66 Vera Connolly, 'Uncle Sam Wants Your Mark,' *Good Housekeeping* 101 (December 1935): 152

67 *Finger Printing – For What? A Memorandum on the Movement for Voluntary and Compulsory Finger-printing* (New York: American Civil Liberties Union 1936), p. 1

68 *Thumbs Down!* p. 12

69 *Finger Printing – For What?* p. 4

70 *Thumbs Down!* p. 6

71 J. Arthur Piers, 'Finger-printing for Protection,' *Canadian Magazine* 90, no. 6 (December 1938): 58

72 CACP, CCAC Minutes, 34th Annual Convention, pp. 113–4. Emphasis added.

73 NA, RG 18, vol. 3754, file G-516-26-1, minutes of Chief Constables' Association for 1927 and 1929

74 NA, RG 18, vol. 3754, file G-516-26-1, minutes of Chief Constables' Association for 1926 and 1928; *Canadian Police Bulletin*, 1928, p. 71

75 NA, RG 18, vol. 3754, file G-516-26-1, minutes of Chief Constables' Association for 1927 and 1929

76 CACP, CCAC Minutes, 27th Annual Convention, p. 77

77 RCMP Access 87HR 1386, Edwards to RCMP Commissioner, 18 April 1934, and Jennings to Edwards, 3 May 1934

78 RCMP Access 87HR 1386, extract of communication, Meller to Director of Criminal Investigation, 23 July 1937

79 Barbara Roberts, *Whence They Came: Deportation from Canada, 1900–1935* (Ottawa: University of Ottawa Press 1988), p. 134. The cause for deportations changed dramatically in the years in which finger-printing became widely used by Canadian police. From 1903 to 1910 the number deported for criminality averaged only 4 per cent. The percentage deported for medical reasons was extremely high, reaching a peak of 80 per cent in 1906. But beginning in 1910 the criminal deportations, which had been single digit percentages throughout the period from 1903, suddenly jumped to 17 per cent and grew to a

height of 56 per cent in 1921. Thereafter, it fell off, to be replaced by the cause of becoming a public charge, which reached a peak of 69 per cent in 1933. It is likely more than coincidence that criminal deportations were highest in the decade in which fingerprinting gained official sanction and was adopted by the Canadian police. See Roberts, *Whence They Came*, p. 46, table IV.

80 CACP, CCAC Minutes, 27th Annual Convention, p. 77
81 NA, King Papers, MG 26, J2, vol. 157, file J-157, Jones to King, 31 May 1938
82 CACP, CCAC Minutes, 33rd Annual Convention, p. 95
83 NA, RG 76, vol 568, file 812274, Scott to Perry, 26 Jan. 1920; Scott to Ragimbal, 15 July 1920. Emphasis added.
84 RCMP, *Fifty Years of Fingerprinting*, p. 13
85 H.R. Butchers, 'Fingerprint Identification in Wartime,' *RCMP Gazette* 6, no. 30 (26 July 1944): 2
86 NA, RG 18, vol. 3754, file G-516-26-1, minutes of Chief Constables' Association for 1926
87 H.R. Butchers, 'How National Finger Printing Would Benefit the General Public,' *RCMP Quarterly* 2, no. 4 (April 1935): 16
88 RCMP historian William Beahen to author, 30 June 1993, citing RCMP file GL302-14-1, W.W. Watson memo of 17 April 1939
89 Krishnalal Shridharani, *War without Violence: A Study of Gandhi's Method and Its Accomplishments* (New York and London: Garland Publishing 1972), pp. 75–9
90 *Thumbs Down!* p. 13
91 *Ibid.*, p. 18
92 NA, RG 18, vol. 3754, file G-516-26-1, Reports on the annual meetings of the Chief Constables' Association for 1926 to 1929; *Canadian Police Bulletin*, 1928, pp. 70–4
93 William Banks, 'Why Fingerprint the Immigrant,' *Saturday Night*, 3 November 1928
94 Piers, 'Finger-Printing for Protection,' p. 58
95 Canada, House of Commons, *Debates*, 22 May 1929, p. 2755
96 Canada, Senate, *Debates*, 12 June 1931, p. 257
97 NA, King Papers, MG 26, J2, vol 157, file J-157, Jones to King, 31 May 1938. Emphasis added.
98 *Canadian Congress Journal*, February 1939, p. 8

99 RCMP Access 87HR 1386, extract of communication, St Pierre to Campbellton Subdivison, 6 April 1934. Emphasis original.
100 Canada, House of Commons, *Debates*, 5 April 1935, p. 2448
101 RCMP Access 87HR 1386, extract of communication from Blake, 9 April 1935
102 *Ibid.*; extract of communication, Jennings to Edwards, 20 April 1935

CHAPTER 3 The birth of state vetting

1 Charles Rivett-Carnac, *Pursuit in the Wilderness* (Boston and Toronto: Little, Brown and Co. 1965), p. 293
2 Stephen Harris, *Canadian Brass: The Making of a Professional Army, 1860–1939* (Toronto: University of Toronto Press 1988), p. 169
3 Canada, House of Commons, *Debates*, 1 August 1931, p. 4453; 3 May 1932, pp. 2591–2
4 Sawatsky, *Men in the Shadows*, p. 58
5 Roberts, *Whence They Came*, pp. 81–2, 84
6 Avery, *'Dangerous Foreigners,'* p. 75
7 Roberts, *Whence They Came*, pp. 80, 83
8 Nora Kelly and William Kelly, *The Royal Canadian Mounted Police: A Century of History, 1873–1973* (Edmonton: Hurtig Publishers 1973), p. 147
9 S.W. Horrall, 'The Royal North-West Mounted Police and Labour Unrest in Western Canada, 1919,' *Canadian Historical Review* 61, no. 2 (June 1980): 172
10 Sawatsky, *Men in the Shadows*, p. 56
11 McDonald, *Commission of Inquiry*, vol. 1, p. 56
12 A. Ross McCormack, *Reformers, Rebels, and Revolutionaries: The Western Canadian Radical Movement, 1899–1919* (Toronto: University of Toronto Press 1977), pp. 130–1
13 Charles K. Talbot, C.H.S. Jayewardene, and Tony J. Juliani, *The Thin Blue Line: An Historical Perspective of Policing in Canada* (Ottawa: Crimcare 1983), p. 26
14 Horrall, 'The RNWMP and Labour Unrest,' pp. 174–5
15 *Ibid.*, p. 174
16 Gregory S. Kealey, 'State Repression of Labour and the Left in Can-

ada, 1914–20: The Impact of the First World War,' *Canadian Historical Review* 73, no. 3 (September 1992): 301

17 Horrall, 'RNWMP and Labour Unrest,' pp. 177–8, 184
18 *Ibid.*, p. 174
19 Betke and Horrall, 'Canada's Security Service,' p. 330
20 Canada, House of Commons, *Debates*, 20 March 1934, p. 1663
21 McDonald, *Commission of Inquiry*, vol. 1, pp. 58–9, 64
22 Horrall, 'RNWMP and Labour Unrest,' pp. 188–9
23 Sawatsky, *Men in the Shadows*, pp. 59–60
24 Betke and Horrall, 'Canada's Security Service,' pp. 387–8
25 *Ibid.*, p. 387; Gregory S. Kealey, 'The Early Years of State Surveillance of Labour and the Left in Canada: The Institutional Framework of the Royal Canadian Mounted Police Security and Intelligence Apparatus, 1918–1926,' *Intelligence and National Security* 8, no. 3 (July 1993): 134
26 Ivan Avakumovic, *The Communist Party in Canada: A History* (Toronto: McClelland and Stewart 1975), p. 21
27 *Ibid.*, p. 15; Avery, *'Dangerous Foreigners,'* p. 139
28 Canada, House of Commons, *Debates*, 3 May 1932, p. 2592
29 Canada, *Statutes*, 1914, 4-5 Geo. 5, c. 44
30 Roberts, *Whence They Came*, p. 71, and *passim*
31 Avery, *'Dangerous Foreigners,'* p. 118; NA, RG 18, Acc 85-86/574, box 9, file G-537-1, Watson to Douglas, 7 August 1926
32 *Ibid.*, Jennings to Officer Commanding, Headquarters Division, 11 March 1935
33 Canada, *Second Report, Commission of Inquiry Concerning Certain Activities of the Royal Canadian Mounted Police* (McDonald Commission), vol. 2, *Freedom and Security under the Law*, Part VI (Ottawa: Ministry of Supply and Services 1981) (hereafter McDonald, *Commission of Inquiry*, vol. 2), p. 829
34 NA, RG 76, vol. 568, file 812274, Blair to Smith, 24 November 1922
35 Avery, *'Dangerous Foreigners,'* p. 88
36 Roberts, *Whence They Came*, p. 134
37 *Ibid.*, pp. 92–3
38 J.E. Hodgetts *et al.*, *The Biography of an Institution: The Civil Service Commission of Canada, 1908–1967* (Montreal: Institute of Public

Administration of Canada and McGill-Queen's University Press 1972), pp. 51–2

39 *Ibid.*, p. 96
40 I owe this observation to Reg Whitaker.
41 RCMP, *Annual Report*, 1931, pp. 18, 56
42 In doing this the CSC was following the path of the New York State CSC, which had inaugurated fingerprinting in the United States in 1902. See FBI, *Fingerprint Identification*, pp. 4–5, 9.
43 CSIS Access 89-A-31. These records indicate that screening of CBC employees began after 1945.
44 CSIS Access 87-A-39, Foran to Starnes, 28 February 1931; Starnes to Foran, 10 March 1931; Foran to MacBrien, 28 September 1931; MacBrien to Foran, 9 November 1931
45 RCMP, *Annual Report*, 1935, p. 33
46 In 1947 the Security Panel reasoned that 'the terms of the Civil Service Act are sufficiently broad to permit rejection of an applicant for employment on security grounds' (NA, MG 26, J1, vol. 429, Security Panel Document 22, 9 Sept. 1947). This is the only justification of civil service security screening I have been able to unearth. Section 4(a) of the act stipulates that one of the duties of the Civil Service Commission is 'to test and pass upon the qualifications of candidates for admission to ... the civil service ...' (*RSC*, 1927), Aside from this broad mandate, the act says nothing which would specifically permit security screening, and it contains no mention of fingerprinting.
47 RCMP, *Annual Report*, 1932, p. 131; 1934, p. 30; 1936, pp. 37, 118; 1937, p. 34; 1938, p. 34; 1939, p. 37
48 Hodgetts *et al.*, *Biography of an Institution*, p. 500
49 NA, RG 76, vol. 446, file 675985, pt. 1, Blair to District Supt. of Immigration, Winnipeg, 26 Sept. 1939.
50 Lawrence Aronsen, 'Some Aspects of Surveillance: "Peace, Order and Good Government" during the Cold War: The Origins and Organization of Canada's Internal Security Program,' *Intelligence and National Security* 1, no. 3 (September 1986): 364–5
51 CSIS Access 87-A-39, extract of communication, Mercer to the Commissioner, 4 March 1938
52 RCMP, *Annual Report*, 1932, p. 48

53 *Ibid.*, p. 69
54 'Automated Fingerprint Processing – A Step Forward,' *FBI Law Enforcement Bulletin*, October 1970, p. 3
55 John Shattuck, 'Computer matching is a serious threat to individual rights,' *Communications of the ACM* 27, no. 6 (June 1984): 538
56 Kealey, 'Early Years of State Surveillance,' p. 134
57 RCMP, *Annual Report*, 1921, p. 47
58 Canada, House of Commons, *Debates*, 3 April 1933, p. 3636; Canada, Senate, *Debates*, 12 June 1931, p. 242
59 CSIS Access 89-A-63, Annual Report of the RCMP Intelligence and Liaison Section for 1939
60 AO, MU 7152, file 3, Hill to the Commissioner, 4 October 1938
61 *Ibid.*, file 1, Wood to Wismer, 20 February 1939
62 David Bercuson, *Fools and Wise Men: The Rise and Fall of the One Big Union* (Toronto: McGraw-Hill Ryerson 1978), p. 93
63 RCMP, *Annual Report*, 1931, pp. 27–8
64 S.R. Elliot, *Scarlet to Green: A History of Intelligence in the Canadian Army 1903–1963* (Toronto: Canadian Intelligence and Security Association 1981), pp. 71–2
65 NA, RG 24, vol. 6596, file HQ 1685-4, Sherwood to Adjutant General, 2 April 1917; A/Adjutant-General to Sherwood, 9 April 1917
66 NA, RG 24, vol. 6596, file HQ 1685-4, Wood to Deputy Minister, DND, 27 October 1938; LaFleche to Wood, 3 December 1938
67 Harvison's own RCMP personnel file indicates that he received three lectures on communism, but none on fascism, when he attended an upgrading course at Depot Division in Regina in April 1937. RCMP Access 92ATIP 1550, 0-311, 23 April 1937 report to Officer Commanding, C Division.
68 Betke and Horrall, 'Canada's Security Service,' pp. 436–7
69 *RCMP Quarterly* 3, nos. 1-3 (July and October 1935, January 1936); C.W. Harvison, *The Horsemen* (Toronto: McClelland and Stewart 1967), p. 84
70 Harvison, *Horsemen*, p. 86
71 Betke and Horrall, 'Canada's Security Service,' p. 402
72 Gregory S. Kealey, 'The RCMP, the Special Branch, and the Early Days of the Communist Party of Canada: A Documentary Article,' *Labour/Le Travail* 30 (fall 1992): 170–1

73 Hinsley and Simkins, *British Intelligence*, vol. 4, p. 141; Betke and Horrall, 'Canada's Security Service,' p. 465

74 S.W. Horrall, letter to author, 8 August 1988; Betke and Horrall, 'Canada's Security Service,' p. 510

75 Elliot, *Scarlet to Green*, pp. 80–1

76 NA, MG 26, J4, vol. 230, 13 December 1939, memo

77 Betke and Horrall, 'Canada's Security Service,' pp. 386–7, 405

78 *Ibid.*, pp. 407–8, 465a

79 *Ibid.*, pp. 501–2

80 CSIS Access 117-91-61, Minutes of the Western Hemisphere Intelligence Conference, 3 August 1942, p. 1

81 Betke and Horrall, 'Canada's Security Service,' pp. 393–5

82 *Ibid.*, pp. 397-8

83 Sawatsky, *Men in the Shadows*, p. 60

84 West, *MI5*, p. 138

85 Hollingsworth and Norton-Taylor, *Blacklist*, p. 101. Actor Michael Redgrave was one of the first of several celebrated artists to run afoul of this vetting. In February 1941 he was banned from the air after signing the 'People's Convention,' a communist-sponsored manifesto which called for 'a people's war' and 'a people's peace.' Protests by members of parliament and fellow actors caused the ban to be lifted three weeks later. Michael Redgrave, *In My Mind's Eye: An Autobiography* (London: Weidenfeld and Nicolson 1983), pp. 135–46.

86 Advertisement for conference, 'The Civil Rights of Black-coated Workers,' organized by National Council for Civil Liberties, 18 February 1939

87 Hinsley and Simkins, *British Intelligence*, vol. 4, p. 32

88 Porter, *Plots and Paranoia*, p. 186

89 Peter Wright, *Spycatcher: The Candid Autobiography of a Senior Intelligence Officer* (New York: Viking 1987), p. 122

90 West, *MI5*, pp. 74–6

91 Athan Theoharis, comp., *FBI filing and records procedures*, (Wilmington, Del.: Scholarly Resources, 1983), Section Three, Classification No. 35, 'Civil Service'

92 Athan Theoharis, *FBI Manuals of Instruction, Investigative Procedures and Guidelines, 1927–78* (Wilmington, Del.: Scholarly Resources, 1983), 1936 manual, Section 19, p. 2

93 Connolly, 'Uncle Sam Wants Your Mark,' p. 155
94 Lowenthal, *Federal Bureau of Investigation*, p. 382. Emphasis added.

CHAPTER 4 The infernal machine

1 *Globe and Mail*, 8 March 1941, p. 25
2 *Globe and Mail*, 24 January 1941, p. 11
3 H.R. Butchers, 'Fingerprint identification in wartime,' *RCMP Gazette* 6, no. 29 (19 July 1944): 1
4 NA, RG 28, A, vol. 134, file 44, Development of Industrial Security Branch Department of Munitions and Supply, 15 September 1943, p. 10
5 RCMP, *Annual Report*, 1946, p. 39. At war's end the RCMP's civil fingerprint collection numbered 1.1 million. (Canada, House of Commons, *Debates*, 24 March 1947, p. 1652.) This declaration would corroborate the RCMP *Annual Report* figure, since it is reasonable to estimate that about 100,000 civilian fingerprints were taken before the war and from September 1945 to 1947. It should be acknowledged that some people must have been fingerprinted more than once during the course of the war, so the absolute numbers of fingerprints held by the RCMP exaggerate the number of people fingerprinted and screened.
6 CSIS Access 89-A-63, RCMP Intelligence and Liaison Section Annual Report, 1941; RCMP, *Annual Report*, 1941, p. 56
7 It appears that the pressure of fingerprinting war plant employees and armed forces personnel contributed to a slight reduction in CSC use of the RCMP fingerprinting service during the war. The practice of fingerprinting candidates at CSC examinations fell into disuse, and was revived only in 1946. Nevertheless, CSC candidates had criminal and subversive checks done on them. CSIS Access 86-A-85, McNaughton report, 8 July 1946, and Parsons to DCI, 22 May 1946.
8 The figure 2.3 million represents the number of fingerprint sets sent to the RCMP. Since people changed jobs during the war and hence were fingerprinted more than once, that number does not correspond exactly with the number of individuals fingerprinted. It is impossible to know precisely how many people were fingerprinted, but it was not likely less than 2 million.

9 Robert Bothwell and Jack Granatstein, *The Gouzenko Transcripts* (Toronto: Deneau 1983), pp. 18–9
10 *Globe and Mail*, 18 August 1939, p. 6
11 Kealey and Whitaker, *R.C.M.P. Security Bulletins, 1939–1941*, p. 10
12 NA, RG 35/7, vol. 24, file Civil-Defence, 'Civil Defence in Canada 1936 to 1946'
13 Ramsay Cook, 'Canadian Freedom in Wartime, 1939–1945,' in *His Own Man: Essays in Honour of Arthur Reginald Marsden Lower*, ed. W.H. Heick and Roger Graham (Montreal: McGill-Queen's University Press 1974), p. 38
14 C.P. Stacey, *Arms, Men and Governments: The War Policies of Canada, 1939–1945* (Ottawa: Queen's Printer 1970), p. 111
15 *Canadian Congress Journal*, October 1939, p. 31
16 *Canadian Congress Journal*, October 1940, p. 23
17 *Canadian Unionist*, September 1939, p. 107
18 *Canadian Congress Journal*, June 1940, p. 10
19 *Canadian Unionist*, September 1939, p. 107
20 *Canadian Unionist*, April 1941, p. 265. See also *Canadian Congress Journal* February 1941, p. 6; April 1941, p. 7; June 1941, p. 4; December 1941, p. 9.
21 Bryan Palmer, *Working Class Experience: Rethinking the History of Canadian Labour, 1800–1991*, 2nd ed. (Toronto: McClelland and Stewart 1992), p. 247
22 Avakumovic, *Communist Party in Canada*, p. 140
23 *Clarion*, 23 March 1940, p. 1
24 *Canadian Congress Journal*, January 1940, p. 8
25 *Canadian Unionist*, September 1940, p. 91
26 *Toronto Clarion*, 1 May 1940, p. 4
27 Irving Abella, *Nationalism, Communism, and Canadian Labour: The CIO, the Communist Party, and the Canadian Congress of Labour, 1935–1956* (Toronto: University of Toronto Press 1973), pp. 25, 31, 38, 43
28 *Canadian Unionist*, April 1941, p. 247. Emphasis added.
29 Ontario Hydro Archives (OHA), file 160.01, memo from chief municipal engineer, 20 June 1940; Kealey and Whitaker, *R.C.M.P. Security Bulletins: 1939–1941*, pp. 261, 269; *Globe and Mail*, 10 June 1940, p. 4
30 Robert Keyserlingk, '"Agents within the Gates": The Search for

Nazi Subversives in Canada during World War II,' *Canadian Historical Review* 66, no. 2 (1985): 224

31 NA, RG 76, vol. 446, file 675985, pt. 1, 31 August 1939, report
32 Keyserlingk, '"Agents within the Gates,"' p. 239; Lubomyr Luciuk, *A Time for Atonement: Canada's First National Internment Operations and the Ukrainian Canadians, 1914–1920* (Kingston, Ont.: The Limestone Press 1988), p. 7
33 The internment of some 24,000 Japanese Canadians represents an anomaly to the general trend, a reversion to an earlier policy of mass rather than selective internment of aliens. The forcible transfer of these people, it should be noted, was carried out despite the RCMP's intelligence assessments to the contrary. See Betke and Horrall, 'Canada's Security Service,' p. 477, and Kealey and Whitaker, *R.C.M.P. Security Bulletins, 1942–1945*, p. 20.
34 S.T. Wood, 'Tools for Treachery,' *Canadian Spokesman* 1, no. 2 (February 1941): p. 3
35 Avery, *'Dangerous Foreigners,'* pp. 13, 116
36 Lita-Rose Betcherman, *The Swastika and the Maple Leaf: Fascist Movements in Canada in the Thirties* (Toronto: Fitzhenry and Whiteside 1975), p. 128; Jonathan F. Wagner, *Brothers beyond the Sea: National Socialism in Canada* (Waterloo, Ont.: Wilfrid Laurier University Press 1981), pp. 64–5 and *passim*
37 NA, RG 25, G1, vol. 1964, file 855-E, pt 1, Robertson memo, 6 September 1939
38 Harvison, *Horsemen*, p. 101
39 Kealey and Whitaker, *R.C.M.P. Security Bulletins: 1939–1941*, p. 22
40 NA, MG 26, J4, vol. 372, file 3913, Pickersgill note and analysis, 27 November 1939
41 Horrall, 'Canada's Security Service,' p. 45
42 NA, RG 27, III, B10, vol. 50, file 41, Wood to Lapointe, 25 August 1939
43 Kealey and Whitaker, *R.C.M.P. Security Bulletins: 1939–1941*, p. 22
44 William Lyon Mackenzie King, 'Diaries,' microfiche ed. (Toronto: University of Toronto Press n.d.) (hereafter cited as King Diary), 24 November 1939
45 *Vancouver Sun*, 7 May 1940, p. 4
46 *Saturday Night*, 8 June 1940, p. 1

47 Kealey and Whitaker, *R.C.M.P. Security Bulletins: 1939–1941*, p. 222
48 *Ibid.*, pp. 201, 206, 361, and *passim*
49 AO, RG 33, Series I-1, U.S.A. 1940–1946, Scott to Tamm, 20 May 1940
50 Avakumovic, *Communist Party in Canada*, pp. 141–2
51 *Toronto Clarion*, 26 September 1940, p. 2
52 Peter Hunter, *Which Side Are You on, Boys? Canadian Life on the Left* (Toronto: Lugus Productions 1988), p. 120
53 Avakumovic, *Communist Party in Canada*, p. 144
54 In addition to the first volume of the Second World War bulletins, see Kealey and Whitaker, *R.C.M.P. Security Bulletins: 1942–1945.*
55 Political Bureau of the CPC, 'A National Front For Victory,' as quoted in Kealey and Whitaker, *R.C.M.P. Security Bulletins: 1939–1941*, p. 409
56 *Ibid.*, p. 390
57 Elizabeth Grace and Colin Leys, 'The Concept of Subversion and its Implications,' in *Dissent and the State*, ed. C.E.S. Franks (Toronto: Oxford University Press 1989), p. 65
58 *The Story of Secret Service* ominously forecast that the next war would see saboteurs who would 'detonate, ignite and demolish opponents with vivid effect and quiet contentment.' *The Story of Secret Service* (New York: Literary Guild of America 1937), p. 521. The 1987 National Intelligence Book Center catalogue describes Hitchcock's *Sabotage* (1936) as 'filled with the master's touches, the most famous of which is the innocent boy carrying a bomb set to go off at any moment. Considerable tension.' *The Man Who Knew Too Much* was produced in 1934 and *The Secret Agent* in 1936. A 1942 Hitchcock film, called *Saboteur*, has a plot vividly evocative of wartime political culture: 'Unjustly accused of sabotage, a war worker flees and exposes a spy ring.' National Intelligence Book Center, *Catalogue* (Washington, D.C. spring 1987), p. 95.
59 Cited in Irving Abella and David Millar, eds. *The Canadian Worker in the Twentieth Century* (Toronto: Oxford University Press 1978), p. 272
60 See, for instance, *Daily Clarion*, 2 June 1939, p. 1, and 2 June 1939, pp. 1–2.
61 OHA, file 160.01, chief operating engineer to chief engineer, 22 April 1939

62 Betke and Horrall, 'Canada's Security Service,' p. 478
63 *Globe and Mail*, 13 June 1940, p. 3
64 Canada, House of Commons, *Debates*, 18 June 1940, pp. 853–4
65 *Globe and Mail*, 15 May 1940, p. 4
66 *Vancouver Daily Province*, 27 May 1940, p. 3, and 29 May 1940, p. 5
67 *Ibid.*, 30 May 1940, p. 11. This is an interesting illustration of the blending of fear of nazis and communists. It also reveals that officials used anxiety about a pro-nazi threat to strike at the communists.
68 *Toronto Star*, 23 May 1940, p. 5
69 *Globe and Mail*, 10 June 1940, p. 4
70 *Le Devoir*, 28 May 1940, p. 10; *Canadian Tribune*, 1 June 1940, p. 1
71 Canada, House of Commons, *Debates*, 27 May 1940, p. 223; 30 May 1940, p. 358
72 *Ibid.*, 20 May 1940, p. 21
73 AO, RG 33, Series I-1, file 84.3, Tamm to Scott, 11 Oct. 1940, and Scott to Tamm, 16 July 1940
74 *Ibid.*, file 84.2, Scott to Hood, 16 Jan. 1940
75 *Ibid.*, file 84.3, War Emergency Bulletin No. 3, 20 Oct. 1939; for distribution list see *Ibid.*, file 90.14, Scott to Hipel, 9 July 1940.
76 *Globe and Mail* and *Toronto Star*, September 1939 and June 1940. These two months were chosen because they represent the opening month of the war and the height of the fifth column crisis, a period separated by nine months. March 1941 (see below) was chosen because it falls nine months after June 1940.
77 CSIS Access 117-91-1, Gagnon to the Commissioner, 23 May 1940
78 Kealey and Whitaker, *R.C.M.P. Security Bulletins: 1939–1941*, p. 260
79 *Toronto Star*, 5 June 1940, p. 3; *Le Devoir*, 28 May 1940, p. 1
80 *Le Devoir*, 6 June 1940, p. 2
81 *Globe and Mail*, 14 June 1940, p. 15
82 Canada, House of Commons, *Debates*, 13 June 1940, p. 747
83 *Globe and Mail*, 13 June 1940, pp. 6, 15
84 J.L. Granatstein, *Canada's War: The Politics of the Mackenzie King Government, 1939–1945* (Toronto: University of Toronto Press 1975), pp. 99–101
85 *Globe and Mail*, 12 June 1940, p. 6; 17 May 1940, p. 6; 8 March 1941, p. 6

86 CSIS Access 86-A-85, Tait to Divisional Officers Commanding, 24 March 1941; RCMP, *The Protection of Industry in Time of War* (Ottawa November 1940), pp. 1–2, 11

87 *Toronto Star*, 5 March 1940, p. 19

88 CSIS Access 86-A-85, King to Divisional Officers Commanding, 28 June 1940

89 National registration was also partly a security precaution. Debate in the cabinet war committee on the controversial issue revealed that at least one cabinet minister, Minister of Finance J.L. Ralston, believed that registration would provide a 'careful check upon all elements in the population,' which would help protect against subversive activities. NA, RG 2, 7C, Minutes and Documents of the Cabinet War Committee, vol. 1, 17 June 1940.

90 Canada, House of Commons, *Debates*, 30 May 1940, p. 360

91 *Ibid.*, p. 357

92 Kealey and Whitaker, *R.C.M.P. Security Bulletins, 1939–1941*, p. 232

93 *Ibid.*, p. 234

94 *Ibid.*, p. 361

95 *Ibid.*, pp. 291, 239

96 AO, RG 33, Series I-1, file 10.6

97 CSIS Access 117-91-61, Minutes of the Western Hemisphere Intelligence Conference, 3 August 1942, pp. 10–11

98 Dubois distinguished three types of workers' sabotage: 'those where the object is to destroy machinery or goods ... those which stop production ... and those which reduce the amount of work done ...' Pierre Dubois, *Sabotage in Industry*, trans. Rosemary Sheed (Harmondsworth, Eng.: Penguin 1979), p. 21. Strikes had been fomented by the Germans in the First World War to hamper American munitions production. Witcover, *Sabotage at Black Tom*, p. 119

99 'So far there has been no serious act of sabotage and it has been suggested that this is probably due to the precautions taken immediately upon the outbreak of hostilities when the known leaders of all Nazi organizations, who were considered likely to commit acts of sabotage, were interned.' *Toronto Star*, 27 January 1940, p. 1

100 For example: 'There most certainly has been no attempt to date at the commission of organized sabotage' (AO, RG 33, Series I-1, file 84.4, Tait to Scott, 5 September 1940). 'Due to the excellent precau-

tions taken, there have been no cases of enemy sabotage.' (NA, MG 27, III B10, vol. 23, file 78, Cadiz to Bernier, Oct. 28 1941). At the end of the war the RCMP commissioner acknowledged that 'only a comparatively few cases of intentional harm were brought to light, and it is certain there was no organized system of sabotage in Canada' (NA, RG 18, Acc. 84-85/084, file G509-79, Supplementary memorandum relating to the war Activities of the Royal Canadian Mounted Police, 28 September 1946). See also, RCMP *Annual Report*, 1942, p. 27; 1943, p. 35; 1944, p. 33; 1945, p. 29.
101 *The Eastern Underwriter*, 19 April 1940, p. 25
102 CSIS Access 89-A-63, RCMP Intelligence and Liaison Section Annual Report, 1939
103 CSIS Access 86-A-85, Tait to the Chairman, CSC, 20 May 1940. Voluntary agreement to be fingerprinted was also a condition spelled out in the application for employment form filled out by munitions workers, although the form was slightly deceptive in claiming the fingerprints were for 'record purposes' rather than for identification. See appendix 1.
104 NA, RG 76, vol. 446, file 675985, pt. 2, report of 1 August 1940
105 *Ibid.*
106 AO, RG 33, Series I-1, file 85.13, Quain to Scott, 23 February 1940
107 Because the Access Act allows government agencies to withhold material that has been supplied in confidence from a foreign government, it is possible only to make an informed guess that documents refer to a British agency. But see, for example, CSIS Access 86-A-85, Wood to Bernier, 8 June 1940.
108 RCMP, *Protection of Industry in Time of War*, p. 11
109 J. de N. Kennedy, *History of the Department of Munitions and Supply: Canada in the Second World War*, 2 vols. (Ottawa: King's Printer 1950), vol. I, p. 6
110 *Ibid.*, vol. II, p. 341
111 *Ibid.*, pp. 346–7; OHA, file 160.01, circular from G.K. Shiels, 21 January 1941; RCMP, *Protection of Industry in Time of War*, cover
112 Kennedy, *History of the Department of Munitions and Supply*, vol. II, pp. 345–6
113 AO, MU 7152, file 1, Civil Security Survey General, Harvison to Haultain, 26 July 1939

114 NA, RG 18, Acc. 85-86/048, box 27, file G-585-4-C, Hobbs to O.C. 'C' Division, 28 November 1939

115 Peter Krawchuk, *Interned without Cause*, trans. Pat Prokop (Toronto: Kobzar Publishing 1985), p. 33

116 NA, RG 18, vol. 3656, file G-537-20, Butchers to Kemp, 9 December 1943

117 RCMP, *Annual Report*, 1944, p. 37; 1945, p. 37, and 1946, p. 39

118 Kennedy, *History of the Department of Munitions and Supply*, vol. II, pp. 349, 375

119 NA, RG 77, Acc. 87-88/104, vol. 69, file 36-5-0-10, Eagleson to Fraser and Smith, 12 May 1942; CSIS Access 89-A-63, RCMP Intelligence Section Annual Report, 1942. Department of Transport (DOT) personnel were screened in part because the department was an integral part of the Canadian cryptanalysis effort, which involved intercepting the telecommunications traffic of Vichy France and Japan, interpreting it, and creating political intelligence from it, much of it passed on to the British and Americans. DOT operated interception stations at places like Point Grey in Vancouver, Winnipeg, and Ottawa. The National Research Council, which operated the Examination Unit, was also an integral part of this effort. It was chosen in part because hiring for it was not done through the open Civil Service Commission process. See Peter St John, 'Canada's Accession to the Allied Intelligence Community, 1940–45,' *Conflict Quarterly* 4, no. 4 (fall 1984): 8–12.

120 CSIS Access 89-A-63, RCMP Intelligence and Liaison Section Annual Report, 1941; RCMP, *Annual Report*, 1941, p. 56

121 CSIS Access 89-A-63, RCMP Intelligence Section Annual Report, 1942

122 CSIS Access 117-91-99, Bavin to DCI, 24 October 1940

123 CSIS Access 117-91-99, Bavin to DCI, 29 October 1940

124 CSIS Access 117-91-99, Wood to Mackenzie, 30 October 1940

125 CSIS Access 117-91-99, Scrogg to the Intelligence Officer, 29 January 1941

126 CSIS Access 117-91-99, Rivett-Carnac memo, 10 July 1945

127 Kellock-Taschereau Commission, *Report*, pp. 318, 409

128 CSIS Access 89-A-63, RCMP Intelligence Section Annual Report, 1941

129 *Ibid.*, 1945; RCMP *Annual Report*, 1945, p. 38
130 CSIS Access 89-A-63, RCMP Intelligence Section Annual Report, 1945. The normal problems of establishing identity after a destructive war were compounded by another fear, which had plagued the RCMP and American security intelligence from the 1930s: what use would the Soviet Union make of the thousands of North American passports it had acquired from Spanish Civil War volunteers? See Betke and Horrall, 'Canada's Security Service,' p. 544.
131 NA, RG 24, vol. 3360, file HQ 377-1-5, vol. 1, Bower memo, 29 April 1944
132 CSIS Access 86-A-85, Edwards to Commissioner, 12 August 1941, and Commissioner to Tait, 14 August 1941
133 NA, RG 24, vol. 3360, file HQ 377-1-5, vol. 2, Canadian Bureau of Identification Fourth Annual Report, 31 March 1945
134 NA, RG 76, vol. 446, file 675985, pt. 1, Blair letter, 26 September 1939
135 Order in Council PC 2505, 10 June 1940
136 Justice Access A89-00061, DMS circular
137 CSIS Access 86-A-85, Mead to Air Member for Personnel, 11 September 1942
138 H.R. Butchers, 'Fingerprint Identification in Wartime,' *RCMP Gazette* 6, no. 29 (19 July 1944)
139 CSIS Access 86-A-85, Wood to Divisional Officers Commanding, 29 January 1941
140 *Ibid.*
141 CSIS Access 87-A-39, Drysdale memo, 28 March 1944; CSIS Access 86-A-85, DMS circular, 21 January 1941
142 CSIS Access 86-A-85, Wood to Divisional Officers Commanding, 29 January 1941
143 McDonald, *Commission of Inquiry,* vol. 1, p. 59
144 NA, MG 27, III, B10, vol. 50, file 41, Wood to Lapointe, 25 Aug. 1939; RCMP, *Annual Report*, 1943, p. 73
145 This is an estimate based upon the figures given for the size of the female staff in the FPS. See RCMP, *Annual Report*, 1943, p. 42.
146 See chapter 6.
147 RCMP, *Protection of Industry in Time of War*, p. 8
148 NA, RG 27, vol. 102, file 424.01:276, *The D-H Gazette*, issued by the DeHavilland Aircraft of Canada Limited

149 NA, RG 27, vol. 102, file 424.01:276, Featherstonhaugh to the Minister of Labour, 6 June 1941; Waters to MacDonald, 5 May 1941

150 NA, RG 18, Acc. 85-86/574, vol. 12, file G-15-84, Lemieux memo, 3 April 1947

151 AO, MU 7152, file 1, Harvison to commissioner, 30 December 1938; AO, RG 33, Series I-1, file 84.4, Howe letter, 6 March 1940

152 CSIS Access 86-A-85, Wood to Divisional Officers Commanding, 29 January 1941

153 *Toronto Clarion*, 15 March 1941, p. 9

154 AO, RG 33, Series I-1, file 85.4, Minutes of the 18 February 1941 meeting. Private corporations had maintained blacklists for years, but this is the first case I have encountered in Canada (aside from a shortlived effort in the First World War – see chapter 1) in which the state actively collaborated with such schemes.

155 NA, MG 30, E350, vol. 1, file 9, Philipps to Mead, 6 May 1943; Leopold to Philipps, 11 and 18 May 1943; Philipps to Leopold, 21 May 1943

156 NA, MG 26, J1, vol. 429, Security Panel Document SP-22, 9 December 1947

157 Bryden, *Best-Kept Secret*, pp. 54, 157; Roger Bowen, *Innocence Is Not Enough: The Life and Death of Herbert Norman* (Vancouver/Toronto: Douglas and McIntyre 1986), James Barros, *No Sense of Evil: Espionage, the Case of Herbert Norman* (Toronto: Deneau 1986)

158 Bowen, *Innocence Is Not Enough*, pp. 76–7; Barros, *No Sense of Evil*, pp. 51–2

159 H.S. Ferns, *Reading from Left to Right: One Man's Political History* (Toronto: University of Toronto Press 1983), pp. 138–9

160 John Sawatsky, *Gouzenko: The Untold Story* (Toronto: Macmillan 1984), p. 283

161 NA, MG 30, E 163, vol. 13, file 148, Robertson to Skelton, 9 December 1940

162 Bryden, *Best-Kept Secret*, p. 150

163 Ferns, *Reading from Left to Right*, pp. 182–3

164 Claire Culhane Privacy Act records, 'D' Division report, 11 March 1940; Saunders to Wood, 18 November 1940; 'C' Division report, 27 November 1942; reference card to the Secretary, CSC, 2 December 1942; 'E' Division report, 29 December 1942; Hill to the officer com-

manding, 'C' Division, 6 January 1943; 'E' Division report, 3 March 1944; interview with Claire Culhane
165 CSIS Access 86-A-85, Tait to Divisional Officers Commanding, 22 February 1941; Wood to Bernier, 7 October 1942
166 CSIS Access 86-A-85, Wood to Anderson, 5 December 1940
167 Justice Access A89-00061, Brady report, 15 April 1941
168 NA, MG 26, J4, vol. 328, file 3490, Turnbull to the prime minister, 6 July 1942. It should be noted that even after June 1941 the Canadian state did not uncritically accept communists. In 1944 Norman Robertson denied H.S. Ferns a permanent job in External Affairs because Ferns was a 'Red,' although a disaffected one. Robertson's correct identification of Ferns, however, came not through security screening, but through Robertson's own acutely sensitive political antennae. See Ferns, *Reading from Left to Right*, p. 171.
169 NA, MG 26, J4, vol. 246, R.G.R. to King, 24 May 1947

CHAPTER 5 Reds under the khaki

1 NA, MG 26, J1, vol. 332, McNeil to King, 29 June 1942
2 *Ibid.*, St Laurent to Robertson, 17 July 1942
3 William Repka and Kathleen M. Repka, eds., *Dangerous Patriots: Canada's Unknown Prisoners of War* (Vancouver: New Star 1982), p. 221, and Pierre Berton, *The Great Depression, 1929–1939* (Toronto: McClelland and Stewart 1990), p. 487
4 C.P. Stacey, *The Canadian Army, 1939–1945: An Official Historical Summary* (Ottawa: King's Printer 1948), p. 1; Stacey, *Arms, Men, and Governments*, p. 66
5 Betke and Horrall, 'Canada's Security Service,' p. 435; Elliot, *Scarlet to Green*, pp. 71–2
6 NA, RG 24, vol. 6596, file HQ 1685-4, Sherwood to the Adjutant-General, 2 April 1917, and 9 April 1917 reply
7 *Ibid.*, Adjutant-General to Deputy Minister, 20 June 1938, and Deputy Minister to the Minister, 26 June 1938; Wood to the Deputy Minister, 27 October 1938
8 *Ibid.*, Wood to Deputy Minister, 6 September 1939; Adjutant-General to C.G.S., 11 September 1939. Even as late as January 1941, four months after the government's Interdepartmental Committee for

Co-ordination of Intelligence for War Purposes had recommended that the military introduce fingerprinting, the deputy minister was still publicly disowning it. This could be due to the unpopularity of fingerprinting. See *ibid.*, DesRosiers to Howitt, 4 January 1941.

9 Kealey and Whitaker, *R.C.M.P. Security Bulletins: 1939–1941*, p. 27
10 King Diaries, 23 November 1939
11 NA, RG 24, vol. 83–84/049, box 1624, file 304-113, vol. 1, Cowley to Officer in Charge, Recruiting Centre, 18 December 1939
12 OLL, W.J. Scott, *Sabotage Prevention*, War Emergency Bulletin No. 8, p. 9
13 Elliot, *Scarlet to Green*, pp. 469, 471; CSIS Access 89-A-63, Annual Report of the RCMP Intelligence and Liaison Section, 1941; NA, RG 24, vol. 2748, file HQS 6265–14, vol. 1, Acland to G.S.O.1 Intelligence, 1 November 1941
14 Kealey and Whitaker, *R.C.M.P. Security Bulletins: 1939–1941*, p. 202
15 CSIS Access 89-A-63, Annual Report of the RCMP Intelligence and Liaison Section for 1942
16 Whitaker, 'Official Repression of Communism during World War II,' p. 151
17 AO, RG 33, Series I-1, file 85.4, Minutes of 17 December 1940 meeting of the Co-ordinating Committee for Security
18 *Ibid.*
19 William Beeching and Phyllis Clarke, eds., *Yours in the Struggle: The Reminiscences of Tim Buck* (Toronto: NC Press 1977), pp. 150–1
20 NA, RG 24, vol. 6596, file HQ 1685-4, Coleman to A.G., 30 December 1940
21 NA, RG 76, vol. 446, file 675985, pt. 2, 1 August 1940 report
22 *Ibid.*
23 NA, RG 24, vol. 5376, file HQC 45-24-20, vol. 1, Atherton memo, 12 November 1940; RG 24, vol. 3360, file HQ 377-1-5, vol. 1, Bower memo, 29 April 1944
24 NA, RG 24, vol. 3360, file HQ 377-1-5, vol. 1, Bower memo, 29 April 1944
25 NA, RG 25, vol. 2663, file 7348–40, Carteret to Under-Secretary of State for External Affairs, 12 December 1941
26 NA, RG 24, vol. 5376, file HQC 45-24-20, vol. 1, Middleton memo, 7 July 1941

27 NA, RG 24, vol. 5376, file HQC 45-24-20, vol. 1, Booklet No. 2, appendix D, and Evans to RCAF Records Officer, 20 March 1943

28 NA, RG 24, vol. 3360, file HQ 377-1-5, vol. 1, Bower memo, 29 April 1944. See chapter 7 for an explanation of the function of this tabulating equipment.

29 *Ibid.*

30 CSIS Access 87-A-39, Claxton to Ilsley, 14 August 1947

31 NA, RG 24, vol. 3360, file HQ 377-1-5, vol. 2, Canadian Bureau of Identification Annual Report, 31 March 1945

32 NA, RG 24, vol. 3360, file HQ 377-1-5, vol. 1, Goodfellow to Adjutant General Branch, 10 July 1943

33 *Ibid.*, minutes of 13 June 1941 meeting re identification bureaus; minutes of meeting of naval service, army and air force officers, n.d.

34 NA, RG 24, vol. 2748, file HQS 6265-14, vol. 1, Acland to G.S.O.1 Intelligence, 1 November 1941; Acland to G.S.O.1 Intelligence, 28 April 1942; Acland to D.M.O.&I., 9 June 1942; Acland to DMI, 29 July 1942; Special Observation Report Form; *ibid.*, vol. 2, Military Security Bulletin No. 2, 22 November 1941

35 NA, RG 24, vol. 2748, file HQS 6265-14, vol. 2, Acland to DMI, 3 March 1943; Elliot, *Scarlet to Green*, p. 473

36 NA, RG 24, vol. 2748, file HQS 6265-14, vol. 1, Acland to DMI, 29 July 1942; Special Observation Report Form; Acland to G.S.O.1 Intelligence, 1 November 1941; Acland to D.M.O.&I., 9 June 1942

37 *Ibid.*, Acland to G.S.O.1 Intelligence, 1 November 1941. There is no indication of how many of these subversives were communists.

38 Elliot, *Scarlet to Green*, p. 472

39 *Ibid.*

40 St John, 'Canada's Accession to the Allied Intelligence Community, 1940–1945,' pp. 6–11

41 NA, RG 24, vol. 2748, file HQS 6265-14, vol. 2, Acland to DMI, 3 March 1943; Elliot, *Scarlet to Green*, p. 472

42 NA, RG 24, vol. 2748, file HQS 6265-14, vol. 1, Acland to G.S.O.1 Intelligence, 1 November 1941

43 Elliot, *Scarlet to Green*, p. 472; CSIS Access 86-A-85, Mead to Divisional Officers Commanding, 15 March 1943, and Instructions for Character Investigations

44 Gary Marcuse, *Cold War in Canada* (Toronto: CBC Ideas Transcripts 1984), p. 7
45 NA, RG 24, vol. 5376, file HQC 45-24-20, vol. 1, Orde memo, 23 September 1946
46 NA, RG 24, vol. 3360, file HQ 377-1-5, vol. 1, untitled [RCAF] report evaluating proposal for joint services identification bureau
47 NA, MG 27, III, B11, vol. 39, Canadian Bureau of Identification Annual Report for 1946
48 NA, RG 24, vol. 3360, file HQ 377-1-5, vol. 2, Canadian Bureau of Identification Annual Report, 31 March 1945
49 Department of National Defence (DND), Directorate of History, file 74/10, RCAF Provost and Security Services History; NA, RG 24, vol. unknown, file HQS 7236-0-1, Under-Secretary of State for External Affairs to the Deputy Minister, DND, 2 February 1945; NA, RG 24, vol. 5376, file HQC 45-24-20, vol. 1, Edwards to Liaison Officer, RAF and RNZAF, 11 January 1941. However, Ralph Pearcey, a Canadian army prisoner of war, recalls being fingerprinted by the Germans (interview with Ralph D. Pearcey, Vancouver, 27 August 1991).
50 CSIS Access 86-A-85, Brand to Wood, 14 March 1942, and Tait to Brand, 24 March 1942
51 NA, RG 24, Acc. 83-84/167, box 1950-24-12, vol. 1, Rankin to D/DNI, 21 August 1946
52 *Ibid.*, Butchers to Secretary, Naval Board, 15 November 1943
53 NA, RG 24, Acc. 83-84/167, box 1950-24-12, vol. 1, Saunders to Mills, 1 December 1944
54 NA, RG 24, Acc. 83-84/167, box 1950-24-12, vol. 1, Roberts to DNI, 18 January 1944
55 Betke and Horrall, 'Canada's Security Service,' pp. 518–19
56 The Smith Act also made it illegal to advocate the overthrow of government by force. Theoharis, *Spying on Americans*, p. 42
57 NA, RG 25, vol. 2785, file 627-40, vol. 2, U.S. Department of Justice statement, 13 January 1941
58 NA, MG 30, E 163, vol. 13, file 147, Mahoney to Secretary of State for External Affairs, 24 June 1940
59 NA, RG 25, vol. 2808, file 978-40, vol. 1, Application for Merchant Seaman's Identity Certificate

60 PC 9166, 26 November 1941

61 NA, RG 12, vol. 2831, file 306-10, pt. 1, 'Seamen's Identity Certificates: General Instructions to Shipping Masters'

62 William Kaplan, *Everything That Floats: Pat Sullivan, Hal Banks, and the Seamen's Unions of Canada* (Toronto: University of Toronto Press 1987), pp. 32–3; CSIS Access 89-A-63, 1941 Annual Report of the RCMP Intelligence and Liaison Section

63 Frederick B. Watt, *In All Respects Ready: The Merchant Navy and the Battle of the Atlantic, 1940–1945* (Scarborough, Ont.: Prentice-Hall Canada 1985), p. 63

64 *Ibid.*, p. 214

65 NA, RG 25, vol. 2808, file 978-40, vol. 1, M.W. to Read, 28 October 1940

66 NA, RG 12, vol. 2831, file 306-10, pt. 1, minutes of conference of 23 October 1940

67 NA, RG 25, vol. 2808, file 978-40, vol. 1, M.W. to Read, 28 October 1940

68 NA, RG 25, vol. 2808, file 978-40, vol. 1, Guttery memo, 26 July 1940

69 Watt, *In All Respects Ready,* p. 128

70 *Vancouver Sun,* 23 November 1991, p. B8

71 Watt, *In All Respects Ready,* pp. 128–31

72 NA, RG 76, vol. 463, file 708755, pt. 1, minutes of 21 January 1941 meeting

73 *Ibid.*

74 *Ibid.*, minutes of 27 January 1941 meeting of subcommittee re alien seamen refusing to sail

75 *Canadian Tribune,* 31 May 1941, p. 1

76 NA, RG 76, vol. 463, file 708755, pt. 2, minutes of 2 October 1945 meeting of interdepartmental committee

77 *Ibid.*, file 708755, pt. 1, minutes of 5 February 1943 meeting of interdepartmental meeting

78 Watt, *In All Respects Ready,* p. ix

79 *Ibid.*, p. x

80 NA, RG 76, vol. 463, file 708755, pt. 1, High Commissioner telegram, 6 February 1941

81 NA, RG 18, Acc. 84-85/084, file G-509-64 Supp 'A, ' Standing orders

and Instructions for the guidance of Security Control Operatives, 7 December 1943

82 Hinsley and Simkins, *British Intelligence,* vol. 4, p. 72

CHAPTER 6 'Gathering information regarding communistic chaps'

1 By contrast, in 1948, soon after security screening was officially introduced, the cabinet issued specific guidelines on how to implement it, known as Cabinet Directive Number 4. Privy Council Access 108-2/897015, Circular No. 4 and Circular No. 4A.

2 NA, RG 13, A2, vol. 2028, file 143931, Spalding to Wood, 28 April 1942

3 *Ibid.,* Spalding to Wood, 14 April 1942

4 NA, RG 13, A2, vol. 2028, file 143931, Howe to St Laurent, 6 November 1943

5 *Ibid.*

6 Reg Whitaker, 'Official Repression of Communism during World War II,' *Labour/Le Travail* 17 (spring 1986): 152–3, 155

7 NA, RG 13, A2, vol. 2028, file 143931, Kennedy to Varcoe, 1 September 1942. Mere accident prevented this proposal from going to cabinet as part of a draft consolidation of the DOCR. The proposed amendments providing for searching, fingerprinting, and photographing of munitions workers did not reach the Department of Justice before the draft consolidation had been set in type. See *ibid.,* Varcoe to Kennedy, 31 October 1942.

8 Granatstein, *Canada's War,* p. 10

9 *Ibid.,* p. 149; J.L. Granatstein, *A Man of Influence: Norman A. Robertson and Canadian Statecraft, 1929–1968* (n.p.: Deneau 1981), pp. 85, 90

10 NA, RG 25, vol. 2663, file 7348-40, Robertson to Deputy Minister of National Defence, 6 December 1943

11 NA, MG 27, III, B10, vol. 25, file 87, Wood to Lapointe, 15 July 1941

12 CSIS Access 87-A-39, Wilson to Shakespeare, 21 March 1947

13 Justice Access A89-00061, Brady report, 15 April 1941; Canada, House of Commons, *Debates,* 10 March 1941, p. 1469

14 J.J. Deutsch, 'Some Thoughts on the Public Service,' *Canadian Journal of Economics and Political Science* 23, no. 1 (February 1957): 84

15 Bryden, *Deadly Allies,* p. 13

16 Betke and Horrall, 'Canada's Security Service,' pp. 426–8
17 Christopher Andrew and David Dilks, 'Introduction,' in *The Missing Dimension: Governments and Intelligence Communities in the Twentieth Century,* ed. Andrew and Dilks (London: Macmillan 1984), p. 6
18 *Ibid.*, p. 9
19 *Ibid.*, pp. xvii–xviii
20 Betke and Horrall, 'Canada's Security Service,' p. xvi. If it were true that the RCMP had never strayed beyond the bounds of strict adherence to the law and obedience to the government, it would be a rare case among western intelligence agencies. As Bernard Porter suggests about the British security intelligence community, intelligence officers at least occasionally 'saw their loyalties as transcending their political masters, especially if those masters were Labour, and attaching to something – an ideal or principle or an interpretation of the "national interest" – which could override their allegiance to mere governments.' Porter, *Plots and Paranoia*, p. 163.
21 NA, RG 18, Acc. 84-85/084, file G 509-79, Wood's supplemental memo, 28 September 1946
22 AO, RG 33, Series I-1, file 10.6, Gov't Defence, 1942–44, address by J. Howe
23 CSIS Access 86-A-85, Tait to Officer Commanding, 'O' Division, 20 September 1941
24 RCMP, *Annual Report*, 1942, p. 10, 1943, p. 42
25 AO, RG 33, Series I-1, file 85.13, Quain to Scott, 9 March 1940, and Scott to Quain, 11 March 1940
26 H.R. Butchers, 'Fingerprint Identification in Wartime,' *RCMP Gazette* 6, no. 29 (19 July 1944): 2
27 McDonald, *Commission of Inquiry*, vol. 2, pp. 782–3
28 AO, RG 33, Series I-1, file 85.4, Minutes of 17 December 1940 meeting
29 Lowenthal, *FBI*, p. 90
30 Wood, 'Tools for Treachery,' pp. 1–3
31 Reg Whitaker, 'Left-wing Dissent: Canada in the Cold War Era,' in *Dissent and the State*, ed. C.E.S. Franks (Toronto: Oxford University Press 1989), pp. 193, 204–5
32 *Ibid.*, pp. 202–3
33 NA, RG 18, Acc. 84-85/084, file G509-79, Wood's supplemental

memo, 28 September 1946; Robertson cited in Whitaker, 'Official Repression of Communism,' p. 150

34 Kealey and Whitaker, *R.C.M.P. Security Bulletins, 1939–1941*, p. 390

35 Harvison, *Horsemen*, p. 149

36 Kealey and Whitaker, *R.C.M.P. Security Bulletins, 1939–1941*, p. 390

37 CSIS Access 89-A-63, Annual Report of the RCMP Intelligence and Liaison Section for 1942

38 CSIS Access 117-91-61, Minutes of the Western Hemisphere Intelligence Conference, 3 August 1942

39 NA, MG 26, J4, vol. 328, file 3490 RCMP 1940–42, Turnbull to the Prime Minister, 6 July 1942

40 CSIS Access 117-91-61, Minutes of the Western Hemisphere Intelligence Conference, 29 January 1942

41 James Rule *et al.* offer a useful definition of social control when they identify it as 'any means of influence by which a person or an organization seeks to render other people's behavior or circumstances more predictable and more acceptable.' James Rule *et al.*, *The Politics of Privacy: Planning for Personal Data Systems as Powerful Technologies* (New York: Elsevier 1980), p. 47

42 Laurel Sefton MacDowell, 'The Formation of the Canadian Industrial Relations System during World War Two,' *Labour/Le Travailleur* 3 (1978): 176

43 Kealey and Whitaker, *R.C.M.P. Security Bulletins, 1939–1941*, p. 73

44 Bryan Palmer, *Working Class Experience*, pp. 237–9

45 Other political parties active in unions – the Co-operative Commonwealth Federation, anarchists, Trotskyists – had no more love for the communists, but they also had no power to implement a state screening system.

46 CSIS Access 89-A-63, Annual Report of the RCMP Intelligence and Liaison Section for 1941; Kealey and Whitaker, *R.C.M.P. Security Bulletins, 1939–1941*, pp. 361–2

47 *Ibid.* Original emphasis.

48 CSIS Access 86-A-85, Fraser memo, 8 November 1940

49 A.F.W. Plumptre, *Mobilizing Canada's Resources for War* (Toronto: Ryerson Press 1941), p. 271

50 NA, RG 2, 7C, vol. 4, minutes of CWC, 5 May 1941

51 H.R. Butchers, 'Fingerprint Identification in Wartime,' *RCMP Gazette* 6, no. 30 (26 July 1944): 1

52 Kennedy, *History of the Department of Munitions and Supply,* vol. II, p. 359

53 CSIS Access 86-A-85, Application for Employment form. Significantly, the minister of labour publicly rebuked a company which asked on its employment form whether the applicant had ever been a member of a labour organization. Questioned about it in the House of Commons by CCF MP Angus MacInnis, Norman McLarty read out a letter to the company, which declared 'I regard it as unfortunate that such a form should be used by any Canadian industry ... The searching character of the information requested is resented on the part of labour.' Clearly union membership was a subject about which the state exercised some care. Yet the official RCMP and DMS application form continued to demand that a person acknowledge membership in other organizations. Canada, House of Commons, *Debates,* 12 March 1941, p. 1469.

54 William Spinrad, *Civil Liberties* (Chicago: Quadrangle Books 1970), p. 104

55 H.R. Butchers, 'Fingerprint Identification in Wartime,' *RCMP Gazette* 6, no. 29 (19 July 1944), p. 2. Emphasis added.

56 AO, RG 33, Series I-1, file 85.4, Minutes of 17 December 1940 meeting

57 NA, RG 24, vol. 5376, file HQ 45-24-20, vol. 1, Evans to RCAF Records Officer, 30 March 1943

58 RCMP, *Protection of Industry in Time of War,* pp. 39–40

59 NA, RG 28A, vol. 13, file 44, Johnson to Kennedy, 30 March 1947

60 Kennedy, *History of the Department of Munitions and Supply,* vol. II, p. 353

61 AO, RG 33, Series I-1, file 10.6

62 Howe's comment could be linked to the theory of sabotage prevailing within the RCMP in mid-1942. Assistant Commissioner R.R. Tait identified 'the most insidious types of sabotage' as serious damage which could be disguised as the result of 'carelessness, error of judgment or oversight' (CSIS Access 117-91-61, Minutes of the Western Hemisphere Intelligence Conference, 3 August 1942, p. 11). But this is a far cry from 'slow work.'

63 Dubois, *Sabotage in Industry,* p. 103
64 CSIS Access 117-91-61, Minutes of the Western Hemisphere Intelligence Conference, 3 August 1942, p. 10
65 CSIS Access 86-A-85, Wood to Bernier, 8 June 1940; King to Divisional Officers Commanding, 28 June 1940
66 AO, RG 33, Series I-1, file 85.13, Quain to Scott, 23 February 1940
67 NA, MG30, A94, vol. 31, file 2921, 18 June 1941 meeting minutes
68 Kennedy, *History of the Department of Munitions and Supply,* vol. I, p. 311
69 CSIS Access 86-A-85, Johnson to the Commissioner, 15 December 1942; Cadiz to Director General, ISB, 18 December 1942
70 Interview with W.C. Bryan, Victoria, B.C., 13 October 1988
71 *Globe and Mail,* 24 April 1992, p. A1

CHAPTER 7 Engineers of conduct

1 Interview with R.W. Wonnacott, Kamloops, B.C., 25 May 1988
2 NA, RG 18, Acc. 85-86/574, box 9, file G-537-1, Wood to the Minister of Justice, 15 September 1939; Bavin to the Director, CIB, 15 September 1939; memo from Hann, 28 November 1939; supplementary list of temporary positions, Ronson to the Commissioner, RCMP, 20 January 1940
3 CSIS Access 86-A-85, King to Officer Commanding, 'C' Division, 19 July 1940
4 *Ibid.*
5 AO, RG 33, Series I-1, file 86.1, Scott lecture, 2 April 1941
6 Kennedy, *History of the Department of Munitions and Supply,* vol. II, p. 350
7 CSIS Access 86-A-85, Butchers to Divisional Officers Commanding, 13 April 1942
8 NA, RG 28A, vol. 13, file 44, DMS History, 'Development of Industrial Security Branch, Department of Munitions and Supply,' 15 September 1943, p. 9
9 NA, RG 18, vol. 3656, file G-537-20, Wood to the Director, CIB, 27 November 1943
10 Butchers, 'Fingerprint Identification in Wartime,' *RCMP Gazette* 6, no. 29 (19 July 1944): 2
11 RCMP, *Annual Report,* 1942, p. 10; 1943, p. 42. The evidence about

exactly when women were introduced as fingerprint searchers is somewhat contradictory. A postwar memo from Inspector R.W. Wonnacott, officer in charge of the Identification Branch, dates the use of civil servants as fingerprint searchers from 1940. See NA, RG 18, Acc. 85-86/574, box 13, file G-537-21-HQS-1953, Wonnacott to DCI, 4 January 1952.
12 RCMP, *Annual Report*, 1943, p. 42
13 NA, RG 18, vol. 3656, file G-537-20, Wonnacott to the Director, CIB, 18 November 1943
14 *Ibid.*, Kemp to Wood, 19 November 1943
15 *Ibid.*, Butchers to the Director, CIB, 9 December 1943
16 *Ibid.*, Kemp to the Deputy Commissioner, 22 December 1943
17 *Ibid.*, Butchers to the Director, CIB, 9 December 1943
18 *Ibid.*, Kemp to the Deputy Commissioner, 22 December 1943
19 Butchers, 'Fingerprint Identification in Wartime,' *RCMP Gazette* 6, no. 29 (19 July 1944): 3
20 IBM Archives (Valhalla, N.Y.), Anonymous [William Cashin], *Finger Print Identification through Automatic Search* (n.p., n.d. [c. 1938]), p. 15
21 IBM, *Business Machines*, 9 December 1937, p. 1
22 CSIS Access 86-A-85, Wood memo, 29 January 1941
23 NA, RG 18, vol. 3656, file G-537-20, Wonnacott to the Director, CIB, 18 November 1943
24 *Ibid.*, Butchers to the Director, CIB, 9 December 1943
25 Butchers, 'Fingerprint Identification in Wartime,' *RCMP Gazette* 6, no. 29 (19 July 1944): 3
26 NA, RG 18, vol. 3656, file G-537-20, Wonnacott to the Director, CIB, 18 November 1943
27 IBM Archives, International Business Machines, 'Chronology'
28 Graham S. Lowe, 'Mechanization, Feminization, and Managerial Control in the Early Twentieth-Century Canadian Office,' in *On the Job: Confronting the Labour Process in Canada*, ed. Craig Heron and Robert Storey (Kingston and Montreal: McGill-Queen's University Press 1986) p. 190
29 John C. McDonald, *Impact and Implications of Office Automation*, Occasional Paper no. 1, Economics and Research Branch, Department of Labour (Ottawa 1964), p. 3

30 Robert Sobel, *I.B.M.: Colossus in Transition* (New York: Times Books 1981), p. 80

31 *Ibid.*, pp. 80–1

32 Marcel Coté, Yvan Allaire, and Roger-Émile Miller, *IBM Canada Ltd.: A Case Study*, Royal Commission on Corporate Concentration, Study No. 14 (Ottawa: Ministry of Supply and Services 1977), pp. 16–17

33 Sobel, *I.B.M.*, p. 104

34 NA, RG 28A, vol. 144, file 3-L-1, vol. 3, Couper to Deputy Minister of Labour, 28 July 1941; RCMP, *Annual Report*, 1942

35 RCMP, *Annual Report*, 1943, p. 42

36 Block, *Fingerprinting*, pp. 119–20; NA, RG 18, vol. 3564, file C11-19-3, Cadiz to Hoover, 16 September 1942

37 Butchers, 'Fingerprint Identification in Wartime,' *RCMP Gazette* 6, no. 29 (19 July 1944): 3; 'Automated Fingerprint Processing – A Step Forward,' *FBI Law Enforcement Bulletin*, October 1970, p. 3

38 U.S. Department of Justice, Freedom of Information Act Request 305,558 and 305,560, IBM to Hoover, 21 August 1934

39 *The IBM Record*, 29 July 1953, p. 2

40 *Business Machines*, 9 December 1937, p. 1

41 IBM, *IBM Sales Manual*, 1 June 1944, pp. 5–6

42 Gary Marx and Nancy Reichman, 'Routinizing the Discovery of Secrets: Computers as Informants,' *American Behavioral Scientist* 27, no. 4 (March/April 1984): 425

43 CSIS Access 86-A-85, Johnson to the Commissioner, RCMP, 22 December 1942

44 Justice Access A89-00061, Tait to Deputy Minister, 2 April 1941

45 CSIS Access 86-A-85, Wood to Divisional Officers Commanding, 29 January 1941

46 CSIS Access 86-A-85, Tait to Divisional Officers Commanding, 24 March 1941. Surprisingly, after years of campaigns by police to have the right to fingerprint vagrants, Tait did not deem that a serious charge. This suggests that the state's criterion of who constitutes a political risk periodically shifts. In the 1920s and 1930s the itinerant worker without visible means of support represented a political challenge to capitalism and a potential convert to communism. In 1941, facing different conditions and new threats, the state was prepared to forgive the decade-old transgressions of these former

dangerous drifters. The threat was in the factories of industrial Canada, not in the now-deserted hobo camps on the margins of Western cities.

47 CSIS Access 86-A-85, Mead to Johnson, 27 July 1943

48 NA, MG30, D211, vol. 10, file Civil Liberties, Canadian Cases 1931–50, citing *Montreal Daily Star*, 21 June 1934

49 I owe this observation to Reg Whitaker.

50 Kealey, 'State Repression of Labour and the Left in Canada, 1914–20,' p. 301; Kealey, 'The Early Years of State Surveillance of Labour and the Left in Canada,' p. 134

51 The single important exception to this was the 1931 prosecution of eight Communist party leaders. And there, although RCMP information and witnesses were central to the crown's case, it was the Ontario government that initiated the proceedings.

52 Porter, *Plots and Paranoia*, p. 133

53 Jean-Paul Brodeur, 'High Policing and Low Policing: Remarks about the Policing of Political Activities,' *Social Problems* 30, no. 5 (June 1983): 511, 513–14

54 Betke and Horrall, 'Canada's Security Service,' pp. 322, 380

55 Kealey and Whitaker, *R.C.M.P. Security Bulletins, 1939–1941*, p. 260

56 Marx and Reichman, 'Routinizing the Discovery of Secrets,' p. 442

57 CSIS Access 86-A-85, Wood to the Secretary, Civil Service Commission, 1 December 1941, and Wood to Bernier, 7 October 1942; *Toronto Star*, 5 March 1940, p. 19

58 NA, RG 25, vol. 3468-40, pt. 1, file 3007, Rose to Robertson, 23 March 1942; *Toronto Clarion*, 5 April 1941, p. 3

59 Ericson and Shearing, 'Scientification of Police Work,' p. 133

60 Kennedy, *History of the Department of Munitions and Supply*, vol. II, p. 350

61 Ericson and Shearing, 'The Scientification of Police Work,' p. 134

62 *Ibid.*

63 *Ibid.*, p. 138

64 G. Bohme, 'The Knowledge-Structure of Society,' in *Knowledge, Policies, and the Traditions of Higher Education*, ed. G. Bergendal, cited by Ericson and Shearing, 'Scientification of Police Work,' p. 158 n39

65 Granatstein, *Canada's War*, p. 101; NA, RG 28A, vol. 144, file 3-L-1, vol. 3, Couper to Deputy Minister of Labour, 28 July 1941

66 Brodeur, 'High Policing and Low Policing,' p. 513
67 *Ibid.*, pp. 513–14

CHAPTER 8 Security affairs

1 CSIS Access 117-91-71, Tait and Mead to Commissioner, 7 February 1942
2 CSIS Access 117-91-71, Robertson to Wood, 15 October 1942; Cadiz to Robertson, 20 October; Mead to deleted, 20 October; Cadiz to deleted, 20 October; Robertson to Wood, 21 October; Cadiz to Robertson, 24 October 1942
3 Wesley Wark, 'The Evolution of Military Intelligence in Canada,' *Armed Forces and Society* 16, no. 1 (fall 1989): 86
4 St John, 'Canada's Accession to the Allied Intelligence Community, 1940–45,' *passim*
5 David Stafford, *Camp X: Canada's School for Secret Agents, 1941–45* (Toronto: Lester and Orpen Dennys 1986)
6 Hinsley and Simkins, *British Intelligence*, vol. 4, p. 5; Betke and Horrall, 'Canada's Security Service,' p. 401
7 Vernon A.M. Kemp, *Without Fear, Favour or Affection: Thirty-five Years with the Royal Canadian Mounted Police* (Toronto: Longmans, Green 1958), p. 162
8 NA, MG 27, III, B10, vol. 50, file 41, Wood to Lapointe, 25 August 1939
9 Hinsley and Simkins, *British Intelligence*, vol. 4, p. 142
10 *Ibid.*
11 Betke and Horrall, 'Canada's Security Service,' pp. 523–5
12 *Ibid.*, pp. 528–31
13 Hinsley and Simpkins, *British Intelligence*, vol. 4, p. 144
14 *Ibid.*
15 *Ibid.*, p. 187. Robert Bothwell points out that BSC vetting was not always adequate. Physicist Bruno Pontecorvo, for instance, was approved by the BSC to work on the Canadian nuclear energy program but in 1950 defected to the Soviet Union. Robert Bothwell, *Nucleus: The History of Atomic Energy of Canada Ltd* (Toronto: University of Toronto Press 1988), pp. 30, 78.
16 Hinsley and Simpkins, *British Intelligence*, vol. 4, p. 145

17 *Ibid.*, pp. 32, 247–8
18 *Ibid.*, pp. 83–4, 285
19 *Ibid.*, p. 285
20 *Ibid.*, pp. 65, 73–4, 285–7
21 NA, RG 24, vol. 2748, HQS 6265-14, vol. 1, Lake to Baxter, 4 March 1941
22 Hinsley and Simkins, *British Intelligence*, vol. 4, p. 146
23 NA, RG 2/18, vol. 45, file D-15-3, Wood to Robertson
24 NA, RG 25, vol. 2945, file 3042-40, vol. 1, Pearson to Mackenzie, 21 March 1942; Johnson to Robertson, 24 March 1942
25 NA, RG 25 A-12, vol. 2116, file AR 418/130, Robertson to Massey, 30 April 1943. In September 1943 Inspector C.W. Harvison also visited MI5 and returned with an MI5 booklet entitled 'Instructions for Security Control Officers at Home, Sea and Air Ports in War,' indicating that at least part of the purpose of his journey was to discuss port security. RCMP Access 92ATIP 1550, 0-311, Harvison file, Harvison to Commissioner, 22 October 1946.
26 RCMP, *Annual Report*, 1944, p. 9; Kemp, *Without Fear, Favour or Affection*, p. 236
27 Canadian Association of Chiefs of Police, CCAC, *Proceedings*, 1943, p. 37. During Inspector Harvison's 1943 visit to MI5, the RCMP ordered him to examine intelligence-gathering systems and file systems, paying 'particular attention to how information is handled with the view of bringing it before the officers concerned quickly.' RCMP Access 92ATIP 1550, 0-311, Harvison file, Introduction and Mead to Officer in Charge, Intelligence Section, 24 September 1943.
28 Hinsley and Simkins, *British Intelligence, vol. 4*, p. 146
29 Betke and Horrall, 'Canada's Security Service,' p. 601, and app. C
30 NA, RG 2/18, vol. 45, file D-15-3, T.A.S. to Robertson, Wrong and Heeney, 5 March 1943
31 *Ibid.*
32 *Ibid.*
33 *Ibid.*, T.A.S. to Robertson and Robertson reply, 22 October 1942
34 *Ibid.*, T.A.S. to Robertson, Wrong, and Heeney, 5 March 1943
35 NA, RG 24, vol. 2750, HQS-6403-9, Director of Military Intelligence memo, 29 April 1946
36 AO, RG 33, Series I-1, file 84.2, Hood to Scott, 16 January 1940; CSIS

Access 89–A-63, Annual Report of the RCMP Intelligence and Liaison Section for 1941; RCMP, *Protection of Industry in Time of War*, p. 37

37 NA, RG 24, vol. 11249, file 10-2-1, vol. 4, Tait to Stethem, 24 November 1941

38 CSIS Access 89-A-63, Annual Report of the RCMP Intelligence and Liaison Section for 1941

39 NA, RG 25, vol. 83–84/351, box 2, file 2821-40, Fraser to Commissioner, 29 July 1941, and Cadiz to Fraser, 7 August 1941

40 *Ibid.*, Burchell to Secretary of State for External Affairs, 6 January 1942, and Dawes to Montgomery, 28 January 1942

41 *Ibid.*, Wild to Burchell, 1 April 1942

42 *Ibid.*, Burchell to Secretary of State for External Affairs, 23 February 1942

43 *Ibid.*, Wood to the Chief of the Air Staff, 10 June 1942

44 *Ibid.*, Burchell to the Secretary of State for External Affairs, 17 September 1942

45 *Ibid.*, Under Secretary of State for External Affairs to Wood, 22 September 1942, and Mead to Keenleyside, 26 September 1942

46 *Ibid.*, Hutchings to Burchell, 30 April 1943

47 Betke and Horrall, 'Canada's Security Service,' pp. 407–8, 465a; Kemp, *Without Fear, Favour or Affection*, p. 162

48 Betke and Horrall, 'Canada's Security Service,' pp. 521–2

49 AO, RG 33, Series I-1, file 84.3, Scott to Tamm, 21 November 1940; NA, MG 30, E163, vol. 13, file 148, 9 November 1940 Press Release

50 AO, RG 33, Series I-1, file 84.1, Scott to Rouse, 28 December 1940

51 U.S., Department of Justice, Federal Bureau of Investigation, *Suggestions for Protection of Industrial Facilities* (Washington, D.C. August 1940); RCMP, *Protection of Industry in Time of War*

52 RCMP, *Protection of Industry in Time of War*, pp. 5–7, 11

53 FBI, *Suggestions for Protection of Industrial Facilities*, p. 8

54 CSIS Access 117-91-71, 26 December 1941 telegram from Canadian Minister in [deleted] to Secretary of State for External Affairs

55 CSIS Access 117-91-71, Minutes of the Western Hemisphere Intelligence Conference, 3 August 1942

56 CSIS Access 117-91-61, Minutes of the Western Hemisphere Intelligence Conference, 3 August 1942

57 Betke and Horrall, 'Canada's Security Service,' app. C, Chronology, n.p.
58 NA, RG 18, vol. 3455, file 0-204, Wood to Commanding Officer, Fredericton, 15 April 1942
59 NA, RG 18, vol. 3566, file C11-19-4-2, vol. 2, Duncan to officers commanding, 28 October 1942
60 CSIS Access 117-91-71, Drysdale to DCI, 19 March 1942
61 CSIS Access 117-91-71, Drysdale to DCI, 25 November 1943
62 NA, MG 30, E 163, vol. 13, file 148, Robertson to Christie, 3 October 1940; Loring to Robertson, 8 October 1940; Robertson to Skelton, 9 December 1940
63 Betke and Horrall, 'Canada's Security Service,' p. 531
64 U.S. National Archives, RG 407, box 35, 91-SCI-0.3, Northwest Service Command, First Semi-Annual Progress Report, January 1944
65 Kennedy, *History of the Department of Munitions and Supply,* vol. II, p. 352
66 Schaar, *Loyalty in America,* p. 133
67 FBI, *Annual Report,* 1942, pp. 7, 14
68 *Ibid.,* p. 14
69 *Ibid.,* p. 15
70 FBI, *Annual Report,* 1945, p. 21
71 FBI, *Annual Report,* 1942, p. 7
72 FBI, *Annual Report,* 1943, p. 8
73 FBI, *Annual Report,* 1944, p. 8, and *Annual Report,* 1945, p. 9
74 NA, RG 18, vol. 3754, file 516-26-1, supp A. vol. 2, 18 October 1946 letter from Assistant Commissioner, New Scotland Yard, to the Finger Print Section, RCMP
75 Cherrill, *Finger Print System at Scotland Yard,* p. 9; FBI, *Fingerprint Identification*m pp. 4–5, 9. The migratory nature of Canadians and Americans could also account for the use of fingerprinting as a security-screening device in North America and its absence in Britain. Police and government authorities in North America were convinced that radicals were especially itinerant. Tracking them required technological aids like card indexes and fingerprinting. See chapter 5.
76 CSIS Access 117-91-71, Drysdale to DCI, 19 March 1942
77 *Ibid.*

78 NA, RG 28A, vol. 13, file 94, DMS History, 15 September 1943 'Development of Industrial Security Branch Department of Munitions and Supply,' pp. 8–10

79 CSIS Access 86-A-85, Johnson to the Commissioner, RCMP, 4 December 1942

80 CSIS Access 86-A-85, Johnson to the Commissioner, RCMP, 21 July 1943

81 AO, RG 33, Series I-1, file 84.3, Scott to Tait, 24 October 1940

82 Theoharis, *FBI Filing and Records Procedures*, Classification #99, Plant Surveys

83 AO, RG 33, Series I-1, file 84.3, Scott to Tait, 24 October 1940

84 RCMP, *Protection of Industry in Time of War*, pp. 6–7

85 NA, RG 24, vol. 11249, file 10-1-1, Stethem to the Commissioner, RCMP, 5 September 1941; *Ibid.*, Batch to Stethem, 19 September 1941. Although the FBI did not receive the letter, neither did the intended recipient; the original rests in the archives.

86 Eleanor Bontecou, *The Federal Loyalty-Security Program* (Ithaca, N.Y.: Cornell University Press 1953), pp. 10, 166

87 Harold Ickes, *The Secret Diary of Harold L. Ickes* (New York: Simon and Schuster 1954), vol. III: *The Lowering Clouds, 1939–1941*, p. 119

88 CSIS Access 86-A-85, Vernon to the Commissioner, RCMP, 7 May 1942

89 Ickes, *Diary*, vol. III, pp, 297, 308–12

90 *The Nation*, 17 and 24 July 1943

91 AO, RG 23, Series A-2, file 1.17, Chief Inspector to Commissioner, 27 May 1937

92 AO, RG 23, Series A-2, Box 2, file 2.3, McCready to Commissioner, 7 and 10 September 1940; file 2.5, McCready to Commissioner, 13 March 1942

93 *Ibid.*, file 2.6, H.S. McC. to Killing, 29 March 1943

94 AO, RG 3, box 309, Volunteer Service Guard, 1940, Shultz to Hepburn, 6 July 1940, and attached resolution; RG 3, box 301, Conant to Lapointe, 17 November 1939, and news release, 21 November 1939; MU 722, D-1, box 2, pkg 2, Conant speech, 7 June 1940

95 David Lewis, *The Good Fight: Political Memoirs, 1909–1958* (Toronto: Macmillan 1981), p. 282

96 G.M.A. Grube, *The LeBel Report and Civil Liberties* (A *Canadian Forum* pamphlet [1946]), pp. 3, 5, 8–10, 12

97 *Ibid.*, p. 12

98 Jean-François Leclerc and J. Raymond Proulx, 'La Sûreté du Québec des origines à nos jours: Histoire administrative et professionnelle, 1870–1988' (unpublished manuscript, Sûreté du Québec, 1989), p. 257

99 B.C., Provincial Police, *Report of the Commissioner of Provincial Police, 1932* (hereafter BCPP, *Report of the Commissioner*), p. 11

100 BCPP, *Report of the Commissioner, 1933*, p. 20

101 British Columbia Archives and Records Services (BCARS), GR 1222, box 26, file 5, 16 April 1939 Intelligence Report

102 BCPP, *Report of the Commissioner, 1939*, Administrative Chart

103 BCPP, *Report of the Commissioner, 1940*, p. 11

104 *Ibid.*, p. 13

105 *Ibid.*, p. 16

106 BCARS, GR 1222, box 26, file 4, Commissioner's radiogram, 28 May 1940

107 BCPP, *Report of the Commissioner, 1940*, Administrative Chart

108 BCPP, *Report of the Commissioner, 1942*, p. 16

109 *Ibid.*

110 BCPP, *Report of the Commissioner, 1943*, p. 14

111 CSIS Access 89-A-63, Annual Report of the RCMP Intelligence and Liaison Section for 1942

112 Wesley Wark, 'Cryptographic Innocence: The Origins of Signals Intelligence in Canada in the Second World War,' *Journal of Contemporary History* 22 (1987): 639 and *passim*; Bryden, *Best-Kept Secret*, pp. 54, 63–89

113 Betke and Horrall, 'Canada's Security Service,' p. xxi

114 Andrew and Dilks, *Missing Dimension*, p. 10

115 Grace and Leys, 'Concept of Subversion,' p. 77

116 Betke and Horrall, 'Canada's Security Service,' p. 519

117 *Ibid.*, p. 541

118 See chapter 4 and Sawatsky, *Men in the Shadows*, p. 93; J.L. Granatstein and David Stafford, *Spy Wars: Espionage and Canada from Gouzenko to Glasnost* (Toronto: Key Porter Books 1990), pp. 26–8

CHAPTER 9 'The first to come under suspicion'

1 Interview with Katie Kisko (a pseudonyn), Port Colborne, Ontario, 29 June 1991; CSIS Access 86-A-85, Wood to the Secretary, Civil Service Commission, 1 December 1941; *Vernon's City of Welland Directory,* 1939, 1941, 1943, 1946. CSIS records released through the Access to Information Act are censored and contain no follow-up information about Kisko. But the 1943 directory shows him as working as a bridgeman on the canal, which suggests he was reinstated. This was confirmed by Mrs Kisko.
2 CSIS Access 86-A-85, S.T. Wood to the Secretary, Civil Service Commission, 1 December 1941
3 *Ibid.,* Wood to the Chairman, CSC, 14 October 1942
4 *Ibid.*
5 CSIS Access 86-A-85, Mead to Nelson, 29 September 1943
6 CSIS Access 86-A-85, extract of communication from Wood to St Laurent, 10 February 1943
7 Interview with W.C. Bryan, Victoria, 13 October 1988. Rosamond 'Fiddy' Greer confirms that lesbian practice led to dismissal from the Wrens. See *The Girls of the King's Navy* (Victoria: Sono Nis 1983), pp. 83–4.
8 Kennedy, *History of the Department of Munitions and Supply,* vol. II, pp. 349, 375
9 *Ibid.,* pp. 349
10 AO, MU 6285, box 1, Scarborough Plant History, Security Department
11 CSIS Access 86-A-85, Cadiz to the Director-General, Industrial Security Branch, DMS, 18 December 1942
12 CSIS Access 86-A-85, Wilson to the Director, CIB, 21 February 1941
13 *Ibid.*
14 *Ibid.,* Cadiz to Johnson, 14 December 1942
15 AO, RG 33, Series I-1, file 85.13, 23 February, 9 March, and 11 March 1940. Emphasis added.
16 CSIS Access 86-A-85, Wilson to Director, CIB, 21 February 1941
17 NA, RG 19, vol. 3656, file G-537-20, Butchers to the Director, CIB, 9 December 1943. This rate, 10.7 per cent, was exceptionally high. In individual corporations, such as Ottawa Car, and larger groups, like

the army, the average proportion of employees with criminal records was about 5 per cent.

18 NA, RG 28A, vol. 13, file 44, DMS History, 'Development of Industrial Security Branch,' 15 September 1943; Kennedy, *History of the Department of Munitions and Supply,* vol. II, p. 353

19 AO, RG 33, Series I-1, file 85.4, Minutes of the Co-ordinating Committee for Security meeting of 17 December 1940

20 *Ibid.*

21 NA, MG 30, E350, vol. 1, file 9, Philipps to Mead, 6 May 1943; Leopold to Philipps, 11 May 1943; Leopold to Philipps, 18 May 1943; Philipps to Leopold, 21 May 1943

22 Berton, *Great Depression,* p. 487

23 Walter Reuther Library (Wayne State University), George Burt Collection, box 1, file 1-1, Minutes of UAW District 26 (Canada) Council Meeting, 29-30 March 1941

24 *Canadian Tribune,* 29 March 1941, p. 1; *Toronto Star,* 21 March 1941, p. 3. No record has been found of the resolution being tabled in the House of Commons.

25 Justice Access A89-00061, 15 April 1941 report from W.M. Brady

26 *Ibid.* For example, the questionnaire asked: 'To what organizations (other than Labour Unions) have you belonged at any time during the past ten years?'

27 *Ibid.*

28 *Canadian Tribune,* 24 May 1941, p. 1

29 CSIS Access 86-A-85, Vernon to the Commissioner, 6 August 1942. Union objections were probably from the B.C. Tel workers. See University of British Columbia Special Collections, Elaine Bernard Papers, Minutes of Directorate of the B.C. Telephone Co. Electrical Employees' Organization, 12 September 1942.

30 *Canadian Forum,* January 1941, p. 306

31 Abella, *Nationalism, Communism, and Canadian Labour,* pp. 69, 139

32 Avakumovic, *Communist Party in Canada,* p. 150

33 *Globe and Mail,* 22 May 1940, p. 7; 24 May 1940, p. 1; 10 June 1940, p. 4

34 *Globe and Mail,* 14 May 1940, p. 4

35 *Saturday Night,* 15 June 1940, p. 3; 31 August 1940, p. 3; Granatstein, *Canada's War,* pp. 99–102

36 Kingsley G. Ferguson, letter to author, 7 July 1991
37 William A. Donohue, *The Politics of the American Civil Liberties Union* (New Brunswick, N.J.: Transaction 1985), pp. 2–3
38 Betke and Horrall, 'Canada's Security Service,' pp. 372–3
39 *Ibid.*, p. 376
40 Suzanne Skebo, 'Liberty and Authority: Civil Liberties in Toronto, 1929–1935' (unpublished MA thesis, University of British Columbia, 1968), p. 99
41 J. Petryshyn, 'Class Conflict and Civil Liberties: The Origins and Activities of the Canadian Labor Defense League, 1925-1940,' *Labour/Le Travailleur* 10 (autumn 1982): 63, and 'R.B. Bennett and the Communists: 1930–1935,' *Journal of Canadian Studies* IX, no. 4 (November 1974): 46-52
42 NA, MG 30, D211, vol. 10, Civil Liberties, 1930–35, Underhill to Stiernotte, 23 November 1932
43 *Ibid.*
44 NA, MG 31, K9, vol. 7, file 133, Cam to Frank (1947); Kealey and Whitaker, *R.C.M.P. Security Bulletins, 1939–1941*, p. 381
45 *Ibid.*, pp. 181, 266–7, 274
46 *Canadian Tribune*, 7 June 1941, p. 2; Kealey and Whitaker, *R.C.M.P. Security Bulletins, 1939–1941*, p. 381
47 *Ibid.*, pp. 266–7; G. Ramsay Cook, 'Canadian Liberalism in Wartime: A Study of the Defence of Canada Regulations and Some Canadian Attitudes to Civil Liberties in Wartime, 1939–1945' (unpublished MA thesis, Queen's University, 1955), pp. 103–4
48 Cook, 'Canadian Liberalism in Wartime,' pp. 168–9, 212
49 NA, MG 30, D211, vol. 10, Civil Liberties Union, 1936–1940, Spry to Scott, 21 December 1936
50 Queen's University Archives, Lower Papers, file 17C, Lower to Pickersgill, 17 February 1940; *ibid.*, Lower to Siverts, 25 February 1940
51 Arthur R.M. Lower, *My First Seventy-five Years* (Toronto: Macmillan 1967), p. 237
52 Cook, 'Canadian Liberalism in Wartime,' p. 168
53 Queen's University Archives, Lower Papers, file 19C, Brewin to Lower, 21 February 1941
54 NA, MG 26, J1, vol. 333, Sandwell to King, 5 February 1942

55 *Ibid.*, King to St Laurent, 23 February 1942
56 *Saturday Night*, 15 June 1940, p. 3
57 NA, MG 26, J1, vol. 333, Summary of meeting of members of the
government with delegation from the Civil Liberties Association of
Toronto, 20 February 1942
58 Neither was it concerned about the relocation of the Japanese Canadians from coastal British Columbia, the policy then being discussed in Ottawa and in the public arena.
59 *Canadian Forum*, November 1940, p. 241
60 *Canadian Forum*, April 1941, pp. 4–5
61 *Canadian Tribune*, 29 March 1941, p. 1, and 24 May 1941, p. 1
62 Lester Phillips, 'Canada's Internal Security,' *Canadian Journal of Economics and Political Science* XII, no. 1 (February 1946): 23. The RCMP
explained the suspension by condemning the paper's 'innuendo,'
which it considered the paper's 'chief weapon.' 'Suspension of the
"Tribune" was not the result of any one misdemeanour but rather of
an accumulation of petty offenses on the border-line of legality that
tended to discourage faith in democracy and retard our war efforts.'
Kealey and Whitaker, *R.C.M.P. Security Bulletins, 1939–1941*, pp.
332–3.
63 In June 1940 the CCF MP for Cape Breton South, Clarence Gillis,
raised a related matter in the House, the case of Walter Camm, a
John Inglis Company worker who was fired for his union activity.
But this was not a discussion of the state's security-screening system. As Gillis declared in the House, 'this specific case proves con-
clusively that *the company* is practising discrimination against
organized labour' (emphasis added). Although the Camm case is
too detailed to discuss here it suggests an intriguing possible motivation for the RCMP and DMS application form: perhaps the state
form was created in order to standardize the employment questionnaire and avoid the unnecessary aggravation caused by the application forms of employers like Inglis, which demanded personal
information that could be interpreted as anti-union. Canada, House
of Commons, *Debates*, 24 June 1940, p. 1010, and *Globe and Mail*, 15
June 1940, p. 9
64 *Canadian Forum*, January 1941, p. 304
65 Canada, House of Commons, *Debates*, 10 March 1941, pp. 1469, 1507

66 Canada, House of Commons, *Debates*, 10 March 1941, p. 1367. Emphasis added.
67 *Canadian Forum*, April 1941, p. 5; *Canadian Unionist*, March 1941, pp. 242–5; *Canadian Congress Journal*, April 1941, pp. 15–16
68 Cook, 'Canadian Liberalism in Wartime,' p. 170
69 NA, MG 30, D211, vol. 10, file Civil Liberties, Montreal Association 1945–1950, Scott to Baldwin, 20 April 1945
70 Cook, 'Canadian Liberalism in Wartime,' p. 278
71 *Ibid.*, pp. 279–81, 286–7
72 Interview with Fred Hicks, Vancouver, 19 April 1989
73 Edgar Friedenberg, *Deference to Authority: The Case of Canada* (White Plains, N.Y.: M.E. Sharpe 1980), pp. 17, 54, 99
74 Doug Owram, *The Government Generation: Canadian Intellectuals and the State, 1900–1945* (Toronto: University of Toronto Press 1986), p. 263
75 F.R. Scott, *Civil Liberties and Canadian Federalism* (Toronto: University of Toronto Press 1959), p. 11
76 Kealey and Whitaker, *R.C.M.P. Security Bulletins, 1939–1941*, pp. 266–7 and 380–1
77 RCMP, *Annual Report, 1940*, p. 75
78 CSIS Access 117-91-1, [name deleted] to King, 22 May 1941
79 *Ibid.*, Civil Liberties Union report, 20 May 1941. Gagnon denied that any members of his division had approached employers to induce them to dismiss people associated with the CCLU. See *ibid.*, Gagnon to Commissioner, 21 May 1941.
80 Interview with Fred Hicks, 19 April 1989
81 CSIS Access 86-A-85, Wilson to Director, CIB, 21 February 1941
82 *Ibid.*, Wilson to Director, CIB, 21 February 1941
83 *Ibid.*, Tait to Officers Commanding, 24 March 1941
84 CCAC, *Proceedings*, 1943, p. 94
85 It is worth noting that the new policy applied only to criminal records obtained from private employers. Full criminal records were made available to government departments. In keeping with the force's strict husbanding of intelligence, details from the force's subversive index were never released in total to employers. See CSIS Access 86-A-85, R.L Cadiz to Director General, Industrial Security Branch, DMS, 18 December 1942, and 8 November 1940 memo from J. Fraser.

86 Justice Access 89A-00061, R.R. Tait to Officers Commanding, RCMP Divisions, 24 March 1941
87 CSIS Access 86-A-85, Wood to Bernier, 7 October 1942
88 *Ibid.*, Wilson to Director, CIB, 21 February 1941
89 Reg Whitaker, *Double Standard: The Secret History of Canadian Immigration* (Toronto: Lester and Orpen Dennys 1987), p. 234
90 Interview with W.C. Bryan
91 CSIS Access 86-A-85, Wood to Anderson, 5 December 1940
92 Queen's University Archives, Lower Papers, file 17C, Fisher to Lower, 7 February 1940
93 *Ibid.*, Lower to Brewin, 1 April 1940; *ibid.*, file 18C, Lower to Waines, 21 May 1940
94 *ibid.*, Lower to Maybank, 14 March 1941, and Brewin to Lower, 21 February 1941
95 Trade unions had also been doing the same for some years, indicating that screening was not the monopoly of the state. But the state commanded far greater resources than private associations in screening and acting upon the results of the screening. I owe this observation to Reg Whitaker.
96 Kealey and Whitaker, *R.C.M.P. Security Bulletins, 1939-1941*, p. 389
97 Cook, 'Canadian Liberalism in Wartime,' p. 208
98 NA, MG31, K9, vol. 8, file 144, National Committee for Democratic Rights minutes and proceedings, conference, 17 May 1942
99 NA, MG31, K9, vol. 7, file 133, Cam (R.A.C. Ballantyne) to Frank (Park)(n.d.); *Canadian Tribune*, 7 June 1941, p. 2, and 21 June 1941, p. 2
100 Lucie Laurin, *Des luttes et des droits: Antécédents et histoire de la Lique des droits de l'homme de 1936 à 1975* (Montréal: Editions du Méridien 1985), p. 35
101 NA, MG31, K9, vol. 7, file 133, Cam (R.A.C. Ballantyne) to Frank (Park) (n.d.); emphasis added.
102 Phillips, 'Canada's Internal Security,' p. 20
103 David W. Ewing, *Freedom inside the Organization: Bringing Civil Liberties to the Workplace* (New York: E.P. Dutton 1977), p. 5

CHAPTER 10 Outcomes, developments, and significance

1 Mackenzie Commission, p. 30

2 CSIS Access 117-91-61, Minutes of the Western Hemisphere Intelligence Conference, 3 August 1942, p. 11
3 NA, RG 24, vol. 5376, file HQ 45-24-20, vol. 1, Evans to RCAF Records Officer, 30 March 1943
4 Foucault, *Discipline and Punish*, p. 227
5 James Littleton, *Target Nation: Canada and the Western Intelligence Network* (Toronto: CBC Enterprises and Lester and Orpen Dennys 1986), p. 166
6 Canada, *Debates*, House of Commons, 24 March 1947, p. 1652
7 RCMP, *Annual Report*, 1949, p. 29
8 *Ibid*, 1952, p. 30
9 I owe this observation to Greg Marquis, 'Creating a Criminal Class: The Identification of Criminals in Twentieth Century Canada,' unpublished paper delivered to the Canadian Historical Association annual meeting, Charlottetown, 1992, p. 22.
10 The figure of 18,000 is an estimate based upon an RCMP file on fingerprints (GL302-14-1) which remains in the possession of the RCMP. In a 30 June 1993 letter to the author, RCMP historian William Beahen explains that 18,128 non-criminal prints were received by the RCMP between 1910 and 1939. 'By implication we may conclude that these prints were all still stored in the fingerprint register, but this is by no means certain.'
11 FBI, *Annual Report*, 1942, p. 14; 1945, p. 21. In 1941, 51 per cent of the fingerprints were civilian; in 1945, 85 per cent of them were civilian.
12 CSIS Access 117-91-99, Rivett-Carnac memo, 10 July 1945
13 RCMP, *Annual Report*, 1946, pp. 38–9
14 Whitaker, 'Left Wing Dissent and the State,' in *Dissent and the State*, p. 196; Kellock-Taschereau Commission, *Report*, pp. 9, 689
15 NA, RG 24, vol. 250, HQS-6403-9, Heeney to Abbott, 6 July 1946
16 Bothwell and Granatstein, *The Gouzenko Transcripts*, p. 19
17 CSIS Access 87-A-39, 22 May 1946 memo from Parsons to the DCI
18 Harvison, *Horsemen*, pp. 216–17
19 CSIS Access 87-A-39, Wonnacott to DCI, 26 January 1949
20 Stafford and Granatstein, *Spy Wars*, p. 74
21 Littleton, *Target Nation*, p. 168

Picture Credits

Index

Acadians 29
Access to Information Act (Canada) 13–15
Acland, Eric 127–8
Adamson, R. 123–4
Alaska Highway 106, 194–6
alien registration (Britian) 23
alien registration (Canada) 32, 88, 179
Alien Registration Act (Britain) 23
Alien Registration Act (Smith Act) (U.S.) 131–2
aliens 23–4, 32, 88–9, 94–5, 97, 107–8, 179
Allason, Rupert 6
Allied War Supplies Corporation 159
American Civil Liberties Union 54–5, 59, 250
American Protective League 27–8
Anderson, R.L. 103, 123, 148–9, 168, 215
Andrew, Christopher 144
Aronsen, Lawrence 8

Avakumovic, Ivan 91

Ballantyne, R.A.C. 236–7
Batch, C. 199
Bavin, E.W. 99, 104, 186, 195
Beaubien, C.P. 74
Bell, Charles 60
Bennett, R.B. 63, 73
Bertillon, Alphonse 45
Bertillon system 45–6
Betke, Carl 143–5, 208
black list 33, 110–11, 136–8, 216–17, 238
Blackwell, John 203
Bloch, Marc 30
Boeing Aircraft 74, 204
Bolshevism and Bolshevik Revolution 7, 19, 24, 33, 35, 39, 64, 66, 82, 241
Borden, Robert 64, 67–8
Bose, R.B.H.C. 45
Bothwell, Robert 85, 111, 252
Boyer, Raymond 105
Brady, W.M. 218
Brand, E.S. 134
Brewin, Andrew 223

British Air Ministry 130
British Army 130
British Broadcasting Corporation
71, 79
British Columbia Provincial
Police 196, 204–5; Criminal
Investigation Branch 204–5;
Special Branch 204
British Nationality, Naturaliza-
tion, and Aliens Act 68
British Security Co-ordination
(BSC) 134, 183, 185–6, 188, 194,
197, 206, 208
Brodeur, Jean-Paul 177, 180–1
Brown, C.C. 42
Brown, Gerald 218
Bruce, W.V.M.B. 194
Bryan, W.C. 212, 233
Buck, Tim 91–2, 124
Business Machines 168, 172
Butchers, H.R. 57–8, 147, 163–7,
215

Cabinet War Committee 140
Cadiz, R.L. 191
Cahan, Charles 64–5
Calgary 94
Camm, Walter 313n63
Camp X 184
Canadian Army Identification
Bureau 106, 126
Canadian Broadcasting Corpora-
tion 71
Canadian Bureau of Identification
107
Canadian Civil Liberties Union
96, 115, 222–3, 230, 236–7

Canadian Congress Journal 60,
86–7, 227
Canadian Congress of Labour
(All-Canadian Congress of
Labour) 86
Canadian Criminal Identification
Bureau 49–51
Canadian Forum 225–7
Canadian Labor Defense League
221–2, 224, 234
Canadian Magazine 59
Canadian Manufacturers' Associ-
ation 146–7, 153, 157
Canadian National Railway 215
Canadian Naval Service 105,
119–20, 129–30, 132
Canadian Pacific Railway 105,
119–20
Canadian Seamen's Union 91,
132, 138
Canadian Security Intelligence
Service 13
Canadian Spokesman 149
Canadian Tribune 91, 111, 216, 224,
226, 228, 236, 313n62
Canadian Unionist 87, 227
Canadian Women's Army Corps
116
Canol pipeline project 106, 195
card indexes 4, 149
Cartwright, Richard 30, 34
Caute, David 26
Central Intelligence Agency 186
Chamber of Commerce (U.S.) 54
Chief Constables' Association of
Canada 48–50, 55–7, 59, 61,
147, 153

Chief Postal Censor 105
Churchill, Winston 187
civil liberties 8, 11–12, 96, 111,
    149, 211–39, 247–51, 253
Civil Protection Committee 178
civil servants and civil service 35,
    70, 80–1; in Britain 79–80;
    screening 5, 6, 8, 9, 11–12, 18–
    21, 25–6, 31, 33, 41, 64, 70–2,
    78–81, 84, 101–2, 104, 107, 109,
    111, 113–14,124, 129–30, 179–
    80, 187, 207, 213, 235, 238, 241–
    2, 249, 252–3; in United States
    80, 196–7
Civil Service Act 70, 145
Civil Service Commission (Can-
    ada) 70–2, 81, 101–2, 104, 108,
    114–15, 117, 129–30, 211–12,
    232, 252
Civil Service Commission (U.S.)
    26, 80–1, 200
Civil Service Rule 1 (U.S.) 26
Clarion 226
Cleaver, Hughes 99
Co-operative Commonwealth
    Federation 203, 221, 223, 226–8
Co-ordinating Committee for
    Security 110, 123, 142, 148, 155,
    168, 215, 239
code-breaking and cryptanalysis
    3–5, 10, 112, 206–7
Cold War 8, 10
Coleman, W.E.L. 124
Cominco Smelter 204
Communist International (Com-
    intern) 7, 33–4, 73, 77, 241
Communist Party of Canada

(communists) 34–6, 41, 56–7,
    69, 85, 87–8, 93, 95–7, 104, 106,
    110–15, 117, 119–21, 130–2, 141,
    160–1, 168–9, 191, 199, 216,
    219, 246; and British Columbia
    Provincial Police 204; civil
    liberties involvement 221–6,
    228, 230, 234–8; cross-border
    travel 77–8; fingerprinting of
    55–7, 148; government and
    RCMP fear of 68, 73–6, 89–92,
    99–100, 116, 148–51, 153, 221,
    242–4, 253; and Ontario Pro-
    vincial Police 202–3
computer matching 73, 172–3
Congress of Industrial Organiza-
    tions (Committee for Industrial
    Organization) 88, 152–3, 203
Connolly, Vera 54
conscription 229, 235
Controller of Aircraft for Canada
    212
Cook, Ramsay 224, 228–9
counter-espionage 6, 10, 24, 27–8,
    32, 192, 194, 207, 209
Creelman, J.J. 94
criminal and political intelligence:
    relationship of 67, 69, 173–82,
    208
Culhane, Claire, see Eglin, Claire

Daily Clarion 93
Dann, T. 185
Davis, David 28
Defence Industries Limited 202
Defence of Canada Regulations
    (DOCR) 85–6, 97, 107, 119,

139–41, 174, 177, 218, 220, 223, 225, 226, 236–7, 239, 248
deference to authority 229, 234, 250–1
DeHavilland Aircraft 110
Democratic Rights Movement 223
Department of External Affairs 13, 112–14, 131, 133, 183, 187, 189, 195, 206–7, 209
Department of Justice 56, 60, 65
Department of Labour 132, 142
Department of Munitions and Supply 84, 98, 102–4, 107, 110, 123, 140, 142, 146, 148, 156, 158–60, 168, 191, 198, 213, 215, 217–18, 242, 244; Industrial Security Branch 140, 196–8, 244; Legal Branch 103
Department of National Defence 74, 76, 101, 104, 107, 126, 141, 204
Department of National War Services, Nationalities Branch 216
Department of Transport 104, 133, 156, 288n119; Central Index Register of Seamen 132
deportation (Britain) 23
deportation (Canada) 29, 39, 57, 65, 68–70, 274n79
desertion 133, 135–7
Dilks, David 144
Directorate of Military Intelligence (DMI) 126
Dominion Bureau of Statistics 171
Dominion Police 49–50, 65–7, 76, 121

Drew, George 203
Drysdale, Alexander 42, 197

Eglin, Claire (Culhane) ix, 114, 130–1, 155
Ericson, Richard 48, 178–9
espionage and spying 5, 8, 9, 10, 80, 102, 105, 132, 150, 188, 190, 241–3, 245, 251
Esquimalt dockyards 75, 114–15, 130
Evans, E.E. 156
Ewing, David 238

Fairchild Aircraft 116, 142, 217
FBI *Annual Report* 200
FBI Manual 80
Federal Bureau of Investigation (FBI) 38–9, 50, 53–5, 59, 73, 78, 80–1, 95, 183, 185–6, 191–201, 206–9, 250; Civil Identification Section 53–4, 81, 250; sharing of fingerprinting knowledge 55, 171–2, 193–4
Fenians 29–31, 221
Ferguson, Kingsley G. 220
Ferns, H.S. 113–14
Ferrier, John 49, 52
fifth column 88, 92–101, 117, 204
fingerprinting 4, 35, 39, 41–61, 69–73, 76, 78–9, 81, 83–4, 102–4, 106–8, 117, 122–6, 129–42, 145–9, 163–74, 177–9, 181, 191–4, 196–7, 199–201, 204–5, 208, 213–20, 222, 225–7, 229–31, 235–9, 242–3, 245–53; civil servants 35, 41, 53–4, 70–2, 78–81,

84, 102, 104–6, 181, 196, 213;
development 43–52; electromechanical tabulating equipment
11, 73, 125, 163, 165, 167–73,
181; industrial workers 83–4,
102–4, 108, 111, 139–42, 145,
147–8, 153–9, 164–5, 172–5,
178–9, 181, 191–3, 196, 200,
213–18, 226–7, 231, 238–9,
242–3, 245–53; military 76,
105–7, 121–6, 129–30, 137, 181,
196, 220; popular image of 56–
61; RCMP members 41–3, 71
firearms registration 171, 179
Flynn, R. 215
forensic science 47
Forke, Robert 59
Foster, Edward 49–51, 55
Foster, George E. 59
Foster, R.M. 155
Foucault, Michel 246, 271n34
Franklin, Benjamin 25, 34
Fraser, R.D. 191–2
Freedom of Information Act (U.S.)
12
French Canadians 229
Friedenberg, Edgar 229, 233,
250–1

Gagnon, H.A.R. 96, 230
Galton, Francis 44
Gandhi, Mohandas K. 58
General Engineering Company
213
General Motors 158
Geneva Convention 130
Gillis, Clarence 313n63

Globe and Mail 83–5, 96–8, 178,
216
Godson, Roy 5
Good Housekeeping 54
Gouzenko, Igor 8, 9, 35, 114, 190,
241–2, 251, 253
Granatstein, J.L. 85, 111, 252
Grasett, Henry 50
Grube, G.M.A. 223
Guthrie, Connop 188
Guthrie, George 57
Guthrie, Hugh 56, 74

Halifax 132, 136, 187–8, 212
Hamilton, C.F. 78
Harvard Business Review 238
Harvey, Jean-Charles 222
Harvison, C.W. 76, 89, 103
Hatch Act 199
Henry, Edward 45, 49
Henry fingerprint classification
system 45–9, 108, 169, 270n18,
270n20
Hepburn, Mitchell 97, 202
Herschel, Sir William 44–5,
269n12
Hicks, Fred 229, 231
Hill, C.H. 115
Hinsley, F.H. 79, 185
Hitchcock, Alfred 92
Hitler, Adolph 83, 92
home guards 103–4, 202, 204
homosexuals 159–60, 212–13
Homuth, Karl 94
Hoover, J. Edgar 38–9, 53–5, 78,
81, 95, 149, 185, 193
Horrall, S.W. 33, 36, 38, 143–5, 208

House of Commons 59–60, 63, 67, 79, 93–5, 97, 99, 117, 142, 217, 226–7
Howe, C.D. 140
Howe, Joseph 100, 146, 157
Hunter, Peter 91
Hydro-Electric Power Commission of Ontario 93, 216
Hyman, Harold 20, 25, 27–8, 34

Ickes, Harold 200–1
identification cards 59–60, 74, 131, 133, 136
Identification of Criminals Act 51–2, 55–6, 59, 145, 243, 249
Ilsley, J.L. 249
immigration and immigrants 4, 6, 29–30, 37, 55–6, 59–60, 64, 69, 74
Immigration Act 69
Immigration Branch 72, 107
Immigration Department 57, 69
Imperial Munitions Board 33
Imperial Oil 74
India 19, 43–5
Industrial Workers of the World 28, 69
infernal machine 11, 95, 248, 253
Ingersoll Rand Company 229
Inglis, John Co. 155, 313n63
Inspection Board of the United Kingdom and Canada 104
Interdepartmental Committee for Co-ordination of Intelligence for War Purposes 102, 124
Interdepartmental Committee on Emergency Legislation 88

International Association for Identification 51–2, 57
International Association of Chiefs of Police 49, 52
International Association of Machinists 116, 142, 217
International Business Machines (IBM) (Hollerith equipment) 11, 73, 106, 108, 125, 163, 165, 167–72, 181, 197
internment 23, 32, 88, 94, 98, 103, 155, 199, 202, 219, 222, 235–6, 245

Jackson, C.S. 155, 219
Jackson, Robert 200–1
Jennings, G.L. 56, 60
Johnson, E.J. 156, 198
Joint Intelligence Committee 131
Jolliffe, E.B. 203
Jour, Le 22

Kananaskis internment camp 103
Kealey, Gregory 66, 176
Keenleyside, Hugh 132
Kellock-Taschereau Royal Commission 35, 85, 105, 112, 251
Kemp, V.A.M. 166–7, 185, 188
Kennedy, John de N. 159
King, C.H. 164–5
King, William Lyon Mackenzie 90, 93, 120, 139, 187, 217, 224–5
Kisko, John 211–12, 310n2
Kostyk, Fred 120, 216

Labour Progressive Party, see Communist Party of Canada

Lapointe, Ernest 90, 93, 97, 122, 141, 185
League of Patriotic Action 178
Leopold, John 78, 151
Lewis, David 203
Liddell, Guy 77
Littleton, James 247
Lockhart, John Bruce 5
London Metropolitan Police (Scotland Yard) 45, 49, 52, 69, 77, 185, 197; Criminal Investigation Branch 45; Finger Print Bureau 49; Special Branch 22–3
Longueuil, Quebec 116, 217
Lowe, Graham 170
Lower, A.R.M. 223, 234
Loyal Legion of Loggers and Lumbermen 27–8
Loyalists 29–30
loyalty testing 3–6, 8, 10, 18–21, 24–6, 28–30, 34, 36, 38

MacBrien, J.H. 41–2, 56, 63–4, 71, 76, 78, 121, 193, 242
McCarthy, Joseph, and McCarthyism 10
McClellan, George 203
Macdonald, John A. 31
McDonald Commission on Security 8, 31, 33
McEwen, Ruth 116
McGill University 104
MacInnis, Angus 95, 226–7
Mackenzie Commission, see Royal Commission on Security
Mackenzie, C.J. 104–5

Mackenzie-Papineau Batallion 75, 103
McLarty, Norman 226–7
McNaughton, Andrew 75, 121–2
McNeil, John 119–20
Manby, A.W. 216
Mann, Daniel 124, 148
Marine Industries 110
Marquis, Greg 50
Mead, F.J. 190, 192, 194
merchant seamen 9, 84, 131–8, 186, 252
Merchant Seamen Order 135
MI5 6, 22–3, 69, 77, 79–80, 136–7, 183, 185–8, 208
MI6 (SIS) 22, 183, 185–6
military intelligence 75, 108, 116, 126, 183, 185
Military Intelligence Section 3 (MI3) 126, 137
Mills, Cyril 188
Ministry of Munitions Labour Intelligence Division (Britain) 23
Ministry of Shipping (Britain) 133
Mitchell, Humphrey 140
Montreal 94, 96–7, 103, 175, 191, 203, 216, 218, 222–3, 228, 230–1, 236–7
Montreal Gazette 86, 230
Mosher, A.R. 88
Murphy, Frank 200

National Committee for Democratic Rights 222, 235
National Council for Civil Liberties 79

National Filling Factory No. 7
17–18, 19, 45
national registration 53, 57, 59,
94–5, 97, 117, 156, 179, 219–20,
225, 229
National Research Council 13,
104–5, 251; Chemical Warfare
Division 104; Examination
Unit 112, 207; Secret Radio
Division 104
National Resources Mobilization
Act 97, 220
National Steel Car Aircraft Division 110
Nationalities Branch, Department of National War Services
111
Nature 47
Naval Boarding Service 136
nazis 87, 89–90, 93, 97, 100, 106,
117, 123, 141, 193
negative vetting 117, 137
Newfoundland 190–2, 201
Newfoundland Rangers 191, 201
Norman, Herbert 112–14
Norman Wells pipeline 194–5
Northwest Service Command
195–6
Noseworthy, J.W. 223
Notes on Industrial Security 74, 77,
102
Nursey, Bill 124

oaths of allegiance and loyalty 4,
7, 20–1, 24–6, 29–32, 34–5,
241
Office of Strategic Services 186

Official Secrets Act (Britain) 13,
22
Ontario Provincial Police 110,
123, 202, 215; Anti-Sabotage
Branch 203; Special Branch
202–3
Orde, E.T.C. 120
Osborne-Dempster, William 203
Oshawa 202
Ottawa 102, 194, 235
Ottawa Car and Aircraft 102, 147,
158, 214–15, 239
Overseas Security Bulletin 190

Padlock Law 60
Paivo, Jules 120
Palmer, A. Mitchell 28
Park, Frank 236
Parliamentary Military Secretary
Department No. 2 23, 37
Pearson, Lester B. 114
Perkins, Frances 200–1
Perry, A.B. 34, 38, 66–7, 176
Petrie, David 188
Phillips, Lester 237
Pickersgill, Jack 90, 114
Plant Protection Manual 193
Popular Mechanics 47
Popular Science 47
port security 187–9, 192, 194,
207
Portecorvo, Bruno 304n15
Porter, Bernard 22–3, 80, 176–7
positive vetting (character investigation) 72, 80, 106, 108, 118,
137
Post Office 71

Power, C.G. 97
Prime Minister's Office 89, 113–14, 117, 151, 209
prisoners of war 194
Protection of Industrial Facilities 193
Protection of Industry in Time of War 102, 109, 156, 193
Public Safety Branch 65

Quain, Redmond 102, 147, 158, 214–15
Quelch, Victor 99

radio communications 194
Ralston, J.L. 286n89
RCMP *Annual Report* 71, 73, 104, 145, 166, 200, 230
RCMP *Gazette* 50
RCMP *Intelligence Bulletin* 89–91, 96–7, 99–100, 114, 122, 145, 150, 230
RCMP Quarterly 47, 58, 76, 109
Red Squad (Toronto) 124, 202
Regan, F.A. 188
Ritchie, David 94
Rivett-Carnac, Charles 63, 78, 105, 109, 251
Robertson, Norman 114, 141, 150, 183, 188–9, 195, 206, 249
Roosevelt, Franklin D. 185
Ross, George 212
Rowan, Richard 92
Royal Air Force 130
Royal Air Force Ferry Command 104, 156
Royal Australian Air Force 130

Royal Canadian Air Force 105–6, 121, 124–5, 130
Royal Canadian Mounted Police 8–9, 12, 13, 34, 38, 41–3, 50–1, 55–8, 60, 63–78, 81–2, 84, 89–117, 120–39, 141, 183, 211–18, 220–2, 225, 227, 229–34, 237, 239, 242–6, 248–53; attitude towards unions 152–3; Central Registry 67–8, 73; Civil Security Branch 74, 146, 213; Civilian Identification Collection in Fingerprint Section 104, 108, 168, 246, 249–50; Criminal Investigation Branch 50, 66–8, 78, 107, 164, 166, 177; Fingerprint Section 41–2, 49, 50, 55, 57, 67, 71, 104, 107–9, 115, 163–72, 177, 215; 'Gestapo reputation' 178, 211, 232, 249; Identification Branch 51, 169; Intelligence (and Liaison) Section 42, 63, 67, 74, 78, 99, 104–5, 108–9, 132, 164, 176–7; relationship with Department of External Affairs and Prime Minister's Office 114, 187, 195, 206; relationship with military intelligence 131; Special Section 252; *see also* RCMP
Royal Canadian Naval Reserve 220
Royal Commission on Security 3–5, 241
Royal New Zealand Air Force 130
Royal North-West Mounted Police 65–7, 69, 77

Russian Workers and Farmers
   Club 94

sabotage 24, 27–8, 32, 75, 77–8,
   90–101, 103, 109, 131–3, 136,
   146, 156–8, 160, 186, 188, 190,
   192–4, 197, 209, 231, 243–6
St John, Peter 184
St John's, Newfoundland 188
St Laurent, Louis 140, 212, 235
Sandwell, B.K. 224–5
Saskatoon 212
Saturday Night 59, 90, 224–5
Sawatsky, John 8
Scarlett, Sam 69
science 4, 7, 11, 34, 45–9, 61, 169,
   178–9, 181
Science 47
Scientific American 47
Scott, C.I. 110
Scott, F.R. 230
Scott, William J. 91, 95, 102, 110,
   165, 214
Scrogg, T.G. 105
security clearance 4, 10
security cooperation (Britain-
   Canada-U.S.A.) 9–10, 38–9, 69,
   76–8, 105–6, 137, 151, 183–209;
   Canada-Britain 50, 69, 77, 105,
   185–93; Canada-U.S. 50, 77–8,
   106, 171, 193–201
Security Executive (Britain) 187–
   8, 190
security officers (private industry)
   108–10, 179, 193, 198
Security Panel 111, 131, 148, 190,
   251–2

security screening: in Britain 6,
   10, 24, 79–80, 186–7; definition 3–5; enforcement of
   morality 159, 246; and industrial workers 21–2, 32–3, 74,
   83–111, 116–18, 139–40, 142,
   164–5, 180, 197–8, 200, 202–5,
   207, 209, 238, 242–7, 252–3;
   and labour mobility 153–4,
   243–4; and military 75–6, 84,
   119–31, 164, 207, 238, 242, 251;
   motive for 242–4; and naturalization 4–6, 68–9, 73, 81, 106,
   204, 241; in United States 10,
   24–8, 80–1, 196–201
Senate 59, 74
Shearing, Clifford 48, 178–9
Sherwood, Percy 50, 76, 121
Shugar, David 105
signals intelligence 206–7
Simkins, C.A.G. 79, 185
sixth column 96
Skebo, Suzanne 221
Skelton, O.D. 77, 195
Smith, Rev. A.E. 222, 235
Sorel, Quebec 110
South Africa 58
Soviet Union 7, 73, 80, 90–1, 93,
   105, 116, 119, 150, 219, 226,
   235–7, 241, 243, 251
Spanish Civil War 75, 103, 120,
   216
Spry, Graham 223
Stacey, C.P. 86
Stafford, David 184
Starnes, Cortlandt 56
Steel Company of Canada 32

Stephenson, William 134, 185–6, 188, 195
Stevens, H.H. 64
Stewart, Alistair 249
Stewart, R.C.C. 75
Stone, T.A. (Tommy) 114, 189
Sullivan, Pat 155, 219
Sûreté du Québec 203–4
Swankey, Ben 120
Swinton, Philip 188

Tait, R.R. 100, 151, 175, 194
Tamm, Edward 95, 193
technology 4, 7, 11, 52, 163–73, 242
telekrypton communication system 194
Thomson, Basil 22–3
Toronto 94, 217
Toronto Civil Liberties Association 223–5, 228, 235
Toronto Clarion 91, 110
Toronto Star 84, 96–9
Trades and Labor Congress 60, 86
Turnbull, W.J. 116

Ukrainian Labor-Farmer Temple Association 94
ul-Haque, K.B. Aziz 45
undercover agents in factories 32–3, 198–9
Underhill, Frank 221–2
United Auto Workers Union 158, 216, 219
United Electrical, Radio and Machine Workers' Union 217, 219

United Nations Relief and Rehabilitation Administration 106, 251
universal fingerprinting movement 54–5

vagrancy 49, 56, 59, 175
Vancouver 56, 94–5, 175, 212, 222
Vancouver Sun 90
Victoria 75, 223
Vulnerable Points Survey 74, 101, 103, 117

Walsh, Bill 129
War Department (U.S.) 200
War Emergency Bulletin 95
Wark, Wesley 8, 10, 184, 206–7
Wartime Prices and Trade Board 212
Washington, D.C. 194, 197
Watt, Fredrick B. 132–3, 136
Webb, Beatrice 22
Webb, Sidney 22
Wershof, M.H. 133
West, Nigel 6
Western Hemisphere Intelligence Conferences 78, 151, 183, 194–5, 206–7, 245
Whitaker, Reg 8, 85, 149, 232, 251
Whitehorse 195
Wilson, A.S. 110
Wilson, Jimmy 103
Wilson, R.S.S. 213–15
Wilson, W.N. 142
Wilson, Woodrow 26, 36
Windsor 94, 218
Winnipeg 119–20, 216, 223

Winnipeg Civil Liberties Association 223, 228, 234
Wolansky, Jim 202
women fingerprint classifiers 166–7
Wonnacott, R.W. 166–9
Wood, R.M. 42
Wood, S.T. 51, 57, 76, 78, 89, 116, 121–2, 128, 141, 149–50, 164–6, 168, 174, 185–6, 188, 190, 192, 194, 211–12, 234, 242

Woodcock, H.F. 94
Woodsworth, J.S. 63–4, 221
Works Progress Administration 54
Wright, Peter 80
Writers, Artists and Broadcasters War Council 111, 216

Yardley, Herbert O. 206–7